The Relational Database

John Carter
Department of Computer Science
University of East London
UK

CHAPMAN & HALL
University and Professional Division

London · Glasgow · Weinheim · New York · Tokyo · Melbourne · Madras

Published by Chapman & Hall, 2–6 Boundary Row, London SE1 8HN, UK

Chapman & Hall, 2–6 Boundary Row, London SE1 8HN, UK

Blackie Academic & Professional, Wester Cleddens Road, Bishopbriggs, Glasgow G64 2NZ, UK

Chapman & Hall GmbH, Pappelallee 3, 69469 Weinheim, Germany

Chapman & Hall USA, One Penn Plaza, 41st Floor, New York NY 10119, USA

Chapman & Hall Japan, ITP-Japan, Kyowa Building, 3F, 2-2-1 Hirakawacho, Chiyoda-ku, Tokyo, Japan

Chapman & Hall Australia, Thomas Nelson Australia, 102 Dodds Street, South Melbourne, Victoria 3205, Australia

Chapman & Hall India, R. Seshadri, 32 Second Main Road, CIT East, Madras 600 035, India

First edition 1995

© 1995 John Carter

Typeset in Great Britain by Columns Design & Production Services Ltd, Reading
Printed in England by Clays Ltd, St Ives plc.

ISBN 0 412 55090 3

A catalogue record for this book is available from the British Library

Library of Congress Catalog Card Number: 94-72634

∞ Printed on permanent acid-free text paper, manufactured in accordance with ANSI/NISO Z39.48-1992 and ANSI/NISO Z39.48-1984 (Permanence of Paper).

Contents

Introduction

This book gives the reader a broad understanding of the main principles involved in relational database design and development. It is suitable for any one or two-semester course in database and covers the material traditionally associated with such courses.

If there is an emphasis in the book, it is on the techniques relating to sound database schema and SQL query design. Many examples and diagrams have been included to illustrate these techniques. The approach has been to provide as comprehensive as possible a coverage of both typical and problem cases in these areas, since it is the author's belief that there is nothing so disappointing in a book as finding that your particular problem has not been covered. To help with the search, an index has been provided which is rather more comprehensive than is usual in a book of this length. Because of this, I believe that practising database designers and programmers will find the book useful.

Chapter 1 introduces the basic idea of using a database and the database approach. The components of typical database systems are described and the stages an organization will go through in developing and using a database are described. The chapter ends by considering the question of what problem characteristics would indicate the use of a database approach.

Chapter 2 begins with a discussion of prerelational databases. This is considered necessary in order to highlight the features and problems associated with these earlier database types so that the motivation for the relational database approach can be justified. There then follows a fairly detailed discussion of E.F. Codd's 12 rules which are perhaps the best way to describe the characteristics of a fully relational database. It is recommended that, in a first reading, these rules are skimmed through and returned to later.

Chapter 3 describes the database logical schema design technique known as Entity-Relationship modelling. It is treated as comprehensively as possible, since in the experience of the author, a poor E-R model is a common source of subsequent problems relating to database accessibility, understandability and performance.

Chapters 4 and 5 describe Normalization techniques. First to Fifth Normal form are discussed. A close relationship exists between Entity Modelling and Normalization, and this is maintained throughout these two chapters.

Chapter 6 moves from database schema design to the question of database access via queries. Relational Algebra is described in a simple way in both its 'Greek' (symbolic) and 'English' forms. Relational Algebra gives an implementation-free way of describing the logic of database queries and, as such, serves as a good benchmark for the SQL in Chapter 7. Relational Algebra is also put to good use in Chapter 9, where Query Optimization is discussed.

Chapter 7 gives a comprehensive introduction to the SQL query language. SQL has become the standard language for querying databases and a full understanding of its power is a definite advantage to database programmers and even some end users. Studying SQL with a sufficiently wide-ranging set of examples is a good way of getting the flavour of what databases are really all about: answering queries.

Chapter 8 follows up the work of Chapters 3 to 5, moving from logical design towards physical representation. Popular database file organizations and indexing methods such as ISAM and B+ Trees are described. How indexes are created in SQL, and the appropriate choice of indexes, are discussed.

Chapter 9 looks at some important tasks normally associated with the Database Administration role. How to choose the file organization for particular application types, how to create Views using SQL and their applicability, security issues and the GRANT command, and Query Optimization are covered.

Chapter 10 discusses Recovery and Concurrency, covering in an introductory manner all of the significant aspects of these issues.

Exercises are liberally distributed throughout the text. Some answers are provided at the end of the book and in many cases answers can be found in the body of the text. In other cases, the exercise is provided in order to stimulate further thought on the particular subject. There might not be a clear answer to some of the exercises. In other cases there may be more than one answer. I hope in any case you find the exercises interesting, rather than just a drill. I hope also that as a result of reading this book you formulate some new questions of your own. Don't be disappointed if you cannot immediately get an answer. Many people find that one of the most satisfying pursuits that they can engage in is to try to find solutions to problems which they have themselves invented! It is in this creative and open-ended spirit that many of the exercises have been set.

To conclude, I hope you find the text interesting and informative. Any questions or comments you may have can be sent to me directly via electronic mail using the following email addresses. I look forward to hearing from you.

John Carter
Dagenham, 1994

john14@bkmain.uel.ac.uk
a27jc@uk.ac.uel.sol1

Chapter 1

The database approach

In this chapter you will learn:

- □ what is meant by the database approach;

- □ to explain the components of a DBMS;

- □ to describe the ANSI/SPARC model;

- □ to define the features to be expected in a 4GL;

- □ to outline the life cycle of a relational database.

The database approach

Centralization

One of the main contributions that the installation of a large shared database management system (DBMS) makes to an organization is to encourage it to consider its data as a resource which is central to its operations and decision making. In non-database installations, where individual applications are developed with specific purposes, an overall system view of the data is unlikely to exist.

Consistency and removal of data duplication

Data in a non-database installation may be fragmented and accessible only by the applications for which it was designed. In some cases, applications are developed in different languages and this may result in data being held in incompatible formats.

Duplication of data may occur, the same fact being held in different data files. If the value of a data fact changes, it is difficult to know where to look in the system to update the fact.

With the database approach, a database schema (an overall design for the database), is produced. This centralized planning, if correctly performed, will result in a database design in which each data fact is stored only once. All the data is in the same format and thus compatible. Instead of the applications being seen as primary, with peripheral data files, the database approach sees the data as central.

The database approach sees data as central and seeks to remove data duplication.

Users may have
different views of the
data.

Consistent world view

The database schema is seen as a data model of that part of the real world in which the organization is interested. Objects (we call them entity types) that are related in the real world are related on the database when it is designed. Because the database is 'like' the real world, it is possible, (using a query language), to make queries, ask questions of the database and get answers to these queries without having to wait for specialized programs to be written, and to ask these questions in a way that relates to the real world. It is also possible for different users to have different views of the same data, to see only the data they need and in a suitable format, for their usual applications.

A major advantage of the database approach is that, via the schema, which is in a sense an 'official' interpretation of the organization's world, all parts of the organization will be 'speaking the same language'. We show in Chapters 3 and 4 how this model is developed. Having an agreed schema diagram and data definitions can improve the communications between different sections within the organization and help prevent confusing differences in terminology arising. In this sense it can increase the cohesiveness of an organization. All the more important then, that the schema should be 'right' at the outset. (In Chapters 3 and 4 we do assume that there is a correct interpretation of the organization's data; the techniques given – entity relationship modelling and normalization are given as a method for discovery of this correct model.)

Exercise 1.1

1. Is there such a thing as a 'correct' view of the world, or is it all a matter of opinion? Perhaps you take a middle view and maintain that some views or models are better than others but none is likely to be perfect. If so, how would you decide one model was better than another? What would be your criteria?

2. How would you translate this into criteria for a 'good' database schema design? What are your criteria? Write a list.

Program–data independence

Minor modifications to data structures on the database can be made without changes to application programs (program–data independence). In a traditional (e.g. COBOL) application, this is not so. A change to a file structure is likely to require editing and recompilation of all applications accessing that file.

Security

When data is centralized, it becomes possible to control access to it. There are several reasons why this might be considered desirable. Accidental

insertion of incorrect data is one reason. If specific classes of user are
restricted in their access to the specific sections of the database that they are
concerned with, the likelihood of incorrect updates is reduced. Secrecy is
another reason. The organization may not want some types of data to be
generally available. It is also possible to reduce the chances of unsolicited
updates occurring. In a relational database the potential for one-off and
undetected access to data facts is greatly increased by the use of a query
language, but built-in security commands ensure that the specified classes of
user can only access (read, insert or change) prescribed data. The measures
that can be taken are described in Chapter 9.

Access to data can be controlled.

Database statistics

Since all data accesses to a database are under the control of a centralized
DBMS, it is possible to keep statistics on the quantities and types of database access. Frequently occurring types of access can be made faster by
introducing appropriate indexes. In a relational database, introducing an
index will not require the user or application program to change its processing style; the same interactive query language commands or application
program code can be used.

Knowledge of database usage patterns can be used to 'tune' the database.

Database administrator (DBA)

Centralization also has the benefit that one person – the DBA, or in some
larger installations a DBA team, can be made responsible for data organization, use of indexes, security, and other 'global' issues. Since all of the relevant information is 'in one head' or at least immediately accessible to a
close-knit group of responsible staff, it is easier to ensure the overall consistency and integrity of the database.

The DBA is an important job role in database installations.

Components of a DBMS

The single most obvious change that occurs when the database approach
is taken, is the purchase and introduction of the DBMS. As we shall see,
there are various broad types of DBMS (hierarchical, network, relational,
object oriented) that can be purchased. This book pays particular attention to the relational DBMS, of which there are in turn several products
on the market. All modern relational DBMSs contain the following
components.

The DBMS controls all accesses to the database.

File manager

The most fundamental part of the DBMS is the file manager. All file crea-
tions, record insertions, deletions and modifications are controlled via the
file manager. Another of its responsibilities is to keep track of where each
item of data is held and its format and the relationships between data.

Query language

Chapter 7: SQL
CREATE & SELECT
Chapter 8: SQL
CREATE INDEX
Chapter 9: SQL
GRANT PRIVILEGE.

Interactive dialogues between user and database are via a query language, two popular examples being QUEL and SQL. SQL has in recent years become the standard query language and it is described in detail in Chapter 7. The essence of interactive query language usage is in the formulation of *ad hoc* queries, in which the user writes a short query to find an immediate answer to a query that he or she has derived. SQL statements can be typed in interactively in this manner, or can be embedded in a host program written in a 3GL (third generation) language such as COBOL, FORTRAN, C or PL/I. The embedded SQL commands define the data to be fetched or modified, and the host program provides formatted user interactions (screens, reports) and decides the conditions under which the SQL commands are to be executed.

See page 297 for
some sample
embedded SQL.

Interactive SQL provides the user with set-oriented access to the database. The database is considered to be a number of sets of data called tables or relations and the user provides conditions in the SQL statement to specify which elements of these sets he or she wants to access.

Embedded SQL provides the host program record-at-a-time access via cursors, which are pointers to the current record in a database table.

4GL facilities

4GL features allow rapid development of database applications.

There is no universally accepted definition of 4GL (fourth generation language). We present here the items which are likely to be called 4GL features.

Screen painters are used for input design.

Starting at the input end, a screen painter may be provided. This allows sophisticated input and update screens to be produced with minimal effort on the part of the programmer. Using this facility, the user is presented with a form on the screen, consisting of a set of fields in which data can be entered or modified. The whole form is accepted or rejected by the system. Some fields may be protected, that is they do not allow data values to be changed. One screen may be used to input or modify data from more than one database table. Screens produced by this method may be embedded in host programs.

Report writers aid fast production of formatted reports.

Another 4GL feature to be expected in a modern DBMS is a report writer. This utility allows formatted reports, derived from one or more database tables, to be easily produced without complex coding. Report writer code may also be embedded in host programs. In fact, once standard screens and forms have been defined they can be placed in a library and inserted in several different programs as required, thus further reducing programming effort.

A code generator is a powerful 4GL tool.

In some applications, it is merely necessary to specify the input and output via screens and reports and the DBMS will generate all the connecting code itself. Such code generation features are common on the more sophisticated relational DBMSs. The generated code is accessible to the programmer, who may then make minor modifications.

In some DBMSs, such as INGRES, a specialized procedural database programming language is provided. The language is, unlike 3GLs, which purport to be general purpose, specifically attuned to database access. Screen definitions, reports, and database queries can all be embedded in code written in this language. In INGRES, this language is called INGRES 4GL. ORACLE has a comparable utility called SQL*FORMS, in which whole procedures can be triggered, depending on the values the user types into specified input fields and the values on the database. In ORACLE, reports are produced by a separate piece of software SQL*REPORT. These two functions can be tied together in 3GL host programs. On the micro front, dBASE and many of its clones contain purpose-built procedural languages in which screens, reports and SQL commands can be embedded.

Integrated CASE tool

In some modern relational DBMSs, the above facilities are supplemented by the use in the package of integrated CASE (Computer Aided Software Engineering) features. The integrated CASE tool allows the database designer to draw entity-relationship diagrams interactively using graphics facilities, and thus to develop the database schema and make changes where necessary. The entity types become, when attributes are added, database table definitions. The CASE tool can then automatically generate the actual database tables from these definitions. Integrity rules (rules which govern the values that attributes can take) can also be defined at this stage. The processes involved in performing these steps are detailed in Chapters 3 to 5.

Integrated CASE tools are becoming common in modern DBMSs.

The ANSI/SPARC model

By 1975, the database approach had gained wide acceptance as a viable and worthwhile approach to solving many data processing problems and a large number of products of different types were coming onto the market. In order to provide some standardization in concepts and terminology, the ANSI/X3/SPARC committee produced in 1978 its final version of what has since become known as the ANSI/SPARC model. ANSI is the American National Standards Institute. ANSI/X3 is its Committee on Computers and Information Processing, and SPARC is that committee's Standards Planning and Requirements Committee. The model concentrates on defining and standardizing the interfaces between the various parts of the DBMS and its various users. The essentials of its recommended database system architecture are shown in Fig. 1.1.

The ANSI/SPARC model shows the architecture of typical DBMS.

Although the terminology shown in Fig. 1.1 is not now in universal use, the essential feature is the three level architecture. At the middle level is the conceptual view of the database, which corresponds closely to what in this book we will call the logical schema, and which in this book we will realize

The conceptual view models the entire system's data.

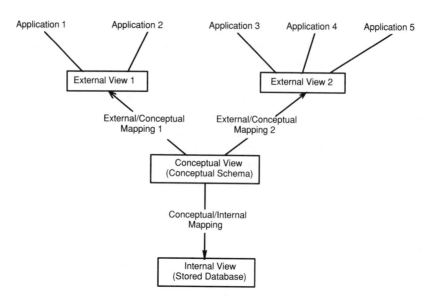

Fig. 1.1   ANSI/SPARC three-level database architecture.

in the form of an entity relationship diagram and a set of normalized relations or table definitions.

External Views give users a simplified view of the data, geared to their individual needs.

As mentioned above, the various classes of user will not all require access to all of the database parts corresponding to the complete logical schema, and will want to have views of the database more closely related to the types of operation they want to perform. Some users for example might never want to be able to access individual records in a delivery table, but will want to see summary data derived from these records. As we shall see in Chapters 3 to 5, data analysis (entity relationship modelling and normalization) tends to split data up into small groups relating to distinct entities in the real world. Some users will want to see reports on screens and paper that contain a combination of data items selected from several tables. The ANSI/SPARC external view level is intended to provide these user-oriented views of the database.

The Internal View reflects the physical storage of data.

Ultimately, the data on a database is represented by binary 1 and 0 bits on a backing storage medium, usually a hard disk. The actual representation of the data on the disk might not appear very similar in structure to the logical schema. For example, the logical schema might on a particular system be represented in a relational way as a set of tables with primary keys and foreign keys, but be represented at a more 'physical' level as a set of files, records and pointers. This level is known in the ANSI/SPARC model as the internal view. These are the three basic levels defined by ANSI/SPARC.

'Mappings' relate the conceptual, External and Internal Views.

Between the levels are mappings, which show, for example, which conceptual schema constructs go to make up an external schema construct, and similarly, how conceptual schema constructs are realized physically.

Logical and physical

The terms logical and physical are in such widespread use in information systems theory and practice that it is worthwhile noting their meanings in this context, particularly since they are so different from normal usage.

Logical is used to describe the user-oriented view of computer usage and physical the computer-oriented view. There is not a clear-cut distinction between the two in practice; rather there is a continuum between them. For example, when designing the database schema, we would use the term logical when describing our ideas about the real-world objects (customers, products, etc.) we want to model, and from that point of view, think of the database itself as tending towards the physical. However, from the point of view of a systems programmer writing a part of the file manager of the DBMS, table definitions would be seen as relatively 'logical' compared to the questions of disk tracks and sectors that he or she is then considering.

Exercise 1.2

See if you can think of a viable explanation of why the logical/physical terminology grew up in computing. Discuss this with colleagues. The more philosophical of you will have an advantage here. You might like to consider in your discussion the following questions. Are people logical? Are they physical? Are they both? Are computers and their applications (e.g. DBMSs) logical? Are they physical? Are they both? Is a conceptual schema logical? Is it physical when it is written down? Is it both? Use the traditional meanings of logical and physical here.

'Logical' and 'Physical' in a database context may not correspond to normal usage of these words.

The life cycle of a relational database

Figure 1.2 shows the stages in the development of a typical database. Notice that on the right of the diagram there is a feedback loop from each stage to every other stage. This represents an admission that a full understanding of a problem and its solution is likely to evolve as the various stages of design and implementation proceed. The designer will often have to go back and refine or alter earlier stages as this understanding develops.

First, the designer must try to obtain as complete as possible an understanding of the real-world problem that is going to be helped by the introduction of a database. This understanding of the nature of the problem and the constraints and outline feasible solutions is often performed using some systems analysis methodology. Many methodologies, such as SSADM and Information Engineering overlap with Fig. 1.2.

Next, an entity relationship diagram is drawn (Chapter 3) and this will serve, perhaps in a modified form, as an essential part of the logical schema. Attributes of the entity types so produced are then added. Primary and

Note the various 'revision' paths in Fig. 1.2.

'SSADM' stands for Structured Systems Analysis and Design Method.

Entity-Relationship modelling is covered in Chapter 3.

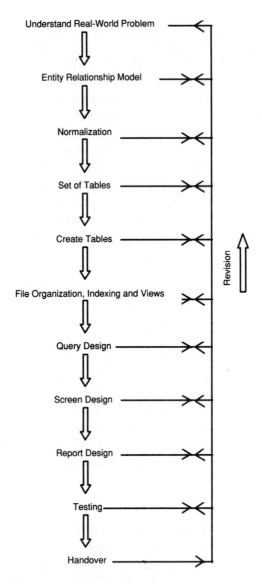

Fig. 1.2   Life cycle of a database.

Normalization is covered in Chapters 4 and 5.

foreign keys are specified. Normalization (Chapters 4 and 5) is then used to check the entity relationship model. Some splitting and even recombination of entity types may result from normalization and the entity relationship model will have to be updated accordingly. The entity relationship model and the table definitions resulting from normalization should be consistent.

CREATE TABLE is covered on page 178.

The database tables can then be created, normally by the DBA (Database Administrator), most probably in the case of a relational database, using SQL CREATE TABLE commands. Primary and even foreign keys and integrity rules can be specified at this stage. Chapter 7 describes the process of creating tables. Chapter 8 discusses how the file organization is decided and also includes details of which indexes should be created. Indexing will in practice be an ongoing process, because which indexes should be created depends to a large extent on the practical performance statistics achieved by the completed database and its applications and these statistics can only be reliably ascertained after implementation.

See page 253 for CREATE INDEX.

Query design is shown as the next stage, although by this stage, probably even from the outset, the designer(s) should have a good idea of the main types of query and report the database will have to accommodate, as a knowledge of the queries and reports will influence earlier stages in the life cycle.

Screen design is partially determined by the data items that must be input and output by particular applications, and partially in HCI (Human Computer Interface) terms. This latter is concerned with aspects of the screen design (colour, fonts, quantity of data per screen, prompts, etc.) and the nature of the dialogue between user and application. Some of the options that may be considered are simple question–answer dialogues (suitable for casual or infrequent users of well-defined applications); menus consisting of several numbered options which can be performed in various orders depending on user needs (more suitable for regular users who understand more about the application); pull-down menus, a variant of the above where a mouse is used to select an option, which then causes a more narrowly defined set of options to be displayed; and windows, a popular approach at the moment which gives the user the opportunity to perform several sub-tasks concurrently. For example, part-way through entering an order in one window, the user may decide to open another window on the database to inspect stock levels, another to check the time on a clock window, and another to send a message to another user. More and more software products, including DBMSs, are adopting this approach and offering versions of their software that are compatible with Microsoft Windows and X Window. However, several vendors already have well established screen-oriented data entry and update utilities and the DBMS in use at the particular installation will have a large influence on the HCI. For maximum speed of data entry, the use of function keys and perhaps a completely specialized keyboard mapping may be implemented. This is most suited to high-volume specialized usage, and can sometimes present obstacles to novice users, although help screens can mitigate this difficulty to some extent. Screen design is best performed in liaison with the prospective users of those screens.

Report design is another area where input from users is paramount. They will specify what they want to see on the reports and the format of the reports and in the case of regular reports, when they should be produced. Most DBMSs have standard report writers which in many cases will suffice. More complex applications may require the use of embedded code, as described above (pages 4–5).

A test database is a
valuable development
resource.

Testing is shown as the next step. Key queries, input and update screens and report programs will serve as the ultimate test of the correctness of the database schema and the viability of the system as a whole. Serious consideration should be given to the creation of a test database (a database with the same schema as the intended 'live' system, but with carefully designed test data). The test database will continue to be useful as a 'testbed' for schema changes and new and modified applications. Before a change or application goes live, it should be thoroughly tested on the test database.

Handover is shown as the final stage. This is the stage where the users receive the finished database and applications and begin data entry. In practice, it is likely that the core of the system will be handed over to users and later extensions to the system will be implemented. Careful testing of the system before handover will minimize the expense of later modifications to the schema and major applications. Faulty applications in particular can introduce incorrect data onto the database which may require considerable time and effort to detect and correct. Fortunately the power and utility of query languages such as SQL can help in this respect and remove the necessity for designing special 'fix-up' programs. In the past it has been known for the fix-up or 'maintenance' programs to become so comprehensive that they ultimately become applications in their own right!

Chapter 10 discusses
Recovery and
Concurrency.

Other considerations that should be addressed are the questions of recovery and concurrency. While the latter is likely to be taken care of by the DBMS itself, there are policy issues to be decided with respect to recovery. These are discussed in Chapter 10.

Is it a database application?

The answer to this question is not always obvious. However, here are some basic points which should help in making this decision. A database application is likely to involve the storage of large numbers of similarly structured objects or entities and relationships between them. Most accounting systems have this attribute. There will be large numbers of customers, and you will want to store the same attributes for each one. The same will be true of invoices that you send them and the payments and orders you receive from them. The relationships between entity types will be of a fixed number and type. The entity types and relationships will be capable of being named.

Data in a relational
database is presented
in a tabular fashion.

There will be few if any 'special cases'. The data should be capable of being presented in a tabular fashion. The structure of the data (vested in the schema) should remain relatively static. A major feature of most applications should be search, that is, scanning through files (tables) for records (rows) that fulfil some criteria.

Here are some applications that are probably not database applications:

* Designing a bridge or an aircraft wing. Here there is only one object. The major effort is in numerical calculation and possibly graphics. CAD

(Computer Aided Design) software, possibly tailored to the particular problem type, is probably indicated.

* Game playing or military strategy. While data will be involved and stored and updated, the emphasis is on problem solving in particular cases.

* Financial planning. A large element of 'what if' exists in this type of problem. Spreadsheets or specialized software are likely to be more suitable than a pure database system.

Exercise 1.3

Produce a list of typical database applications and a list of applications that are not suitable for a database approach, giving reasons. You will probably find that your first list contains many commercial applications. Why? Try to include in this first list as many noncommercial applications as you can. Could the design of a road network or genetic engineering benefit from a database approach? Is it true that some applications are partially database applications? In these cases, how would you interface the database to other software?

Chapter 2

The relational database

In this chapter you will learn:

- ☐ to define the three major types of DBMS;

- ☐ to define the characteristics of the ideal relational database according to Codd's 12 rules.

Introduction

An *n*-ary relation is a table with n columns.

Normal forms are intended to simplify data structures for databases.

SQL has become a universal data manipulation language.

E.F. Codd originated the idea of relational databases in his seminal paper of 1970 (Codd, 1970). In it he proposed a model for data storage based on *n*-ary relations, a normal form for database relations, and the concept of a universal data manipulation language based on relational algebra, a branch of mathematics.

Subsequently, further work on the relational model took two major paths, development of methods of data representation around the definition of further normal forms, and the development of a universal data manipulation language, culminating today in SQL (Structured Query Language), which itself has been realized in several SQL standards.

In Chapters 4 and 5 we look in detail at the various normal forms and in Chapters 6 and 7 at the data manipulation aspects, with particular reference to relational algebra and SQL.

However, we first take a brief look at the kinds of DBMS types that preceded the relational one. Whilst it is true that these earlier types of DBMS still exist, our major purpose here is to consider the shortcomings in these DBMSs that motivated work on the relational model.

Prerelational DBMS types

Two major types of DBMS, the hierarchical and the network DBMSs (the latter formalized in the CODASYL model), preceded the relational approach. We shall not study these in detail, but describe the overall approach. One of the first selling-points for the database approach and the purchase of a DBMS was that, unlike paper-based and other computerized systems of information storage, the DBMS could represent complex relationships between data items. These relationships were represented by pointers. If, for example, you wanted to store data about customers, their invoices, and the payments they had made, you would first create a CUS-TOMER file, an INVOICE file and a PAYMENT file. There were no design rules enforcing this however; prerelational database design was largely intuitive and governed by performance considerations involving prespecified programs. Assuming you had these three files, you would want to show which invoices belonged to which customers and which payments related to which invoices. How this is performed in the hierarchical, CODASYL and relational models is described below.

DBMSs can represent complex relationships.

The hierarchical model

There have been (and are) several hierarchical DBMSs in existence, a notable example being IBM's IMS product. In a hierarchical database, the relationships mentioned above could be implemented by having CUSTOMER, INVOICE and PAYMENT files (sometimes known as record types). The INVOICEs relating to a given CUSTOMER would be held contiguously (together) as part of an INVOICE file and a pointer from a particular CUS-TOMER would give the disk address of the beginning of that customer's invoices in the INVOICE file (Fig. 2.1). An INVOICE pointer would be contained in each CUSTOMER record.

A hierarchy is a tree-like structure.

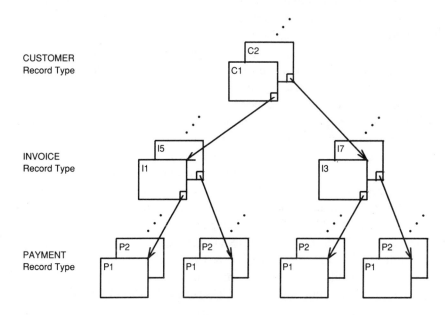

Fig. 2.1 A hierarchy of data in an entity-relationship model.

Fig.2.1 shows typical
accounting data
represented in a
hierarchical manner.

Each INVOICE record would in turn contain a PAYMENT pointer, point-ing to the set of payment records for that invoice in the PAYMENT file. The advantage of the pointers in performance terms was that, for example, given a particular CUSTOMER, you could quickly find the address of all INVOICEs because this address was held in the CUSTOMER record – no need to sequentially search the INVOICE file or indexes. Answering the query:

'Which invoices were sent to this customer?'

would be performed quickly. Unfortunately, answering the query:

'Who was this invoice sent to?'

(or more grammatically 'To whom was this invoice sent?') would not be performed quickly via the pointers because the INVOICE records only con-tained 'downwards' pointers. You would have to search the CUSTOMER file to see which record contained a pointer containing the address of the INVOICE. The program code for performing these closely related queries would be entirely different. This can be called query asymmetry. Provided it was usual in the set of processes at the installation to access 'downwards' through the hierarchy, efficient processing resulted. In fact the placement of pointers was decided on the basis of expected processing needs. If company information needs changed and one or more important processes required

Queries 'up' the tree
are difficult in
hierarchical databases.

accesses 'upwards' through the hierarchy, either major database reorganiza-tion, duplication of data or the introduction of indexes would have to be tried. This signals one deficiency in the hierarchical approach. The system does not have program-data independence. The data structures have been set up with certain processes in mind and when these change or are extended, the data structures have to be altered.

In the example above, the data relationships are inherently hierarchical (although as we have seen this does not mean that all of the required pro-cessing will be). One CUSTOMER (owner or master record type) will have many INVOICES (member or detail record type), but each INVOICE is related to just one CUSTOMER. This is expressed by saying that the rela-tionship between CUSTOMER and INVOICE is a one–many relationship (1:N). Similarly, INVOICE:PAYMENT is 1:N. The whole data structure is tree shaped, much like the 1970s management structure in IBM perhaps. The hierarchical structure involving CUSTOMER, INVOICE and PAY-MENT is shown in the small entity-relationship diagram (more on these in Chapter 3) in Fig. 2.2. The relationships are shown as 1:N by having a crowsfoot at the 'many' end.

In some situations, the data is not inherently hierarchical. Consider for example a situation in which it is possible for one payment to pay several invoices (Fig. 2.3). The relationship between INVOICE and PAYMENT is

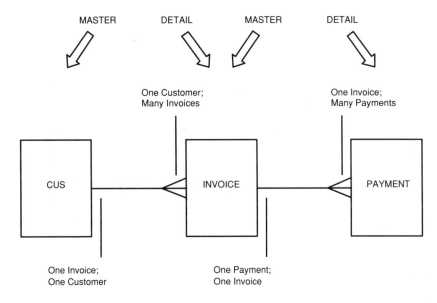

MASTER   DETAIL   MASTER   DETAIL

One Customer;
Many Invoices

One Invoice;
Many Payments

CUS   INVOICE   PAYMENT

One Invoice;
One Customer

One Payment;
One Invoice

Fig. 2.2   A hierarchy of data in an entity-relationship model.

now many–many (M:N), meaning that one INVOICE may be related to many PAYMENTs, and one PAYMENT may be related to many INVOICEs. ('Many' means zero or more.)

A hierarchical DBMS is not inherently suitable for representing this type of data. Different INVOICE records would own the same PAYMENT record, so the structure would no longer be hierarchical. If an attempt were made to put an 'upward' (i.e. 'backward') pointer in the PAYMENT record back to the set of INVOICEs that it paid, it would be found that the INVOICE records would not be in the correct order to show this; if the sequence was correct for one payment, it would not be correct for another payment. If an attempt was made to install a linker record type, such as INV_PMT in Fig. 2.4, answering either of the queries:

'Which payments were made against this invoice?'

or

'Which invoices was this payment for?'

would entail an access against (that is in the opposite direction to) the pointers.

The inability to handle many–many relationships was the main difficulty with the hierarchical model that the CODASYL model was designed to overcome.

> Hierarchical DBMSs have difficulty representing non-hierarchical data, such as that in Fig. 2.3.

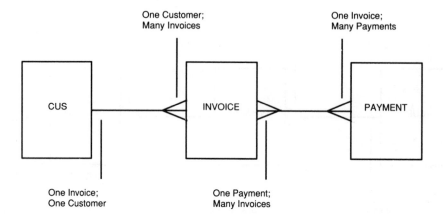

Fig. 2.3   A non-hierarchy between INVOICE and PAYMENT.

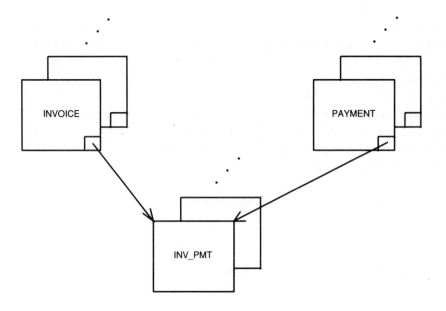

Fig. 2.4   Abortive attempt at representing an M:N via a linker in a hierarchical database.

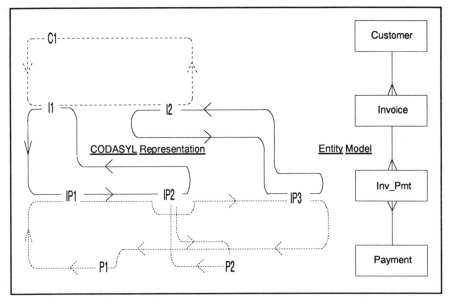

Fig. 2.5   The CODASYL model.

The CODASYL model

In the CODASYL model, every record involved in a relationship contains a pointer for that relationship. For example, in Fig. 2.5, where the records relating to customer C1 are shown, the fact that C1 owns INVOICE 1 and INVOICE 2 (I1 and I2) is represented by a pointer in C1 to I1 and a pointer from I1 to I2. The last INVOICE that C1 owns points back to the owning C1. The owner C1 and the members (here I1 and I2) are together called, in CODASYL parlance, a set. (This does not incidentally coincide with the mathematical meaning of a set, which is simply a collection of distinct elements.) It is this set concept that solves the first type of problem with the hierarchical model mentioned above. The query:

> 'Which invoices belong to customer C1?'

can be answered by following the chain of pointers from C1 to all of its invoices. In the hierarchical model this set of INVOICE records was associated either by proximity, that is, they were stored contiguously, or by a set of pointers. Because a pointer to the next record in the set is stored in each record in a CODASYL DBMS, the records in the set do not have to be held contiguously; a new INVOICE record for example can be stored in the next available space on the disk. The sequence is preserved by the pointer chain. More significantly, the query:

> 'To which customer does I1 belong?'

can be answered by following the pointer chain around (via I2 in this example) until the owner customer record C1 is found.

CODASYL DBMSs can represent many-to-many relationships without data duplication.

The second advantage the CODASYL model has over the hierarchical is that M:N relationships, such as INVOICE:PAYMENT in this example, can be stored, and without duplication. In Fig. 2.5, INVOICE:PAYMENT is represented using the linker record type INV_PMT and its records IP1, IP2 and IP3. The procedure for answering the query:

'Which payments has invoice I1 received?'

is as follows:

To answer queries on a CODASYL database, you have to navigate through the record types via pointers.

1. Fetch the I1 record and follow the pointer in the INVOICE–INV_PMT set around to retrieve record IP1. This will then be the current record in that set.
2. Follow the INV_PMT–PAYMENT set around via the pointers until the PAYMENT (P1) record is retrieved. Output this record. (Notice that P1 also paid I2.)
3. Follow the INV_PMT–PAYMENT set around until the original owner record IP1 is accessed.
4. Go back to the current record in the INVOICE–INV_PMT set (IP1) and fetch the next IP record if it exists, here, IP2.
5. Revert to the INV_PMT–PAYMENT set pointer in IP2 and list out the payment as above.
6. Go back to the current record in the INVOICE–INV_PMT set (IP2) and fetch next in that set. Here, it is the original I1 record, so the query is complete.

A similar procedure can be performed for answering the query:

'Which invoices did payment P1 pay?'

by starting from P1 and working back through the two sets mentioned to output I1 and I2.

While the CODASYL model solves the problems of the hierarchical model we mentioned, it has to be admitted that the procedure outlined above seems rather complex for such simple queries. Writing such procedures for navigating a CODASYL database is thus a detailed task. The model the programmer or analyst has in his or her mind when designing such procedures is physical, that is, close to the actual representation of the data on the physical storage devices.

Navigating a CODASYL database requires complex 3GL (COBOL, FORTRAN, PL/I, C) programs with specialized embedded DML (Data Manipulation Language) statements.

Another disadvantage of the CODASYL model is that the access paths a process must take are contained on the database itself. The logic of the procedure that has to be written depends on the physical organization of the data. For example, if a suitable pointer chain exists, then the procedure will be written one way; if it does not, then the procedure is written with different logic. The CODASYL model then still lacks full program-data independence.

The relational model

The essence of the relational approach is to represent data to the users (end users, analysts and programmers) as a set of relations (also known as tables) in which data is stored. Tables consist of a number of tuples (also known as rows), each row containing the same number of attributes (also known as columns). If you imagine a sheet of paper ruled up into rows (horizontal) and columns (vertical) you have a fair idea of how data is viewed in the relational model (Fig. 2.6). This approach corresponds fairly closely to conventional paper-based methods of data storage and presentation. It is the way we are used to seeing data represented.

The preceding example would be handled in a relational database in a much simpler fashion, as will be shown in later chapters.

In 1985, Codd (1985) published a set of 12 rules which he said any RDBMS (Relational Database Management System) should comply with. While most commercial RDBMSs do not comply with all of these rules, the rules represent an ideal against which the relational 'purity' of any database management system can be measured.

Codd's 12 rules follow.

We now consider these 12 rules, both as a means of specifying the essential nature of relational databases and of introducing the terminology used in this field.

You may wish to skim the rest of this chapter to obtain a preview of terminology and issues to be covered later on and, after having studied the rest of the book, to return to this section and review your understanding of Codd's rules.

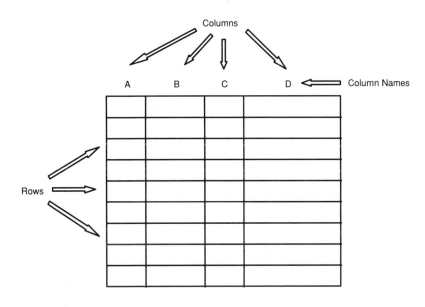

Fig. 2.6 The relational model.

Codd first specifies one overarching rule, Rule Zero:

> For any system that is advertised as, or claims to be, a relational database management system, that system must be able to manage databases entirely through its relational capabilities.

This is Codd's foundation rule. He says that 'Any DBMS that does not satisfy this Rule Zero is not worth rating as a relational DBMS'. This rule is not as stringent or specific as the combination of the 12 rules below. Rule Zero is saying that it should not be the case in a relational database that some database management functions can be performed using a relational approach, but that others must be performed by other means.

Rule 1: The information rule

> All information in a relational database is represented explicitly at the logical level and in exactly one way – by values in tables.

The 'logical level', as we saw in Chapter 1, is the view the users of the database get of the data in the database. This should always be in the form of values in tables. Other lower-level concepts such as pointers, sets, etc. should not be apparent to the users, even if they are used at the physical level. Appendix A shows several such database tables, which we shall be using as examples throughout this book. Note that all data is represented by values in rows and columns.

Rule 2: Guaranteed access rule

> Every datum (atomic value) in a relational database is guaranteed to be logically accessible by resorting to a combination of table name, primary key value, and column name.

The term 'datum' is the singular of 'data'. An atomic value is a datum which is not normally split, it is normally considered as a whole. Each intersection of a row and column in a table is an atomic value. For example the SNAME (Surname) of C_NO 4 in the CUS table in Appendix A is the atomic value Dziduch.

Every table has a unique (and hopefully meaningful) name. All tables in Appendix A have a unique name: CUS, INVOICE, PAYMENT, PRODUCT, etc.

A primary key is a set of one or more columns in each relation whose value uniquely identifies a particular row. For example, the primary key in the table CUS is C_NO. No two rows in CUS have that same value. Hence C_NO 4 uniquely identifies the row for Mr Dziduch. The primary key in table INVOICE is INV_NO. IN PAYMENT the primary key consists of the

Primary key values identify rows. Each row stores data about one real-world entity.

two columns INV_NO with PMT_NO. Neither of these columns on its own can be guaranteed to have unique values (there are in the sample data shown two rows with INV_NO 940 and two rows with PMT_NO 1). However, the two columns together should always have a unique value. Such a primary key is called a composite primary key.

By quoting the table name CUS, the primary key (C_NO) value 4, and the column name CRED_LIM, we are able to access the value 100, which is Mr Dziduch's credit limit. In a relational database, we should need no other concepts (such as indexes, pointers, pages, disk addresses, etc.) to retrieve this datum. Table name, primary key value, and column name are sufficient to access any data item.

Rule 3: Systematic treatment of null values

Null values (distinct from the empty character string or a string of blank characters and distinct from zero or any other number) are supported in a fully relational DBMS for representing missing information and inapplicable information in a systematic way, independent of data type.

When inserting rows into a table, some values may occasionally not be known. It is up to the database designers to decide what should be done in such a case. For example, when the row for C_NO 6 in the CUS table was inserted, the value of CRED_LIM had not yet been decided. The policy of the designers was to allow the program to input all the other values, but to place a null value in this field until the credit limit was known, at which point the field could be updated.

'Null values' is a special value intended for this kind of purpose. If it were not used, and any missing value in a field depended on the column name, for example '−1' for a missing credit limit (numeric data), and 'xxxxx' for a missing postcode (string data), etc., then this would be extra information that end users, analysts and programmers would have to know about the database. It has to be said however, that detecting a null value in a field does not in itself indicate what it means in that particular position. In the CRED_LIM column, our database designers have decided that it means 'as yet unknown'. In some other database it could mean 'this customer shall have no credit limit; he can owe us as much as he likes'. These are different meanings and will have to be generally agreed on in each position in which a null is allowed.

It should be possible to place a null in a field of any data type: string, numeric, date, logical, etc. One important question arising when a null is placed in a numeric column such as CRED_LIM is what should happen when an aggregate function such as MAX, MIN or AVG is applied to the column. In our particular case, if we wanted to calculate the AVG (average) value of CRED_LIM for the six customers in the CUS table, what should we do about C_NO 6, where CRED_LIM is null? Clearly, the best policy is

Null values may be used to 'mean' different things, but should be treated consistently by the DBMS.

SQL's treatment of NULL is discussed on page 186.

not to include C_NO 6's CRED_LIM in the calculation at all and divide the sum of the CRED_LIMs for customers 1 to 5 by five rather than six. This is how nulls are treated with aggregate functions in the SQL query language. The DBMS should have such systematic policies with respect to null built in. The primary key should never be nullable, since two rows with a null value for the primary key may not be otherwise distinguishable, and identical rows are not allowable in a relational database. The primary key is the only guaranteed mechanism for preventing identical rows.

The primary key should not be NULL-able.

Exercise 2.1

If the designers had decided that a null in CRED_LIM meant 'this customer shall have no credit limit; he or she can owe us as much as they like', and we asked the system to list the MAX (maximum) value of CRED_LIM that any customer has, what should be output? What should be output if we wanted to list the CUS rows for the customer or customers with the maximum credit limit? Find out what happens on your system. Assuming you have created a CUS table as in Appendix A, type the following SQL statements to find out:

See page 185 for details of SELECT syntax.

```
1 SELECT MAX(CRED_LIM)
2 FROM CUS;
1 SELECT *
2 FROM CUS
3 WHERE CRED_LIM =
4 (SELECT MAX(CRED_LIM)
5 FROM CUS);
```

Details of SQL syntax and usage are given in Chapter 7.

Rule 4: Dynamic on-line catalogue based on the relational model

The database description is represented at the logical level in the same way as ordinary data, so that authorized users can apply the same relational language to its interrogation as they apply to regular data.

The DBMS Data Dictionary contains information about the structure of the database.

Many 'relational' databases (the quotes mean DBMSs marketed as relational) contain a data dictionary. In a true relational database, according to this rule, the database description should itself be in tabular form. This is held usefully in an on-line data dictionary accessible via SQL, as with all the other tables.

In ORACLE, for example, every time you create a table, say CUS, there is a row automatically put into a data dictionary table called ALL_TABLES which shows details of the new CUS table. ALL_TABLES is itself a table and can be accessed in the same way that CUS can. By simply querying ALL_TABLES, you can find out details of the structure of the CUS and any other table on the database.

Exercise 2.2

Become familiar with the data dictionary in your relational database by checking the manuals. Typically, such information will be found in the DBA manual. Much useful information about tables, columns, views, users, and access privileges can be found in the data dictionary. In an ideal world, these data dictionary tables would be in the same standard format in all relational DBMSs but this is unfortunately not yet the case.

In ORACLE, the Data Dictionary can be accessed directly by SQL.

Rule 5: Comprehensive data sublanguage

A relational system may support several languages and modes of terminal use (for example, the fill-in-the-blanks mode). However, there must be at least one language whose statements are expressible, per some well-defined syntax, as character strings and that is comprehensive in supporting all of the following items:

SQL provides many of the requirements of Rule 5.

- data definition;
- view definition;
- data manipulation (interactive and by program);
- integrity constraints;
- authorization;
- transaction boundaries (begin, commit and rollback).

Even though there may be several ways of accessing the database, such as filling in screen forms for data entry, report writers for routine reports, query languages such as SQL and embedded code, there should be at least one language consisting of typed commands that can perform all of the above database functions.

Data definition is the process of defining the structure of the database tables: their names, their column names and types, their primary keys, permissible values, etc. In some DBMSs there is a special-purpose DDL (Data Definition Language) to define tables.

View definition is similarly the process of defining the tables and their columns and the selection criteria for the rows that go into a view. Views are described in more detail in Chapter 9.

Data manipulation is the process of inserting, deleting and accessing the rows and columns of the database tables. In some DBMSs there is a special-purpose DML (Data Manipulation Language).

Integrity constraints are the rules which govern such things as the values that can be placed in primary keys, the necessity of a foreign key value existing as a primary key value elsewhere, and the values of calculated fields. In some databases, these integrity rules and the associated procedures that ensure they are carried out, are defined in the database itself, rather than being left up to individual programs to implement.

Authorization relates to the access rights (read, update, insert, delete) that individual users and classes of user are allowed to have with respect to rows, columns and whole tables. These can be defined using the GRANT PRIVILEGE commands of SQL and are described in Chapter 9 (page 280).

Transaction boundaries are associated with database recovery and concurrency, which are discussed in Chapter 10. A transaction is an indivisible unit of database update activity which, if only partially completed, would result in database inconsistency. A transaction is committed when it has satisfactorily completed and rolled back (undone) if an error is detected during the transaction.

This rule is saying that all of these functions should be executed in the same language: a data sublanguage. Most of these functions are in fact included in most versions of SQL.

Rule 6: View updating

There should be no artificial constraints upon updating via views.

All views that are theoretically updatable are also updatable by the system.

Most DBMSs place restrictions on the updates to base tables (tables that actually exist on the database) that are allowable via a view. Since a view is, roughly speaking, a combination of subsets of rows and columns of one or more base tables, questions such as the following (and more complex ones) arise. Suppose we have the base table CUS as defined in the Appendix, and we also have a view defined on CUS called CUS_BASIC, which contains only the columns C_NO, SNAME and BALANCE. Should we be allowed to insert via this view? If so, what should happen to the values of the other fields such as TITLE, INITS, etc.?

By 'theoretically updatable' Codd means updates which could go ahead according to current, agreed, established theory. Some DBMSs will of course lag behind such theory, and worse, some may even contravene it. The problem is that a complete theory of view updates has not yet been universally agreed. This rule is saying that DBMSs which are claimed to be relational should not lag behind such theory.

Rule 7: High-level insert, update and delete

The capability of handling a base relation or a derived relation as a single operand applies not only to the retrieval of data but also to the insertion, update and deletion of data.

Instead of first defining the row to be updated and then updating it, using a row-by-row approach, the table or view should first be defined as a single operand in one command, and the update values and criteria sent for the whole update. A simple SQL example involving the PRODUCT table in Appendix A follows:

You can update a whole table using one SQL command.

```
1 UPDATE PRODUCT
2 SET PRICE = PRICE * 0.9
3 WHERE QIS > 2 * REORDQ;
```

This single command implements a 10% price cut on all rows in the PRODUCT table where there is plenty of stock, i.e. QIS (Quantity in stock) is over twice REORDQ (Reorder quantity – the stock level below which the company reorders more stock). Here, many updates are occurring and only one command has had to be issued. It would be slower, and in the case of a remote database, incur greater communications costs, if a separate command had to be issued for the update of each row.

Rule 8: Physical data independence

Application programs and terminal activities remain logically unimpaired whenever any changes are made in either storage representation or access methods.

We have previously called this program-data independence. If a change is made to the physical organization of the database, by for example deleting a set in a CODASYL database, then many programs and queries may have to be rewritten. In a fully relational database, this rule is saying, this should not be necessary. A clear distinction between the physical representation of data and the logical view presented to the user (via the 'mappings' in ANSI/SPARC terms – see Chapter 1, Fig.1.1) should be made. The user view of the data and hence the logical processing involved in a program or query should not have to be changed when such physical changes are made. In a relational database, a change to the physical storage sequence of records or the introduction or removal of an index should (and usually does) have no effect on the code of programs and queries and the corresponding database contents and output. Some performance differences such as access time (hopefully reduced) may of course result from such physical changes.

Changing file organization (page 235) or indexes (page 253) should not require changes to programs and SQL queries.

Rule 9: Logical data independence

Application programs and terminal activities remain logically unimpaired when information-preserving changes of any kind that theoretic-ally permit unimpairment are made to the base tables.

An example of an 'information preserving change' is to split a table by rows or columns for, say, performance reasons. The data content will still be the same. Say for example we split the CUS table by rows such that all London customers were in CUS_LON and all others in CUS_REST. It should then be possible to define a view with the original name CUS on these new base tables so that all processes which previously accessed CUS can still access it without change. This can be done in SQL for example by:

Users now access CUS as a view rather than a base table. This should be transparent to the user.

```
1 CREATE VIEW CUS AS
2 SELECT * FROM CUS_LON
3 UNION
4 SELECT * FROM CUS_REST;
```

after redistributing the rows of the original CUS table to CUS_LON and CUS_REST and dropping the CUS base table. As far as the users are concerned, CUS still exists; it is however now a view rather than a base table.

Rule 10: Integrity independence

Integrity constraints specific to a particular relational database must be definable in the relational data sublanguage and storable in the catalog, not in the application programs.

INGRES allows integrity constraints to be implemented via rules and procedures which are held on the database itself.

In Chapter 4, a database rule and an associated procedure are given which ensure that before an INVOICE row can be entered, a CUS row exists whose C_NO primary key value is the same as the C_NO foreign key value in INVOICE. (This is an example of the referential integrity rule – see Chapter 4.) The rule and procedure are stored in the database catalog as an integral part of the database itself, rather than in each application program that inserts an INVOICE row. This is desirable, since any modifications to a rule then only have to be made once, rather than updating all the copies in the programs. This feature is available in the latest versions of INGRES. The language used to incorporate such integrity rules and procedures is similar to SQL.

Rule 11: Distribution independence

A relational DBMS has distribution independence.

The user should not have to know where the data is physically located.

This means that even if data in different tables or even rows or columns in one table are geographically distributed at different sites, as far as the user is concerned, the data all appears to be at one site. The user should not have to know where the data is or how it is distributed. Even if data is redistrib-uted several times among different sites, this should remain transparent to the user. No changes to programs or interactive queries and updates should have to occur. Relational databases have a natural advantage in this respect. Relationships between tuples are via logical (real-world) values contained in primary and foreign keys. When a tuple is relocated, the values do not change, and so the relationship between, say, a CUS record in London for C_NO 1 and an INVOICE record in Aberdeen for C_NO 1 remain, even if either of the records is subsequently moved. In a hierarchical or CODASYL database, relationships are represented by physical device address pointers and hence movement of records from one site to another is inclined to present problems. With a relational database, upgrading from a single-site database to a distributed database (of the same vendor preferably), should present no problems due to distribution dependence.

Rule 12: Nonsubversion

> If a relational system has a low-level (single-record-at-a-time) language, that low level language cannot be used to subvert or bypass the integrity rules and constraints expressed in the higher level relational language (multiple-records-at-a-time).

In most commercial RDBMSs, it is possible to perform record-by-record processing using a host-language program and embedded query language statements. These embedded query language statements should be (and usually are) subject to the same constraints as the interactive use of the query language. In particular, it should not be possible to bypass the integrity constraints governing the database. For example, it should not be possible to insert a duplicate row, or a row with a duplicate or null primary key value, or (in the example above), an INVOICE with no 'owning' CUS row.

3GL procedural programs interface to the database via embedded SQL commands.

Fully relational databases

If a DBMS complies with all 12 of the above rules, it qualifies, according to Codd, as being fully relational. In practice, not all features of all of the DBMSs that are marketed as being relational fully obey all of these rules. The rules represent a standard and relational DBMSs are gradually coming closer to the ideal they represent. In the following chapters, the ideas presented here are further developed.

Chapter 3

Entity-relationship modelling

In this chapter you will learn:

- ☐ to explain the need for entity-relationship modelling;

- ☐ to explain the terms entity-relationship model, entity-relationship diagram;

- ☐ to define the terms entity type, entity, attribute, attribute value, primary key, relationship, relationship type, inverse relationship type;

- ☐ to explain ways of classifying relationship types;

- ☐ to define the terms unary, binary, ternary, degree, cardinality and optionality with regard to relationship types;

- ☐ to define mutually exclusive relationship types;

- ☐ to show alternative entity-relationship diagramming conventions;

- ☐ to show how many–many relationship types can be split into one–many relationship types;

- ☐ to give various examples of entity-relationship modelling.

Introduction

When a relational database is to be designed, an entity-relationship diagram is drawn at an early stage and developed as the requirements of the database and its processing become better understood. Drawing an entity-relationship diagram aids understanding of an organization's data needs and can serve as a schema diagram for the required system's database. Nearly all systems analysis and design methodologies contain entity-relationship diagramming as an important part of the methodology and nearly all CASE (Computer Aided Software Engineering) tools contain the facility for drawing entity-relationship diagrams. An entity-relationship diagram could serve as the basis for the design of the files in a conventional file-based system as well as for a schema diagram in a database system.

The details of how to draw the diagrams vary slightly from one method to another, but they all have the same basic elements: entity types, attributes and relationships. These three categories are considered to be sufficient to model the essentially static data-based parts of any organization's information processing needs.

Entity types

An entity type is any type of object that we wish to store data about. Which entity types you decide to include on your diagram depends on your application. In an accounting application for a business you would store data about customers, suppliers, products, invoices and payments and if the business manufactured the products, you would need to store data about materials and production steps. Each of these would be classified as an entity type because you would want to store data about each one. In an entity-relationship diagram an entity type is shown as a box. In Fig. 3.1, CUSTOMER is an entity type. Each entity type is shown once. There may be many entity types in an entity-relationship diagram. The name of an entity type is singular since it represents a type.

> An entity type is any type of object we wish to store data about.

An entity type is considered to be a set of objects. For this reason some people use the alternative term entity set. An entity is simply one member or example or element or instance of the type or set. So an entity is one individual within an entity type. For example, within the entity type CUSTOMER, J. Smith might be one entity. He is an individual entity within the type, an element in the set, an instance of the type 'customer'.

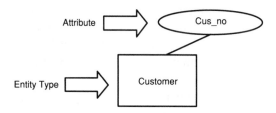

Fig. 3.1 Representing entity types and attributes on an entity-relationship diagram.

Attributes

The data that we want to keep about each entity within an entity type is contained in attributes. An attribute is some quality about the entities that we are interested in and want to hold on the database. In fact we store the value of the attributes on the database. Each entity within the entity type will have the same set of attributes, but in general different attribute values. For example the value of the attribute ADDRESS for a customer J. Smith in

> Every entity in an entity type has the same set of attributes.

a CUSTOMER entity type might be '10 Downing St., London' whereas the value of the attribute 'address' for another customer J. Major might be '22 Railway Cuttings, Cheam'.

There will be the same number of attributes for each entity within an entity type. That is one of the characteristics of entity-relationship modelling and relational databases. We store the same type of facts (attributes) about every entity within the entity type. If you knew that one of your customers happened to be your cousin, there would be no attribute to store that fact in, unless you wanted to have a 'cousin-yes-no' attribute, in which case nearly every customer would be a 'no', which would be considered a waste of space.

Primary key

A primary key is used to identify each entity.

Attributes can be shown on the entity-relationship diagram in an oval. In Fig. 3.1, one of the attributes of the entity type CUSTOMER is shown. It is up to you which attributes you show on the diagram. In many cases an entity type may have ten or more attributes. There is often not room on the diagram to show all of the attributes, but you might choose to show an attribute that is used to identify each entity from all the others in the entity type. This attribute is known as the primary key. In some cases you might need more than one attribute in the primary key to identify the entities.

In Fig. 3.1, the attribute CUS_NO is shown. Assuming the organization storing the data ensures that each customer is allocated a different cus_no, that attribute could act as the primary key, since it identifies each customer; it distinguishes each customer from all the rest. No two customers have the same value for the attribute cus_no. Some people would say that an attribute is a candidate for being a primary key because it is 'unique'. They mean that no two entities within that entity type can have the same value of that attribute.

A composite primary key contains more than one attribute.

As already mentioned, you may need to have a group of attributes to form a primary key, rather than just one attribute, although the latter is more common. For example if the organization using the CUSTOMER entity type did not allocate a customer number to its customers, then it might be necessary to use a composite key, for example one consisting of the attributes SURNAME and INITIALS together, to distinguish between customers with common surnames such as Smith. Even this may not be sufficient in some cases.

Primary keys are not the only attributes you might want to show on the entity-relationship diagram. For example, in a manufacturing organization you might have an entity type called COMPONENT and you want to make it clear on the entity-relationship diagram that the entities within the type are not single components but a component type such as a BC109 transistor. There are thousands of BC109s in stock and any one will do for any application. It is therefore not necessary to identify each BC109 differently (they all look and work the same). However you might want to distinguish BC109s from another transistor type BC108. To make it clear that you are considering all the BC109s as one entity and all the BC108s as another entity, you might put the attribute QIS (quantity in stock) on the entity-relationship diagram as in Fig. 3.2. This makes it clearer at the entity-relationship model level that each entity in the entity type is in fact a stock item of which there will be several in stock. Any doubts on this point should be resolved by inspecting the entity description, which shows all the attributes of the entity type and (ideally) their meaning. The primary key might be STOCK_NO and one of the attributes QIS, which should remove any doubt on this point.

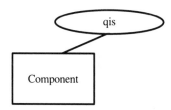

Fig. 3.2 A well-placed attribute may clarify the meaning of an entity-type.

In a quality control situation however you might be interested in individual components ('pieces') and you would then consider each piece as an entity within the entity type BC109. STOCK_NO would not then be an adequate primary key.

Object Oriented Analysis, which is sometimes considered as an alternative to entity-relationship modelling, focuses on this distinction between object and type, making it clear that it is possible for an item to be both an object (instance, entity) and a type (class, entity type) at the same time. There is generally no problem in coping with this in entity-relationship modelling provided the modeller makes clear what he or she means. In this example we have seen that the simple placing of a well-chosen attribute on the entity-relationship diagram helps clear up any ambiguity. It is an important skill of the systems analyst and database designer to be able to recognize and control such ambiguities where they arise. Careful naming of entity types is another device to enhance clarity and reduce ambiguity. Changing the name of COMPONENT to COMPONENT_TYPE would be a further improvement.

Fig. 3.3(a) uses the idea of a card file and individual cards within it as being analogous to an entity type and an entity respectively. In Fig. 3.3(b) the set – element model is used to show the same thing, and in Fig. 3.3(c)

Careful naming can make the 'meaning' of an entity type clearer.

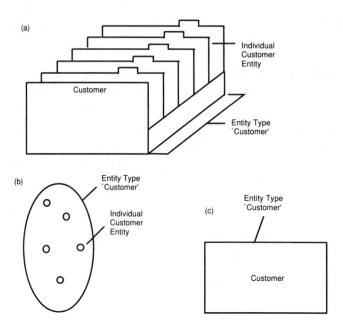

Fig. 3.3   Three ways of thinking of an entity type.

the entity-relationship model for the same situation is shown. These are three different models of the same phenomenon. Notice that the entity-relationship model version does not explicitly show individual entities. You are meant to know that 'within' the entity type CUSTOMER there are lots of customer entities.

Apart from serving as an identifier for each entity within an entity type, the primary key also serves as the method of representing relationships between entities. The primary key becomes a foreign key in all those entity types to which it is related in a one–one or one–many relationship type. The concept of foreign keys is discussed in detail in Chapter 4.

Relationship types

Relationship types link the entity types.

The first two major elements of entity-relationship diagrams are entity types and attributes. The final element is the relationship type. Sometimes, the word 'types' is dropped and relationship types are called simply 'relationships' but since there is a difference between the terms, one should really use the term relationship type.

Real-world entities have relationships between them, and relationships between entities on the entity-relationship diagram are shown where appropriate. An entity-relationship diagram consists of a network of entity types and connecting relationship types. A relationship type is a named association between entities. Individual entities have individual relationships of the type between them. An individual person (entity) occupies (relationship) an individual house (entity). In an entity-relationship diagram, this is generalized into entity types and relationship types. The entity type PERSON is related to the entity type HOUSE by the relationship type OCCUPIES. There are lots of individual persons, lots of individual houses, and lots of individual relationships linking them.

There can be more than one type of relationship between entities. For an example of three different relationship types between two entity types see Fig. 3.31(a). Figure 3.4 shows a single relationship type 'Received' and its inverse relationship type 'Was_sent_to' between the two entity types CUSTOMER and INVOICE. It is very important to name all relationship types. The reader of the diagram must know what the relationship type means and it is up to you the designer to make the meaning clear from the relationship type name. The direction of both the relationship type and its inverse should be shown to aid clarity and immediate readability of the diagram. The tense of the relationship type should also be clear from its name.

Every relationship type has an inverse.

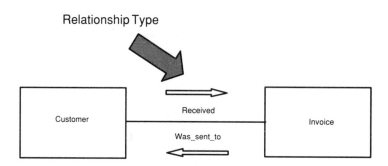

Fig. 3.4   Representing a relationship on an entity-relationship diagram.

In the development of a database system, many people will be reading the entity-relationship diagram and so it should be immediately readable and totally unambiguous. When the database is implemented, the entity-relationship diagram will continue to be used by application programmers and query writers. Misinterpretation of the model can result in much lost time going down wrong tracks. There is little harm in putting redundant information into your entity-relationship model. What seems redundant to you can sometimes remove potential ambiguities for other users of your diagram. Get your user to explain your entity-relationship model to you! Then you will see how clear it is.

You should name all relationship types.

In Fig. 3.4 what is being 'said' is that customers received invoices and invoices were_sent_to customers. How many invoices a customer might have received (the maximum number and the minimum number) and how many customers an invoice might have been sent to, is shown by the degree of the relationship type. The 'degree' of relationship types is defined below.

In Fig. 3.5 three different ways of illustrating the existence of a relationship type are shown. In (a), in which the CUSTOMER and INVOICE entity types are represented by index cards, it can be seen that there is a 'received' relationship type between customer number 2 and invoice numbers 7 and 9. Customer number 2 has 'received' these two invoices. These two invoices 'were_sent_to' customer number 2. In (b) the same information is shown using set notation with the relationship type 'received' and inverse relationship type 'was_sent_to' linking customer entities and invoice entities. Figure 3.5(c) is the entity-relationship diagram version and information about individual entities and which entity is linked to which is lost. The

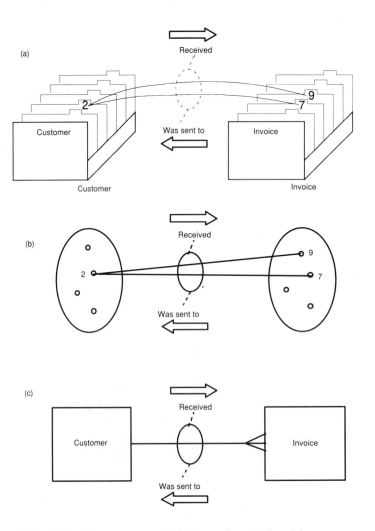

Fig. 3.5   Three ways of thinking of a relationship.

reason for this is simply that in a real database there would be hundreds of customer and invoice entities and it would be impossible to show each one on the entity-relationship diagram.

It was mentioned earlier that there is in fact a distinction between relationships and relationship types. In Fig. 3.5(a) and (b) there are in fact two relationships shown: one between customer 2 and invoice 7 and one between customer 2 and invoice 9, so strictly speaking 'received' is a relationship type consisting of a number of relationships between entity types. However, this distinction is sometimes dropped (it frequently is in this book), and both are given the name 'relationship'.

> The word 'type' is often dropped.

Finally, note that relationships between entity types are represented in a relational database using foreign keys. The value of the primary key of one entity is placed in every entity of the second type to which it is related. This is discussed in detail in Chapter 4.

Ways of classifying relationships types

A relationship type can be classified by the number of entity types involved, and by the degree of the relationship type, as is shown in Fig. 3.6. These methods of classifying relationship types are complementary. To describe a relationship type adequately, you need to say what the name of the relationship type and its inverse are, and their meaning (if not clear from their names) and you also need to declare the entity type or types involved and the degree of the relationship type that links the entities. We now discuss the latter two items.

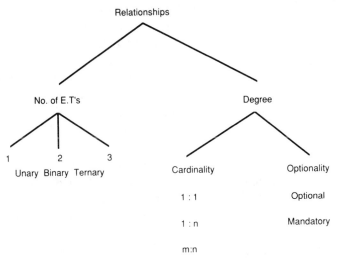

Fig. 3.6 Two ways of classifying relationships.

The purpose of discussing the number of entity types is to introduce the terms unary relationship type, binary relationship type, and ternary relationship type, and to give examples of each. The number of entity types in the relationship type affects the final form of the relational database.

The purpose of discussing the degree of relationship types is to define the relevant terms, to give examples, and to show the impact that the degree of a relationship type has on the form of the final implemented relational database.

Number of entity types

Unary relationship types are also called 'recursive' and 'involuted'. They link entities in just one entity type.

If a relationship type is between entities in a single entity type then it is called a **unary** relationship type. One example is the relationship 'friendship' between entities within the entity type PERSON. If a relationship type is between entities in one entity type and entities in another entity type then it is called a **binary** relationship type because two entity types are involved in the relationship type. An example is the relationship 'Received' in Fig. 3.4 and Fig. 3.5 between customers and invoices. Another example of a binary relationship type is 'Purchased' between entity types CUSTOMER and PRODUCT. Two entity types are involved so the relationship is binary.

Binary relationship types link entities in two entity types.

It is possible to model relationship types involving more than two entity types. For example a LECTURER 'recommends' a certain TEXT on a certain COURSE. Here the relationship type is 'recommends'. This relationship type is said to be a **ternary** relationship type since three entity types are involved. Examples of unary, binary and ternary relationship types are shown in Fig. 3.7.

A relationship type involving 3 or more entity types can be replaced by a new entity type.

It is sometimes possible to replace higher-order relationship types (ternary and above) by a collection of binary relationship types linking pairs of the original entity types. However this is not always possible (although as we shall see, the high-order relationship can always be redefined, with suitable renaming, as an entity type). In the example cited above concerning lecturers recommending textbooks on courses, it is not possible to replace the ternary relationship type 'recommends' with two or even three binary relationship types because information would be lost. Figure 3.8(a) shows the ternary relationship type 'recommends' linking LECTURER, TEXT and COURSE.

In Fig. 3.8(b) an attempt has been made to replace the ternary relationship type with two binary relationship types. LECTURERs 'recommend' TEXTs and TEXTs 'are_used_on' COURSEs. The fact that a lecturer recommends a text and that text is used on a course does not necessarily mean that lecturer recommended that text for that course. The text might be used on the course and recommended by someone else, whereas our lecturer does recommend that text but for a different course.

In Fig. 3.8(c) it is possible to tell which texts a lecturer recommends and which courses he or she teaches on, but not which texts are used on a course

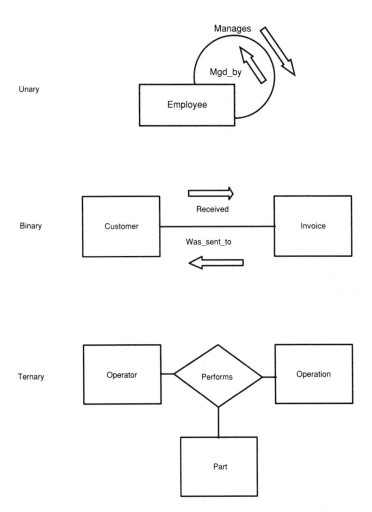

Fig. 3.7 There can be one, two, three or more entity types involved in a relationship.

or which courses use a given text. The fact that a lecturer recommends a text and teaches a course does not imply that he or she recommends that text for that course.

In Fig. 3.8(d) it is possible to tell which courses a lecturer teaches and which texts a course uses but not which texts a teacher recommends. Only if every course had only one lecturer would (d) be satisfactory because then the fact that a course used a text implies who recommended it. Otherwise (d) is unsatisfactory.

In Fig. 3.8(e) it is possible to tell who recommends which texts, who teaches which courses, and which texts are used on which courses. However it is still not possible to ascertain, in general, the answers to questions like:

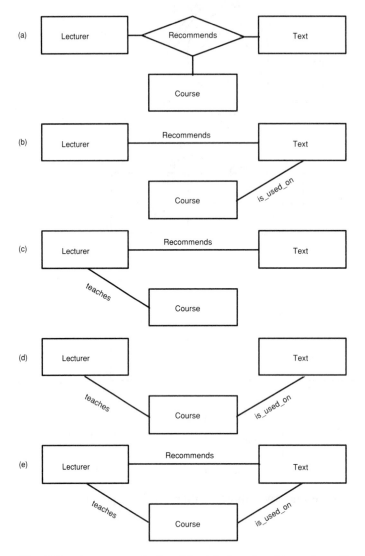

Fig. 3.8   A ternary relationship (a) that should not be split.

'Which text does Mr Smith recommend for the 4th year Database course?'

The reason is that even though Mr Smith may recommend text1 and Mr Smith teaches on 4th year Database, it is not known whether it was Mr Smith who recommended the text for the course, because he may have recommended the text for another course, and another lecturer on the 4th year Database course may have recommended text1. The only satisfactory relationship type is that shown in Fig. 3.8(a).

Removing ternary relationship types

It is advantageous to remove ternary and higher order relationship types. One reason is that it might be considered more 'natural' to think of entity types having attributes than relationship types having them. It is in fact always possible to remove these high-order relationship types and replace them with an entity type. A ternary relationship type is then replaced by an entity type and three binary relationship types linking it to the entity types which were originally linked by the ternary. A quaternary relationship type would be replaced by an entity type and four relationship types and so on.

In Fig. 3.8(a), the ternary relationship type 'recommends' (verb) can be replaced with an entity type 'recommendation' (noun), and a binary relationship between it and each of the entity types LECTURER, TEXT and COURSE (three binary relationships in all). It is natural to think about the attributes of a recommendation but not so natural to think about the attributes of a relationship type 'recommends'. Typical non-key attributes of the RECOMMENDATION might be DATE_RECOMMENDED and STATUS (whether the recommendation has been approved or not). Another advantage of replacing the ternary relationship type is that a ternary or higher-order relationship type cannot in any real sense have a direction. Another is that in Fig. 3.8(a) it is not clear from the diagram (without pre-existing contextual knowledge) what is recommending what to what. Does a lecturer recommend a course in a text? Or does a lecturer recommend a text for a course?

There are several advantages in replacing relationship types linking more than two entity types.

When the single ternary relationship type has been replaced by three binary relationship types, each of the relationships and their inverses can be named, lending considerably more semantic information to the diagram. Clearly, replacing the ternary has allowed us to convey more semantics about the real-world situation than before.

The general conclusion then is that the only relationship types that should be shown on the entity relationship diagram should be either unary (involving one entity type) or binary (involving two entity types).

As stated, the naming of the new entity type and the new relationship types is important. Inappropriately naming the entity type or omitting or inappropriately naming the relationship types will lead to misunderstanding and consequent incorrect processing of data (possibly caused by programmers misunderstanding the 'meaning' of the database schema) and incorrect data appearing on the database. As a general guide entity types should have noun names (e.g. RECOMMENDATION) and relationships should have the form of a verb (e.g. 'made' or 'concerned' or 'was_for').

Exercise 3.1

1. Produce an entity-relationship diagram equivalent to Fig. 3.8(a), replacing the `Recommends' relationship type with a RECOMMENDATION entity type as discussed above. Carefully name all relationship types.

2. Think of an example where, in replacing the ternary relationship type with an entity type and three relationship types and naming those relationships, it is discovered that one of the relationship types is many–many.

The degree of a relationship type

Terminology varies.
The second way of classifying relationship types is to state their degree. As stated in the preceding section, the number of entity types and the degree both have an important impact on the final design of the relational database. The use of terminology related to the degree of a relationship type varies between different authors (Fig. 3.9). The terminology adopted here is the most conventional usage.

Diverse Terminology

Source	Number of e.t's in the relationship	Minimum number of participants	Maximum number of participants
Date			Degree
IEW		Optionality	Cardinality
D.C.C.		Optionality	Degree
Ashworth			Degree
Eva		Optionality	Cardinality and degree
Kroenke	Degree	Minimum Cardinality	Maximum Cardinality
Bamford			Degree

Fig. 3.9   Various usages of entity-relationship terminology.

The degree of a relationship type concerns the number of entities in each entity type it can link.
The degree of a relationship type concerns the number of entities within each entity type that can be linked by a given relationship type. Figure 3.10 shows how this degree is shown on an entity-relationship diagram. There are two directions of a relationship type. Each is named and each has a minimum degree and a maximum degree.

Cardinality and optionality

The maximum degree is called cardinality and the minimum degree is called optionality. In another context the terms 'degree' and 'cardinality' have different meanings. In Date (1986, p.240) 'degree' is the term used to denote the number of attributes in a relation while 'cardinality' is the number of tuples in a relation. Here, we are not talking about relations (database tables) but relationship types, the associations between database tables and the real world entity types they model.

There are three symbols used to show degree. A circle means zero, a line means one and a crowsfoot means many. The cardinality is shown next to the entity type and the optionality (if shown at all) is shown behind it. Refer to Fig. 3.10(a). In Fig. 3.10(b) the relationship type R has cardinality one-to-many because one A is related by R to many Bs and one B is related (by R's inverse) to one A. Generally, the degree of a relationship type is described by its cardinality. R would be called a 'one–many' or a 'one-to-many' or a '1:N' relationship type. To describe fully the degree of a relationship type, however, we should also specify its optionality.

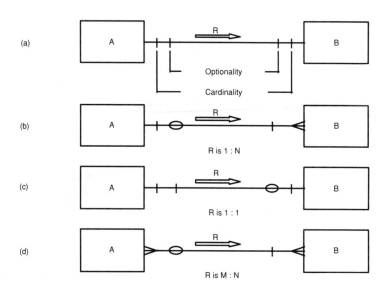

Fig. 3.10   Relationship degree.

The optionality of relationship type R in Fig. 3.10(b) is one as shown by the line. This means that the minimum number of Bs that an A is related to is one. A must be related to at least one B. Considering the optionality and cardinality of relationship type R together, we can say that one A entity is related by R to one or more B entities. Another way of describing the optionality of one, is to say that R is a mandatory relationship type. An A must be related to a B. R's optionality is mandatory. With optionality, the opposite of 'mandatory' is optional. In Fig. 3.10(b) the inverse of R happens to be optional, as shown by the circle. The inverse of R is an optional relationship type. This means that one B might not be related (by the inverse of R) to any A. There may be a B entity not related to any A entity. Considering the optionality and cardinality of the inverse of R together, we can say that a B entity is related (by the inverse of R) to zero or one A entities.

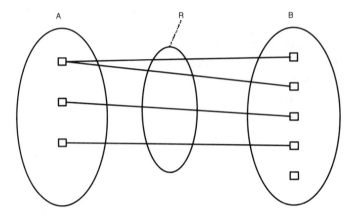

Fig. 3.11   A set diagram representation of Fig. 3.10(b).

The case of Fig. 3.10(b) is shown in the form of a set diagram in Fig 3.11. The two entity types A and B are shown as sets (the oval shapes). The entities are shown as small boxes: elements in the sets. The relationship type R links A entities to B entities. It shows which A entities are related to which B entities. Notice that it is possible for an A entity to be related to one or more B entities. The maximum number of Bs for a given A is 'many' (for example the first A entity is related to two Bs) and the maximum number of As for a given B is one. This establishes the one-many cardinality of R. The minimum number of Bs for a given A is 1. (There are no A entities without a B entity). This establishes mandatory optionality of R. There can exist a B that is not related to any A; for example the last B entity. This establishes the 'optional' optionality of the inverse of R.

Figure 3.12 summarizes the terminology in another example.

Exercise 3.2

Draw example set diagrams for each of the entity relationship diagrams in Fig. 3.10 and Fig. 3.12. This will demonstrate your understanding of relationship degree.

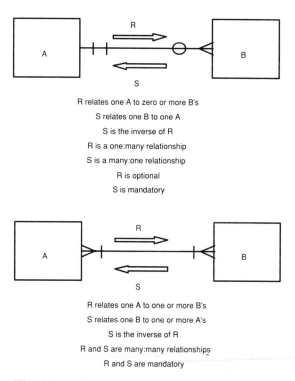

R relates one A to zero or more B's

S relates one B to one A

S is the inverse of R

R is a one:many relationship

S is a many:one relationship

R is optional

S is mandatory

R relates one A to one or more B's

S relates one B to one or more A's

S is the inverse of R

R and S are many:many relationships

R and S are mandatory

Fig. 3.12   A summary of our relationship degree terminology.

Deriving a one–many relationship type

In Fig. 3.13 the procedure for deriving the degree of a relationship type and putting it on the entity relationship diagram is shown. The example concerns part of a sales ledger system. Customers may have received zero or more invoices from us. The relationship type is thus called 'received' and is from CUSTOMER to INVOICE. The arrow shows the direction. The minimum number of invoices the customer has received is zero and thus the 'received' relationship type is optional. This is shown by the zero on the line. The maximum number of invoices the customer may have received is 'many'. This is shown by the crowsfoot. This is summarized in Fig. 3.13(a). To complete the definition of the relationship type the next step is to name the inverse relationship type. Clearly if a customer received an invoice, the invoice was sent to the customer and this is an appropriate name for this inverse relationship type. Now consider the degree of the inverse relationship type. The minimum number of customers you would send an invoice to is one; i.e. you wouldn't send it to no one. The optionality is thus one. The inverse relationship type is mandatory. The maximum number of customers you would send an invoice to is also one so the cardinality is also one. This is summarized in Fig. 3.13(b). Figure 3.13(b) shows the completed relationship.

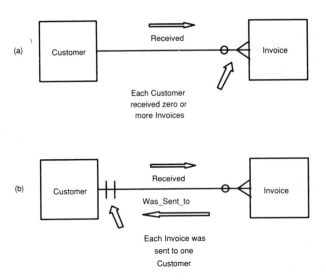

Fig. 3.13 Deriving a 1:N (one–many) relationship.

You must answer TWO
questions when
deciding the degree of
a relationship type.

A word of warning is useful here. In order to obtain the correct degree for a relationship type (one–one or one–many or many–many) you must ask two questions. Both questions must begin with the word 'one'. In the present case (Fig. 3.13), the two questions you would ask when drawing in the relationship line and deciding on its degree would be:

Question 1: One customer received how many invoices?
Answer: Zero or more.

Question 2: One invoice was sent to how many customers?
Answer: One.

This warning is based on observations of many student database designers getting the degree of relationship types wrong. The usual cause of error is only asking one question and not starting with the word 'one'. For example a student might say (incorrectly): 'Many customers receive many invoices' (which is true) and wrongly conclude that the relationship type is many–many. The second most common source of error is either to fail to name the relationship type and say something like 'Customer to Invoice is one-to-many' (which contains very little meaning) or to give the relationship type an inappropriate name. The example of Fig. 3.31(a) on page 64 illustrates the importance of naming all relationships.

Deriving a many–many relationship type
Figure 3.14 gives an example of a many–many relationship type being derived.

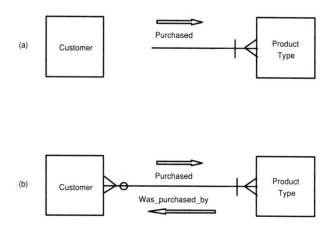

Fig. 3.14   Deriving a M:N (many–many) relationship.

Question 1: One customer purchased how many product types?
Answer: One or more.

Question 2: One product type was purchased by how many customers?
Answer: Zero or more.

Note that the entity type has been called PRODUCT TYPE rather than PRODUCT which might mean an individual piece that the customer has bought. In that case the cardinality of 'was_purchased_by' would be one not many because an individual piece can of course only go to one customer. This point is another common source of error: the tendency to call one item (e.g. an individual 4″ paintbrush) a product and the whole product type (or 'line') (e.g. the 4″ paintbrush product type) a product. You should make the meaning clear from the name you give the entity type. (This was also covered on page 39.)

We have assumed here that every customer on the database has purchased at least one product; hence the mandatory optionality of 'purchased'. If this were not true in the situation under study then a zero would appear instead. The zero optionality of 'was_purchased_by' is due to our assumption that a product type might as yet have had no purchases at all.

In practice it is wise to replace many–many relationship types such as this with a set (often two) of one–many relationship types and a set (often one) of new, previously hidden entity types. This is covered on page 59.

Deriving a one–one relationship type
Figure 3.15 gives an example of a one–one relationship type being derived. It concerns a person and his or her birth certificate. We assume that everyone has one and that a certificate registers the birth of one person only.

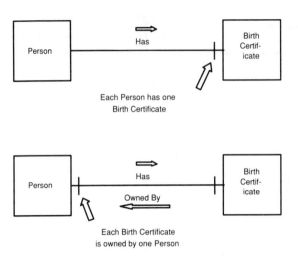

Fig. 3.15 Deriving a 1:1 (one–one) relationship.

Question 1: How many birth certificates has a person?
Answer: One.

Question 2: How many persons is a birth certificate owned by?
Answer: One.

Sometimes you will
want to merge entity
types which are linked
only by a 1:1
relationship type.

Where there is a one–one relationship type we have the option of merging the two entity types. The birth certificate attributes may be considered as attributes of the person and placed in the person entity type. The birth certificate entity type would then be removed. There are two reasons for not doing this. Firstly, the majority of processing involving PERSON records might not involve any or many of the BIRTH_CERTIFICATE attributes. The BIRTH_CERTIFICATE attributes might only be subject to very specific processes which are rarely executed. The second reason for not merging might be that the BIRTH_CERTIFICATE entity type has relationship types to other entity types that the PERSON entity type does not have. The two entity types have different relationship types from other entity types.

Mutually exclusive relationship types
In some cases the existence of one kind of relationship precludes the existence of another. Entities within an entity type A may be related by a relationship type R to an entity in entity type B or entity type C but not both. The relationship types are said to be mutually exclusive. Usually both relationship types will have the same name, as in the following example. In Fig. 3.16 a fault report may have been for a computer or a printer but not both. The fact that it might not have concerned a computer is shown by the zero optionality of the upper 'was_for' relationship type between FAULT

REPORT and COMPUTER. The fact that it might not have concerned a printer is shown by the zero optionality of the lower 'was_for' relationship type between FAULT REPORT and PRINTER. However a fault report must have been for either a computer or a printer (in this example). The zero optionality cannot apply for both. Both this and the fact that the fault report can have been for a maximum of one of the two entity types is indicated by the arc on the diagram linking the two relationship types. In summary then, the arc shows that a fault report can be for a maximum and a minimum of one entity from the types COMPUTER and PRINTER.

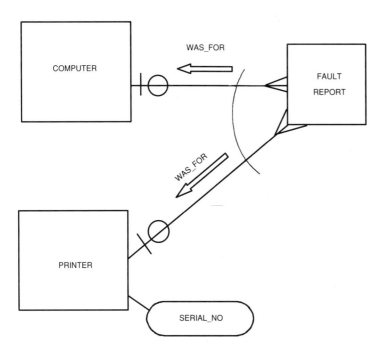

Fig. 3.16 A mutually exclusive relationship 'was_for'.

The set of relationship types is normally assumed to be exhaustive in one sense (i.e. there are not any other relationship types) because it is customary to put all relationships of interest on the diagram. However the set of relationship types might not be exhaustive in the sense that a given entity A might not be related to an entity in any of the other entity types in the group marked by the arc. This second type of exhaustiveness (or lack of it) cannot be shown using this arc device.

Another limitation of the arc device is that it cannot show excluded and mandatory combinations of permitted relationships. For example, it might be the case that an entity in type A might be related to some subset of entities from types B, C and D. It might be that if it is related to a B and a C then it cannot be related to a B entity. It might be that if it is related to a B then it must also be related to either a C or D but not both.

A further constraint type that may be required in practice is that an entity of type A may legally be related to any *n* entities from a selection of *m* entity types.

The suggestion being made here is that current methods for drawing entity relationship diagrams could be extended to allow these types of relationship constraints to be shown on the diagram.

Exercise 3.3

1. Think of a situation in which the relationship types are mutually exclusive but do not have the same name.

2. Think of a situation in which the relationship set indicated by the arc is mutually exclusive but not exhaustive in the second sense mentioned above.

3. Think of examples where excluded and mandatory combinations are required.

4. Think of an example where the 'any *n* of *m*' constraint is required.

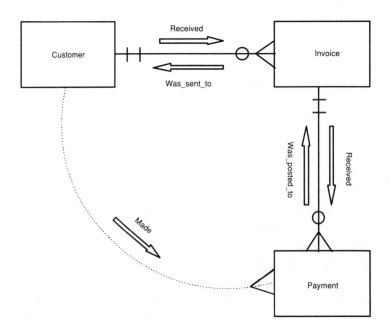

Fig. 3.17   The 'made' relationship is redundant.

Redundant relationship types

In Fig. 3.17 there is a 'received' relationship type between CUSTOMER and INVOICE and an 'obtained' relationship type between INVOICE and PAYMENT. It is possible via 'received' to find which invoices have been received by a given customer. It is possible to find the customer an invoice was sent to via the 'was_sent_to' relationship type (the inverse of 'received'). Using the 'obtained' relationship type it is possible to find the payments that a given invoice has received and via its inverse 'was_posted_to', the invoice that a payment was posted to. Using the composition of 'received' and 'obtained' (that is, using one relationship type followed by the other), it is possible to find all the payments that a given customer has made. By navigating from CUSTOMER to INVOICE and thence to PAYMENT this can be done.

> A loop in your entity-relationship diagram might indicate a redundant relationship.

Similarly, it is possible to find the sender of a payment using the composition of the two relationship types 'was_posted_to' and 'was_sent_to', navigating from PAYMENT to INVOICE to CUSTOMER.

If an extra (direct) relationship type from CUSTOMER to PAYMENT were to be implemented it would be redundant. If it showed only which customer sent a payment and (via its inverse) which payments a customer made, it would be unnecessary because it shows nothing that cannot be shown using compositions of the other two relationship types.

In general, when there are loops in your entity-relationship diagram, be on the lookout for the possibility of breaking the loop at some point by removing a relationship type that can be synthesized from the composition of other relationship types on the diagram. This is often not possible because of the nature of the relationships i.e. their meaning, in which case the loop should be retained.

Exercise 3.4

Find an example in which a loop in an entity-relationship diagram is necessary, and another one in which one of the relationship types in a loop is unnecessary. There can be any number of entity types in the loop.

Note that in some rare cases you might consider it advisable to introduce a logically redundant relationship type simply out of consideration of efficiency.

Figure 3.18 shows the entity-relationship diagram for a relatively simple accounting system. The top grouping of entity types and relationship types constitute a sales ledger ('accounts receivable' and 'debtors ledger' are two other names for this). The whole diagram will be used as a schema for the database holding such data and the sales ledger entity types and relationship types will be called the sales ledger subschema. The bottom subschema is

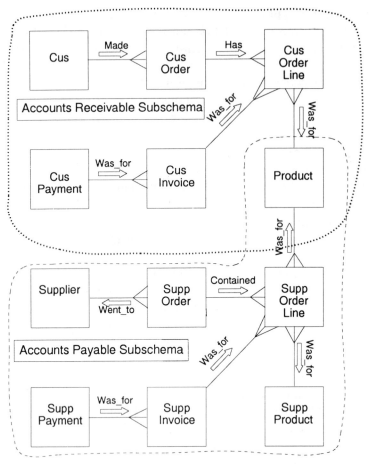

Fig. 3.18 Entity-relationship diagram for a small accounting system.

the accounts payable subschema (also called the 'purchase ledger'). Notice that subschemas may overlap, as here. The PRODUCT entity type is used in both contexts; sales and purchasing. Products are purchased and they are sold. Notice that in this case owing to space limitations only one direction of each relationship type is named. This is acceptable in this case because the inverse relationship type names are pretty obvious. If they are not, they should be included.

Returning to the subject of redundant relationship types, let us consider placing a 'redundant' relationship type between the entity type CUS and the entity type CUS_PAYMENT. There are many queries that could be answered using the schema shown, including:

'List all payments made by customer X.'

A 'redundant' relationship may simplify some queries.

The problem with this query is that to answer it, it is necessary to navigate via four relationship types. Using the first relationship type 'made', all the customer orders are accessed. For each order, 'has' is used to access every order line. For each order line, the customer invoice (if any; an invoice might not yet have been sent. This could be shown using an 'optional' circle at the left-hand end of the relationship type) is accessed and the payment retrieved and listed. The pseudo-code for this could be written as shown in Fig. 3.19.

```
RETRIEVE CUS record
OBTAIN customer's account number
RETRIEVE first CUS_ORDER record for this account
DOWHILE not end of CUS_ORDERs
     OBTAIN order's order number
     RETRIEVE first CUS_ORDER_LINE record for this order number
     DOWHILE not end of CUS_ORDER_LINEs
         OBTAIN order line's invoice number
         IF invoice number is not null
             RETRIEVE CUS_INVOICE record for this inv no
             OBTAIN invoice's payment number
             IF invoice's payment number is not null
                 RETRIEVE PAYMENT record for this pmt no
                 LIST payment details
             ENDIF
         ENDIF
             RETRIEVE next CUS_ORDER_LINE record for this order no
     ENDWHILE
     RETRIEVE next CUS_ORDER for this account number
ENDWHILE
```

Figure 3.19 Pseudo-code for 'List all payments made by customer x'.

This pseudo-code assumes that a customer order line that has not yet been invoiced is indicated by a null value for the invoice number attribute in the order line and that an invoice that has not yet been paid is indicated in a similar way using a null value for the payment number in the invoice record. It must be noted also that this pseudo-code may be considered rather 'physical' since it talks about records rather than real-world entities. However in general every entity of interest will be modelled by a database record. Also, in a relational database, the relationship types are shown using foreign keys such as invoice number in CUS_ORDER_LINE and payment_no in CUS_INVOICE. In other types of database, in particular the older network (CODASYL) and hierarchical databases, foreign keys are not used so the details of the pseudo-code in Fig. 3.19 would be different. How relationship types are represented, including a discussion of foreign keys, is covered in Chapter 4.

The pseudo-code might be considered rather complex for such a simple query. It can be considerably simplified by adding a 'redundant' direct relationship type from CUS to CUS_PAYMENT. A foreign key (the customer's account number) would be placed in CUS_PAYMENT as an extra attribute. While unnecessary, as we have said, this relationship type is advantageous in that the pseudo-code for the query is now as shown in Fig. 3.20, which is much simpler.

```
RETRIEVE CUS record
OBTAIN customer's account number
RETRIEVE first CUS_PAYMENT record
DOWHILE not end of CUS_PAYMENTs
        RETRIEVE PAYMENT record for this account number
        LIST payment details
        RETRIEVE next CUS_PAYMENT for this account number
ENDWHILE
```

Fig. 3.20 Simplified pseudo-code for 'list all payments made by customer x'.

In summary, redundant relationship types should be identified and in general removed. However, implementing a redundant relationship type into the database schema may make the programming of some queries, reports and updates simpler. The major disadvantage of having redundant data on the database is that it may lead to inconsistency. The redundant one–many relationship type we are considering putting between CUS and CUS_PAY-MENT would be implemented by placing a foreign key (the customer's account number) into the CUS_PAYMENT entity type. If this value was different from the value obtained by navigating back via the long route (CUS_PAYMENT, CUS_INVOICE, CUS_ORDER_LINE, CUS_ORDER, CUS) then this would constitute an inconsistency.

Alternative ways of drawing relationship types

The method we have adopted for drawing entity-relationship diagrams is based on the methodology known as Information Engineering (IE) and implemented in the CASE tool IEW (Information Engineering Workbench). Avison and Fitzgerald (1988) give more detail on the history of the Information Engineering approach. ORACLE*CASE, which is an advanced integrated CASE tool used with the ORACLE DBMS, and SSADM, the widely propagated systems analysis method use a different convention and that is discussed next. Following that, Chen diagrams are described. Both are compared and contrasted with our adopted method.

SSADM convention

In the Systems Analysis method known as SSADM (Structured Systems Analysis and Design Method) a different convention for drawing in the relationship types between entity types is adopted. Instead of denoting the name of a relationship type and its inverse, that is, thinking of both directions of a relationship type, SSADM shows one end of a relationship type and the other end. This is closely analogous to using directions as we have done, but it leads to a rather curious effect. The cardinality of a relationship type is shown at one end of the relationship line and the optionality at the other!

The SSADM convention draws relationships differently.

This is illustrated in Fig. 3.21. In (a) the usual method of representing a relationship type has been shown. Note that R is a one–many optional relationship type and its inverse S is mandatory. R is optional because an A can be related to zero or more Bs. S is mandatory because a B can be related to a minimum of one As.

In (b), the SSADM method of showing the same relationship type is

SSADM doesn't have `directions' of a relationship; it has `ends'.
It also has `may' and `must' in place of zero and one optionality.

Using our conventions :

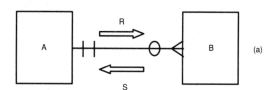

means that :
    Each A is related by R to zero or more B's
    Each B is related by S to one A.

Using the corresponding SSADM conventions for this example :

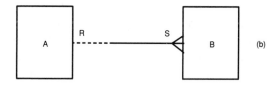

means that :
    Each A   *may* be related by R to one or more B's
    Each B   *must* be related by S to one A

Fig. 3.21   Using the SSADM LDS conventions (one–many).

In SSADM, relationship *ends* are considered instead of relationship *directions*.

shown. A may be related to one or more Bs by relationship R. The word 'may' is denoted by the dotted line. It is meant to convey the idea that an A might not be related to any B. That is shown at the left end of the relationship type. The right end of the relationship type has a crowsfoot meaning 'one or more', so A can be related to zero, one or more Bs and this is expressed by the sentence 'an A may be related to one or more Bs'. Two features of this notation are:

- the minimum number of Bs related to an A is shown at one end and the maximum at the other;
- to say that A may be related to one or more Bs is equivalent to saying that A is related to zero or more Bs.

Another example of the SSADM convention for representing relationship types is shown in Fig. 3.22. In (a) we can see that R is a many–one optional relationship type and S is mandatory. In (b) this results in a dotted crowsfoot at the R end, even though R is mandatory. The conventions shown are those of SSADM version 4. In version 3 of SSADM the treatment of

Be careful when using the SSADM conventions for representing relationship types.

optionality was subtly different. [See for example Ashworth and Goodland (1990, p.27)]. In version 3, a relationship either existed or it didn't. Optionality was shown at the centre of the relationship line and it was impossible to distinguish between one direction of a relationship type being optional and the other direction being optional. So for version 3 the sentence 'A boy can eat zero or more ice-creams' was equivalent to the sentence 'An ice-cream can be eaten by zero or more boys'. In version 4 the first sentence reads 'A boy may eat one or more ice-creams'. These are predictable sources of error. In general, the IE method seems less likely to result in such errors.

Another difference between our terminology and that of SSADM is that SSADM speaks of entities taking part in a number of relationships rather than being related to a number of other entities by a relationship (type). Look at Fig. 3.23. There are several sources of possible confusion here and it is instructive to go through them. Having a loan participating in a current loan relationship type is a bizarre idea. The truth is (probably) that the borrower (entity type) has made (relationship) one or more (degree) loans (entity type) some of which are current (attribute).

You should be able to 'read' an entity-relationship model. The sentence 'A borrower has made one or more current loans' makes sense. The sentence 'A borrower current loans one or more loans' does not. If this basic SUBJECT-VERB-OBJECT structure is not present in your entity-relationship model then it will be difficult to understand and will lead to error.

The confusion in Fig. 3.23 has probably arisen because the designer was thinking about the number of current loan relationships the borrower was involved in rather than the number of loans a borrower may have made. Rather than thinking how many relationships an entity is involved in, you had better ask how many entities the given entity is related to.

Note that with the SSADM convention, optionality is shown at one
end of the relationship, cardinality at the other

Using our conventions :

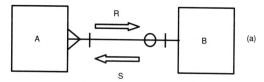

means that :
Each A is related by R to zero or one B's
Each B is related by S to one or more A's.

Using the corresponding SSADM conventions for this example :

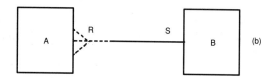

means that :
Each A   *may* be related by R to one B
Each B   *must* be related by S to one or more A's.

Fig. 3.22   Using the SSADM LDS conventions (many–one).

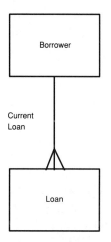

Fig. 3.23   A poorly named relationship.

Exercise 3.5

1. Redraw Fig. 3.23 adopting the IE conventions used in this chapter.

2. Here are two English sentences:

   'The customer may receive a refund.'
   'A refund may be given to a customer.'

   (a) Model these sentences using the SSADM convention. Comment on the difficulty of placing the optionality.
   (b) Model the same sentences using the IE convention. Note that this would require you to convert the sentences into:

   'A customer receives zero or more refunds.'
   'A refund is given to a customer'.

   (c) In the light of this example, discuss the following proposition:

   'The SSADM version 4 convention on LDS optionality is more likely to lead to error than the IE convention since the former may reproduce ambiguities in the English descriptions of optionalities.'

Chen diagram convention

Chen diagrams show relationships as diamonds.

One other convention for drawing relationships uses diamonds to show the relationship name. This is the convention used by P. Chen, the inventor of entity-relationship diagrams [Ref. 9]. A Chen diagram is shown in Fig. 3.24 with the equivalent using our conventions below. Note that Chen allowed many–many relationship types to go unresolved (possibly losing 'hidden' entity types) and allowed these many–many relationship types to have attributes. He also allowed ternary and higher order relationship types to remain as relationship types and often named relationship types just by listing their associated entity types (he called them entity sets). The role that an entity took with respect to a relationship can be shown on a Chen diagram (see for example 'worker' in Fig. 3.24 indicating that the role a worker has to the 'project-worker' relationship is that of a worker).

Chen diagrams have weak entity relations, weak relationship relations and existence dependencies.

Figure 3.25 shows a larger Chen diagram. Note the many–many relationship types, the ternary relationship type SUPP-PROJ-PART, and the unary 'relationship' COMPONENT. The double box around the DEPENDANT entity type indicates that DEPENDANT is a weak entity relation, meaning that, in this example, an employee's dependants are not identified solely by one or more of their own attributes, but via their relationship (EMP-DEP) with their employee parent. Part of the primary key for DEPENDANT would thus be the primary key for EMPLOYEE. If DEPENDANT were related to some other entity type, the relationship would be a weak relationship relation because the link between DEPENDANT and the new entity

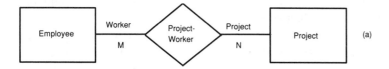

Fig. 3.24 Using the Chen entity-relationship conventions.

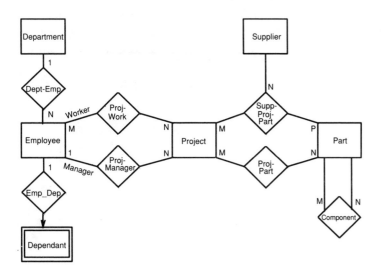

Fig. 3.25 A larger example using the Chen entity-relationship conventions.

type would contain the primary key of EMPLOYEE also. Any update to that key value or deletion in EMPLOYEE would have knock-on effects on DEPENDANT and the new entity type because, in the case of the deletion for example, there would be 'floating' dependants not any longer linked to an employee, and probably no longer of any interest to the users of the database. This existence dependency of DEPENDANTS on EMPLOYEEs is shown in Fig. 3.25 by the arrow between the EMP-DEP relationship type and the weak entity relation DEPENDANT. The ideas of weak entity and relationship relations and existence dependency have implications with regard to data integrity, which is the completeness and lack of redundancy and inconsistency in the database as a whole.

The direction of binary and unary relationship types is not shown on a Chen diagram. Neither are inverse relationship types. The direction of ternary relationship types is meaningless, but if the ternary were replaced by a meaningful entity type (if appropriate - see page 39) then the directions of the new binary relationship types could be shown as could their names and those of their inverses.

Using our conventions for drawing entity-relationship diagrams, the SUPP-PROJ-PART ternary relationship type shown in Fig. 3.25 might be redrawn as in Fig. 3.26. Note that redrawing it in this way calls into question the name of the new entity type and thus the nature of the old relationship. One possible meaning for the relationship type SUPP-PROJ-PART might have been that a SUPPLIER is committed to a CONTRACT ITEM which involves a commitment to supply certain parts for certain projects. (The actual meaning could only be found by resort to the real world situation that the schema is modelling.) The quantities and relevant dates would be attributes of the CONTRACT ITEM. This would also call into question the existence of the CONTRACT in the real world, which itself may have attributes that should be modelled, for example the date that the contract was signed.

Finally, optionality is not shown on the original Chen diagram.

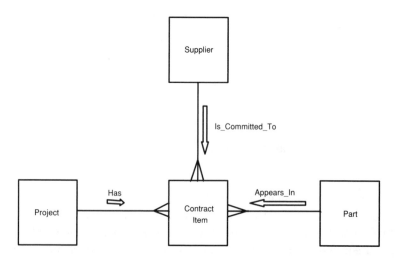

Fig. 3.26   Using our entity-relationship conventions for part of Fig. 3.25.

Exercise 3.6

Redraw Fig. 3.25 using the IE conventions used in this chapter.

Splitting many–many relationship types (hidden entity types)

Wherever a many–many relationship type exists it is advantageous to consider whether it should be split into a number of one–many relationship types (normally two) and a number (normally one) of new entity types. This process is shown in Fig. 3.27. The many–many relationship type R has been replaced by a new entity type X and a one–many relationship type S on one side and one or more one–many relationship types on the other side.

Splitting m:n relationship types may reveal hidden entity types.

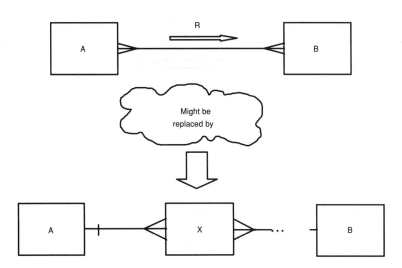

Fig. 3.27   Replacing a M:N relationship.

There are two main advantages in splitting in this way. Firstly, as was mentioned on page 39, it may seem more 'natural' to have attributes of an entity type rather than a relationship type, although as we have seen the original Chen diagrams allowed this. The second and major reason for splitting many–many relationship types is that more than one hidden entity types may emerge.

Figure 3.28 gives an example where this happens. In (a) a many–many relationship type 'purchased' is shown between entity types CUS (customer) and PROD (product). One customer may have purchased many products and

In Fig. 3.28, two entity types are hidden by an m:n relationship type.

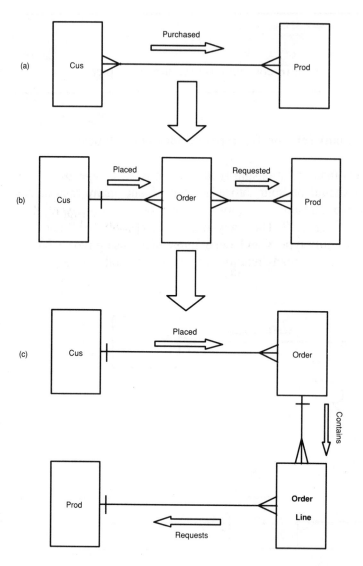

Fig. 3.28   Replacing one M:N introduces two new entity types.

one product may have been purchased by many customers. When splitting the
many–many relationship type, the question is asked:

'What is it in the organization that involves customers purchasing products?'

It occurred to the analyst in liaison with the user representative that what
was 'hidden' in the relationship type was in fact a customer order.
Consequently Fig. 3.28(b) was drawn in which the new entity type ORDER
appears. The relationship types 'placed' and 'requested' were then added

and their degrees considered. The first relationship type 'placed' turned out to be one–many but the 'requested' relationship type was many–many (because an ORDER can request several products and a product can be requested on several orders). The many–many relationship type 'requested' was then split and the new entity type drawn in as in Fig. 3.28(c). To name the new entity type the question was asked:

'What is it that is about ordering and products?'

It was decided on reflection that the hidden entity type was an order line. The two new relationship types were named and their degrees considered. Since they both turned out to be one–many relationship types, the splitting process stopped, the new entity type ORDER_LINE and the new relationship types were added to the model and the attributes of the two new entity types ORDER and ORDER_LINE were considered. If the splitting of the original 'purchased' relationship type had not been performed, the ORDER and ORDER_LINE entity types and their attributes would have remained hidden.

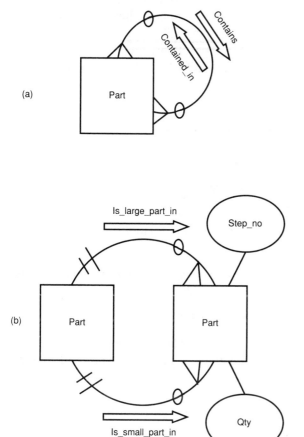

Fig. 3.29   Replacing a unary M:N relationship.

Figure 3.29 gives another example of a many–many relationship type hiding an entity type. This time the relationship type is a unary relationship type, as we have called it, because it relates entities within one entity type. In this instance, parts contain and are contained in other parts. The relationship type is optional in both directions since some parts may have no subparts and some parts might not be contained in any part.

When the many–many relationship type is split, the hidden entity type ASSEMBLY_STEP is revealed. This name was chosen by considering the nature of the relationship, how it had been derived, and what it would be used for. Having found the entity type name, the relationship types were then named and their degrees decided upon. The two attributes of interest 'step_no' and 'qty' were then added. It had not occurred to the data analyst or user that these attributes should go onto the database until the new entity type had been 'discovered'. Since both relationship types are one–many, there was no need for further splitting.

In Fig. 3.30(a) the entity-relationship model is 'about' patients being referred from one hospital to another by doctors. Splitting the many–many unary 'has_referral_to' relationship type reveals a REFERRAL relationship type and two roles for a hospital (shown as relationship type names), the sending hospital and the receiving hospital. Showing the referral as an entity type rather than a relationship type allows important relationships from DOCTOR (who made the referral) and PATIENT (who was referred) to be included.

Exercise 3.7

1. Think of some other examples where important entity types are hidden in a many–many relationship type.

2. Think of some examples where some of the relationship types between the entity types are one–one.

3. Think of some other entity type, not shown, that might be related to the entity type ASSEMBLY_STEP in Fig. 3.29.

4. Referring again to Exercise 3.2 on page 42:

    (a) think of an example where, when replacing a ternary relationship type with an entity type and three relationship types and naming them it is discovered that one of the relationship types is many–many;

    (b) split the many–many to reveal the new set (possibly one) of entity types.

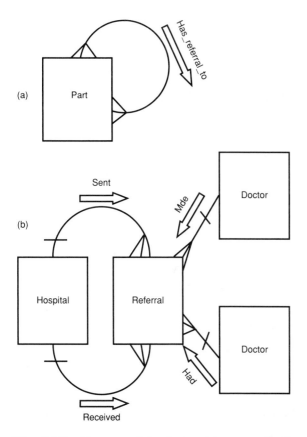

Fig. 3.30 Extra useful relationships may be found by replacing a unary M:N.

More than one relationship type between entity types

It is possible for there to be more than one relationship type between a pair of entity types (and also between entities within the same entity type). Figure 3.31(a) shows three different relationship types between the entity types EMPLOYEE and VEHICLE. Little further comment is required except to say that this is a further demonstration of two points already made. Firstly, every relationship type should be named. The names here distinguish the different relationship types from each other. It would therefore be meaningless to say that 'Employee to Vehicle is one–many' or 'Employee to Vehicle is many–many'. The second point is that the name and meaning of the relationship type determine its cardinality and optionality.

In Fig. 3.31(b) two distinct unary relationship types are shown defined on the one entity type PERSON.

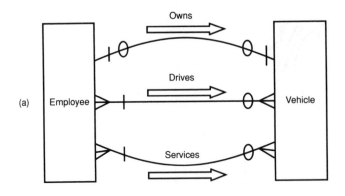

(a)

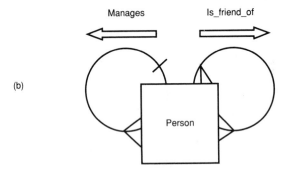

(b)

Fig. 3.31 Parallel relationships: (a) binary; (b) unary.

___

Exercise 3.8

1. Complete the modelling of the EMPLOYEE–VEHICLE model in Fig. 3.31(a) by splitting the two many–many relationship types.

2. Think of another realistic example in which there are two or more unary relationship types defined on an entity type.

3. Complete the modelling of the PERSON model in Fig. 3.31(b) by:

   (a) Splitting the many–many 'is_friend_of' relationship type;
   (b) Naming the new relationship types and determining their degree (cardinality and optionality).

___

Representing trees and networks

Two data structures that occur frequently in applications are the tree and the network. Figure 3.32(a) shows the general structure of a tree represented as a graph. A graph is just a drawing consisting of number of nodes and edges. In the tree of Fig. 3.32(a) there are a number of nodes such as a, b, c, ... and a number of edges (lines) connecting the nodes. The tree is a very general data structure and can be used as a modelling method for many different types of computing application. In the applications we are considering, each node represents an entity and each edge represents a relationship between two nodes or another entity. In Fig. 3.32 the edges represent relationships. This tree diagram shows individual entities whereas the entity-relationship version in Fig. 3.32(b) generalizes this and also shows the name of the relationship type.

Tree data structures of fixed or variable depth can be modelled in an entity-relationship diagram.

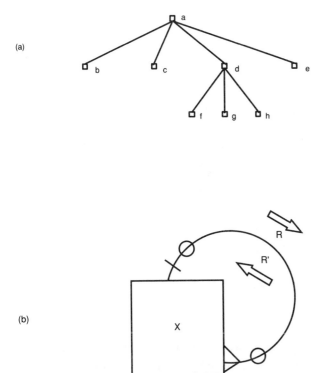

(a)

(b)

Fig. 3.32 A tree structure (a) can be modelled by a unary relationship (b).

In a tree, there are no loops. The graph is 'open'. Along one direction of an edge ('down' the tree), a node can be connected to zero or more other nodes, but along the other direction it can be connected to zero or one nodes only. A typical example of this is shown in Fig. 3.33. The 'root' or

An organization chart is tree-shaped.

top of this tree is employee e1 who manages but is managed by no one. One of the 'leaves' of the tree is e4, who is managed, but manages no one. Node e5 is managed by one employee and manages two others. In a tree of this type, the relationship type is optional in both directions to allow for the existence of a root and leaf nodes.

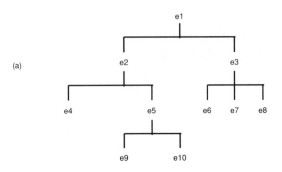

(a)

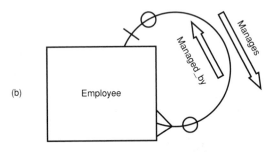

(b)

Fig. 3.33   An example tree structure.

In a network data structure, loops are allowed.

Figure 3.34 shows a simple network, similar to Fig. 3.32, except that node h is connected back to node e, forming a loop. This means that a node may be related to zero or more nodes in both directions. There are loops. An example of a network is shown in Fig. 3.35. This is a particular case in which person A being related to person B implies that B is related to A by the same relationship. It does not however imply that the graph must be a network since for the friendship relationship type, loops do not necessarily occur in particular cases. However, the entity-relationship model allows for the possibility of loops and hence networks by showing a many–many unary relationship type.

(a)

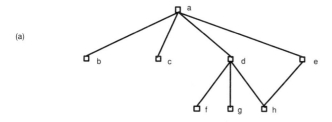

(b)

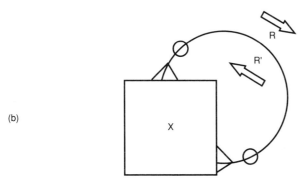

Fig. 3.34 A network (a) can be modelled by a unary relationship (b).

Exercise 3.9

1. Draw a graph of a network in which:
   (a) the optionality is mandatory in one direction;
   (b) the optionality is mandatory in both directions.

2. Think of real-world examples of (a) and (b).

3. Draw both graphs and entity-relationship models of the examples.

4. Think of an example in which the edges of the graph represent entities rather than relationships. *Hint:* A road network is one example.

5. Draw both a graph and the entity-relationship diagram of the example.

6. Think of an example of a network in which more than one entity type is involved and draw the entity-relationship model and the graph of a particular case.

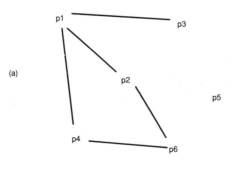

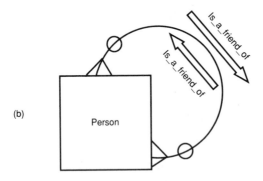

Fig. 3.35   An example network structure.

Navigating the entity-relationship model

When the complete entity-relationship model has been assembled it should be tested by checking it against a comprehensive set of queries and reports that you know the database will have to accommodate. One way of doing this is to document the path through the model that each process will take. This process should be repeated later when all the attributes of each entity type have been finalized after the normalization stages in the design. However, quite a lot can be achieved at this stage. Navigating between the entity types is usually via the relationships shown on the model. If we take the example of the simple accounting system shown in Fig. 3.18, the navigation paths for two queries are shown in Fig. 3.36. The first query is:

> 'What is the address of the customer that invoice number 1234 was sent to?'

The navigation path for this query is shown with white arrows. The CUS_ORDER_LINE entity type contains the invoice number which we

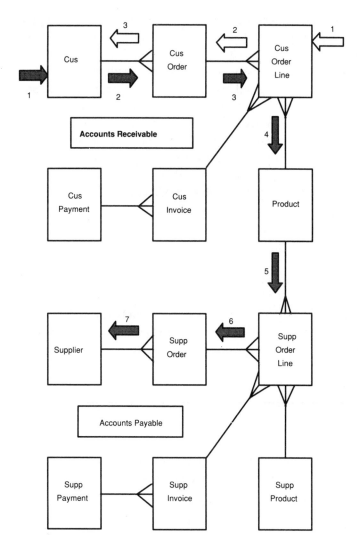

Fig. 3.36   Desk checking two queries.

know (1234) and so this is the starting point for the query(1). We retrieve this record and obtain from it the order number so that we can obtain the order record via the relationship type 'has' (2). The next link in the navigation chain is to retrieve the relevant CUSTOMER entity via the 'made' relationship type (3). Having obtained the customer record, we can list out the address, as required.

The second query is:

'Who is the main supplier of products that our customer J. Smith and Co. buys?'

This is a more complex query because it requires a longer navigation path. We start with what we know, the customer name 'J. Smith'. We must end up with what we want to know, a supplier. The dark arrows show the required navigation path. We can only be sure that this path is viable when we have finalized the attributes of all entity types and their meanings, and the names and meanings of all the relationship types. In some cases there is more than one route from one entity type to another. It such a situation it is not simply a case of using the shortest route. Only one of the routes will be appropriate. The two routes will have a different meaning. If this is not the case, that is, either route could be taken, then there is some redundancy in the entity model which may lead you to redesign parts of it.

In other cases, a query involving more than one entity type might not use any of the established relationships at all. Consider the query, again related to the simple accounting schema of Fig. 3.18:

'Which of our customers are also suppliers of ours?'

This query involves a direct comparison of the attributes (probably name and possibly address also) of entities in the CUSTOMER and SUPPLIER entity types. None of the relationship types shown on the model is required.

Exercise 3.10

1. Write down some other pertinent English queries that the schema of Fig. 3.18 ought to be able to answer and show their navigation paths.

SSADM calls an entity-relationship diagram a 'LDS' (Logical Data Structure).

2. Investigate the SSADM technique known as EAP (Enquiry Access Paths) and describe its use in verifying an entity-relationship diagram. [Downs, Clare and Coe (1992) and Ashworth and Goodland (1990) will help here.]

Entity-relationship modelling – summary

1. An entity type is a type of entity you want to store data about. The data is stored in the form of attributes. An individual within an entity type is an entity. Each entity in an entity type has a different value of the entity type's primary key.
2. Entity types are linked by relationship types. A relationship type is a type of relationship in the real world that you want to represent on the database. An individual within a relationship type is a relationship. Relationships are represented in a relational database by foreign keys.

3. Relationship types are binary or unary. Ternary and higher order relationship types can always be replaced with binary relationship types and new entity types.

4. The degree of a relationship type includes its cardinality and its optionality. Optionality is shown differently in the IE and SSADM conventions and not at all in the Chen convention.

5. Relationship types have two directions, may have degree one–one, one–many or many–many, and may be mandatory or optional in either direction.

6. Redundant relationship types may occasionally be modelled and implemented to improve performance.

7. Many–many relationship types should always be split to reveal entity types and relationship types that might otherwise remain hidden.

8. Relationship types must always be named in both directions. There can be more than one relationship type between entity types. The names distinguish them.

9. It should be possible to 'read' an entity-relationship diagram which should represent a set of simple subject-verb-object sentences. Subject and object are entity types. Relationship types correspond approximately to verbs. An entity-relationship model should explain itself. An unclear or ambiguous model does more harm than good, since it might mislead. The good entity modeller is good at grammar, good at spotting ambiguity, and uses the simplest words.

10. Navigating an entity-relationship diagram with queries is a good way to test it.

11. Entity modelling is followed by normalization to check the design more rigorously.

12. When drawing an entity-relationship model, don't assume anything; rather write a list of questions you would have to find answers to to complete the model. State any assumptions you are aware of having made.

Exercise 3.11 – Cars

Identify all entity types, attributes, relationship types and their degrees in the following case. Draw an entity-relationship diagram.

An organization makes many models of cars, where a model is characterized by a name and a suffix (such as GL or XL which indicates the degree of luxury) and an engine size.

Each model is made up from many parts and each part may be used in the manufacture of more than one model. Each part has a description and an ID code. Each model of car is produced at just one of the firm's factories, which are located in London, Birmingham, Bristol, Wolverhampton and Manchester – one in each city. A factory produces many models of car and many types of part although each type of part is produced at one factory only.

Exercise 3.12 – A university

A university consists of several faculties. Within each faculty there are several departments. Each department may run a number of courses. All teaching staff are attached to departments, each staff member belonging to a unique department. (*Note:* see how many meanings you can assign to this ambiguous sentence.) Every course is composed of subcourses. Some subcourses are part of more than one course. Staff may teach on many subcourses and each subcourse may be taught by a number of staff.

Draw an entity-relationship model for this example. Show both cardinalities and optionalities. Put a question mark where the degree is not clear from the text. Don't assume anything; rather, write a list of questions to which you would have to find answers to complete the model.

Exercise 3.13 – Students and courses (similar to Exercise 12)

Draw an entity-relationship diagram for the following scenario, stating any assumptions you find it necessary to make, and showing unknown cardinalities and optionalities using question marks on the relationship line. Show also the attributes explicitly mentioned in the scenario and underline any you consider suitable candidates for being primary keys.

It is required to keep the following information on students, courses and subcourses. Each student has a name, identification number, home address, term address, and a number of qualifications for which the subject (e.g. maths), grade (e.g. C) and level (e.g. 'A' level) are recorded. Each student is registered for one course where each course has a name (e.g. Information Systems) and an identification number. Record is kept of the number of students registered for each course.

Each course is divided into subcourses where a subcourse may be part of more than one course. Information on subcourses includes the name, identification number and the number of students taking the course.

Exercise 3.14 – Mortgages

Draw an entity-relationship diagram for the following. Produce also a list of questions you would have to have answered in order to complete the model.

In a case study of this kind, and in particular in exam questions, there is not usually the space to completely specify a problem. Remember also that not all the information given in a case study of this type is necessarily relevant. Some information, while relevant to the organization concerned, might not be relevant as far as database design is concerned.

Members of a friendly society invest money in any one of the society's branches. A member may hold a number of investment accounts. Each investment account is associated with the branch where it was opened, but money may be paid in or withdrawn at any branch. For each account, the member holds an account book to record all transactions. A member may also have one mortgage account. All mortgage accounts are associated with the Head Office. Payments may be transferred from any investment account into the mortgage account.

Exercise 3.15 – Sales ledger and stock control

ABC Ltd plans to computerise its sales ordering and stock control system. A feasibility study has strongly suggested that a relational database system be installed. The details of ABC's sales and stock control are as follows:
   Customers send in orders for goods. Each order may contain requests for variable quantities of one or more products from ABC's range. ABC keeps a stock file showing for each product the product details and the preferred supplier, the quantity in stock, the reorder level and other details.
   ABC delivers those goods that it has in stock in response to the customer order and an invoice is produced for the despatched items. Any items that were not in stock are placed on a back order list and these items are usually re-ordered from the preferred supplier. Occasionally items are ordered from alternative sources.
   In response to the invoices that are sent out to ABC's customers, the customers send in payments. Sometimes a payment will be for one invoice, sometimes for part of an invoice and sometimes for several invoices and part-invoices.

Draw an entity-relationship model, stating any assumptions made. Make sure you remove all many–many relationships and replace them with new entity types and relationship types.

Exercise 3.16 – Families

Draw an entity-relationship diagram and list all attributes including the primary key for each entity type, for a database suitable for showing fatherhood, motherhood, brotherhood, sisterhood, cousins, nephews, nieces and nephews, grandparents, in short all family relationships. Remember that it is possible to reproduce without marriage and that marriage does not imply reproduction. It is possible to model this with one entity type.

Show how the model changes if we wish to keep a record of marriage and spouse relationships. Keep the model as simple as possible. There should be no redundant data. It would be redundant for example, to state that persons A and B were brothers and also that they shared a mother; sharing a mother and the fact that they are both male implies that they are brothers (or half-brothers).

The secret in this example is to isolate the most fundamental fact about human reproduction, divorced from artificial social constructions.

Chapter 4

Relational representation and normalization

In this chapter you will learn:

- ☐ to show how the entity-relationship model is represented in terms of relations;

- ☐ to show how relationships are represented using foreign keys;

- ☐ to define the terms entity integrity and referential integrity;

- ☐ to give examples of database procedures and rules;

- ☐ to explain in more detail the notion of primary key;

- ☐ to define the terms candidate key, composite key, compound key, index key, sort key;

- ☐ to define the term repeating group;

- ☐ to define the terms functional dependency, full functional dependency, partial dependency;

- ☐ to define the term transitive dependency;

- ☐ to use the following normal forms;

  - first normal form;
  - second normal form;
  - third normal form;
  - Boyce–Codd normal form.

Introduction

Having produced the entity-relationship diagram, the next step is to represent the entity types, relationship types and attributes in relational form. There are several steps in this procedure. The first is to choose a primary key for each entity type. Secondly, we must represent the relationship types using foreign keys. This takes us one step closer to the design of the

Relational databases represent the data using relations (tables), and primary and foreign keys.

relational database. In this context, the relational integrity issues of entity integrity and foreign key integrity are discussed. Once this step is completed, the resulting relations (see Chapter 2 for the definition of the term 'relation') are normalized to check whether any further splitting of the relations is necessary. In this chapter, four normal forms (1NF, 2NF, 3NF and BCNF) are described. The next chapter describes higher normal forms. The reasons for normalization include program-data independence (changes to physical database structures should not require changes to program structure), and the desirability of detecting and removing both data redundancy (the same data facts repeated in various parts of the database in an uncontrolled way) and update anomalies (added complexities involving insert, delete and update database operations).

Normalization serves as a check on the entity-relationship model.

As a result of the splitting of relations in normalization, the corresponding entity types in the entity-relationship diagram have to be split and the entity-relationship diagram redrawn so that it and the relational model are consistent.

Relational representation

Each entity type in the entity-relationship model will be represented as a relation, and each entity within the entity type will be represented as a tuple. The attributes in the entity-relationship model will remain as attributes (columns) in the relational model. At this point, it is worthwhile summarizing some equivalences in terminology in current use with respect to relational databases. While not exact equivalences in every respect, the table in Fig. 4.1 represents a reasonable guide.

Relationship types are represented in the relational model using foreign keys, but are not named.

ENTITY-RELATIONSHIP	RELATIONAL	SQL	TRADITIONAL
Entity type	Relation	Table	File
Entity	Tuple	Row	Record
Relationship type			
Attribute	Attribute	Column	Field

Fig. 4.1   Equivalences in terminology.

Notice that there is no equivalent in the other terminologies to the 'relationship type' of the entity-relationship model. However, remember that relationship types are represented in relational databases using foreign keys.

Also notice that the term 'relation' has nothing to do with the term 'relationship' or 'relationship type'. A relation is a table and a relationship is a link between tables.

Figure 4.2 shows how an entity type CUSTOMER is represented as a relation. The entity type name becomes the table ('relation') name and the attribute names form the column names. The table name, the attribute names and the definitions of the attributes (width, type, range, etc.) are collectively called the intension of the database and the set of actual values in the rows, the extension. This distinction is made simply to make it clear, when we refer to 'the database', whether we are talking about the structure of the database (intension) or its data contents (extension).

The intension is the description of a table's structure. The extension is the data contained in the table.

Notice in Fig. 4.2 the general point that every entity in a relational database table has to have the same set of attributes (different values of course). If you happened to know that one of the customers in the CUSTOMER table was the Queen, there would be nowhere to record the fact.

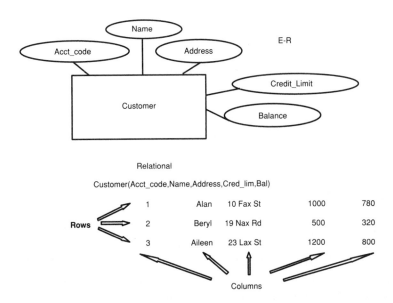

Fig. 4.2   Representing an entity type as a relation.

Candidate keys and the primary key

A subset (often one) of the attributes is chosen as the **primary key**, that is, an identifier of rows. No two rows will have the same value of this key. As mentioned in Chapter 2, in a relational database, no two rows are allowed to be identical. The primary key is a mechanism for realizing that aim. Its other main purpose is that the value of the primary key for a tuple will be

The primary key value is unique to each row.

Foreign key values
show relationships
between table rows.
placed in other tuples as a foreign key to represent relationships between tuples/rows/entities. The primary key is not necessarily the major way of retrieving a record, as is sometimes thought. You may want to retrieve records based on the values of any attributes.

In Fig. 4.3, the account code has been chosen as the primary key because its value is unique to each customer. There is no other attribute or set of attributes that would be quite as satisfactory as ACCT_CODE in identifying customers in this relation. You might try NAME, but that tends to be rather long, perhaps twenty characters. Since the customer's primary key value will appear in all rows in other tables that it is related to, an excessive amount of storage would be used. Also, two customers might have the same name. When trying to retrieve a customer record using the name, one would have to be very careful to type in the correct spelling, punctuation, etc. in order to retrieve the correct record. Using the name plus the address, whilst ensuring uniqueness, would suffer more from space and typing problems.

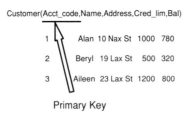

Customer(Acct_code,Name,Address,Cred_lim,Bal)

1   Alan 10 Nax St 1000 780

2   Beryl 19 Lax St   500 320

3   Aileen 23 Lax St 1200 800

Primary Key

Fig. 4.3   The primary key.

A candidate key is a
set of one or more
attributes that is
suitable for use as the
primary key.
It is true that name + address is a candidate key, that is, it could be the primary key because it is 'unique'. Account code is also a candidate key. We choose ACCT_CODE from these two candidate keys to be the primary key. It is compact, and is quickly typed in by computer users when accessing the database. The primary key is underlined with a solid line. No candidate key should be longer than necessary.

Primary keys that consist of just one attribute are called atomic primary keys. It is possible for a primary key (or any other candidate key) to contain more than one attribute, in which case they are compound keys or composite keys. These are discussed below on page 92.

Exercise 4.1

Draw up a list of entity types (things you want to store data about in a database) and against each write a suitable set of attributes, and then write down the candidate keys. Pick one candidate key to be the primary key in each case, giving reasons for your choice. Underline the primary key. In many cases there will be only one candidate key so you will of course pick it to be the primary key.

If you are a good designer, your colleague should be able to understand what the resulting relations mean just by looking at them. The surest way to achieve this is to give each attribute a meaningful name, corresponding to something real. Use abbreviations judiciously and be aware of possible ambiguities (e.g. what does 'm_no' mean?). If in doubt, make the attribute name longer. Remember the end user will not have to type attribute names, just their values. Avoid attribute names like X1, X2, ..., etc. (unless you really want to make your design obscure!).

Foreign keys

Foreign keys are used to link rows of database tables to show some kind of relationship between them. We now consider their use in several situations.

Foreign keys in conventional one-to-many relationships

In Fig. 4.4 we have two tables, CUSTOMER and INVOICE. They are related by the one–many relationship type 'received'. For the sake of simplicity, no inverse relationship or optionalities have been shown on this diagram. The one–many relationship type is represented by placing the primary key attribute ACCT_CODE into the INVOICE table as a foreign key. This is the way relationships are represented in relational databases. There is no other method, and nothing else to learn. It is used to represent any one-to-many or one-to-one relationship. Remember that all many-to-many relationships have been split into one-to-manys by this time.

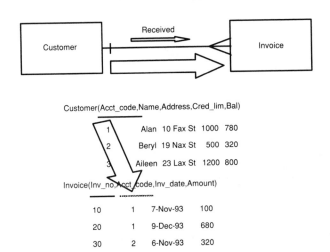

Fig. 4.4 Relationships are represented by foreign keys.

It is important to remember the direction of 'emigration' of the foreign key in a one–many relationship type. The primary key of the 'one' side of the relationship type emigrates to the 'many' side. That is, a copy of the primary key in the entity type at the 'one' side emigrates to (also appears in) the entity type at the 'many' side as a foreign key. In the table at the 'one' end of the relationship line it is called the primary key. In the table at the 'many' end of the relationship line it is called the foreign key.

The foreign key does not identify rows as the primary key does; it is there just to show a relationship between rows. Notice that the name of the relationship ('received') is not shown in the relational model. The foreign key ACCT_CODE in the INVOICE table of Fig. 4.4 is there to show which customer account the invoice belongs to. This particular extension of the INVOICE table shows that the customer with account code 1 received invoices 10 and 20.

A foreign key in one table is a primary key in some (usually different) table.

The foreign key is underlined with a dotted line to show its special significance. When you see an attribute with a dotted underline, you know that it is a foreign key and that it must therefore be a primary key in some other table. Whatever table that is has a one-to-many or one-to-one relationship to this table. The quickest way to find that other table is to look on the entity-relationship diagram. The relationship line will lead you there. SSADM takes this one stage further in its 'RDA LDS' (Relational Data Analysis Logical Data Structure) diagrams, actually showing the primary and foreign keys in the entity type boxes. If the relationship names and optionalities are added (SSADM removes them), a quite useful diagram results (Fig. 4.5). In SSADM, underlining is used to show the primary key and asterisks indicate the foreign keys.

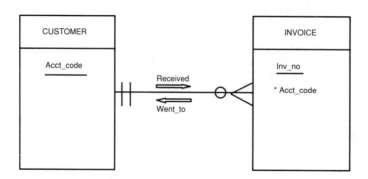

Fig. 4.5   SSADM RDA LDS diagram (with improvements).

Exercise 4.2

1. Invent some situations in which entity types are related in a one-to-many fashion and draw the entity-relationship diagram for each. Then represent each situation in relational form, inventing attributes where necessary and choosing primary keys. Finally represent the one-to-many relationships using foreign keys. You do not have to give the foreign key the same name as the primary key, but it is clearer if you do.

    Remember to make your relation names and attribute names clear, and do the 'colleague test'. If your colleague cannot tell you what your database is about just by looking at the relations then you have failed.

2. Produce a relational representation of the entity-relationship model in Fig. 3.17. Do not include the foreign key from CUSTOMER to PAYMENT, since the 'made' relationship is redundant, as discussed on page 49.

Foreign keys in unary relationships

In the previous example, the rows to be linked using the foreign key were in different tables. With a unary (involuted, recursive) relationship, the rows related by the foreign key are in the same table. In Fig. 4.6, the primary key is EMP_NO and the foreign key is MGR_NO (manager number). Every MGR_NO is in fact an EMP_NO in another row in the table, because every manager is an employee. Note that because the top manager in the hierarchy is not managed by anyone, 'managed by' is optional, and consequently, for this employee, the MGR_NO foreign key will not have a value. This can be handled by placing a special 'null' value in the MGR_NO field or some other special value which the users and the system will recognize as meaning 'this employee does not have a manager'.

In a unary I:N relationship, the foreign key is the primary key of the same table. It is given a different name.

The optionality in the other direction, i.e. the optionality of the 'manages' relationship type, means of course that some employees manage no one. They are the `leaves' of the management hierarchy tree. This is shown in the EMPLOYEE table by the fact that the value of none of these employees' EMP_NOs will appear as a MGR_NO foreign key. Note that the set of manager numbers is a subset of the set of employee numbers. However the allowable range of manager numbers is also the allowable range of employee numbers. This minor point is sometimes expressed either by saying that the two domains MGR_NO and EMP_NO are defined on the same value set (Chen, 1976) or that MGR_NO and EMP_NO are the same domains with different role names.

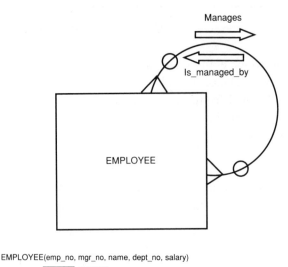

EMPLOYEE(emp_no, mgr_no, name, dept_no, salary)

Fig. 4.6   Foreign key representing a unary relationship.

Exercise 4.3

1. Think of further simple examples of unary one-to-many relationships and produce a relational model for each one.

2. Why is it necessary in a unary relationship to use a different name (a 'role' name) for the foreign key?

3. Everyone has a father. State any religious, political, philosophical or grammatical objections you have to this statement, and then:

   (a) assume it is true;
   (b) model it in an entity-relationship diagram. Remember that girls have fathers, and that no girl can be a father, and that some boys are not fathers;
   (c) model it using a relational representation.

4. Consider the entity type PERSON and the symmetrical relationship 'is the spouse of' under conditions of enforced monogamy. The relationship is one-to-one and optional in both directions. It is symmetrical because A being the spouse of B implies that B is the spouse of A. Assume that you want to store the name of each person in the PERSON entity type.

   Draw an entity-relationship diagram for this unary relationship type, and produce the relational representation for the diagram. Put in a sample extension, showing two or four people in spouse relationships and one or two not in spouse relationships. Is it necessary to duplicate the facts about people's spouses? Remember, one of the main objectives of a fully normalized database is that there should be no duplication of data.

Foreign keys with parallel relationships

If we had more than one relationship between two entity types, (parallel relationships) as in Fig. 4.7, we would in this situation also, have to distinguish between the different roles of the foreign keys by giving them different names. The attributes OWNER_NO and SERVICED_BY are both foreign keys taking values from EMP_NO in EMPLOYEE.

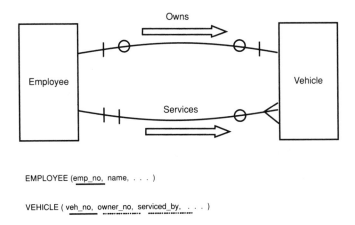

EMPLOYEE (emp_no, name, . . .)

VEHICLE (veh_no, owner_no, serviced_by, . . .)

Fig. 4.7 Representing parallel relationships.

Exercise 4.4

1. Think of further examples involving parallel relationships and produce a relational model for each one.

2. Is it possible to name the foreign keys in such a way that the nature of the relationship is made apparent?

Foreign keys in one-to-one relationships

In a one-to-one relationship, there are several relational representations possible. Which method is chosen depends on circumstances. In Fig. 4.8 we have a one–one relationship between the DRIVING_LICENCE and EMPLOYEE entity types. Notice that the 'has' relationship is optional. To show the relationship, we could consider placing the primary key of the table LICENCE in table EMPLOYEE as a foreign key, or placing the primary key of EMPLOYEE in LICENCE as a foreign key.

If we placed LIC_NO in EMPLOYEE, it would sometimes be null (undefined) since some employees do not have a driving licence. If however we place EMP_NO in LICENCE, no null values are required, since every licence will have an employee owner. So the latter is the preferred option.

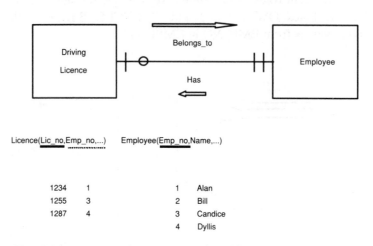

Fig. 4.8   Representing a 1:1 relationship.

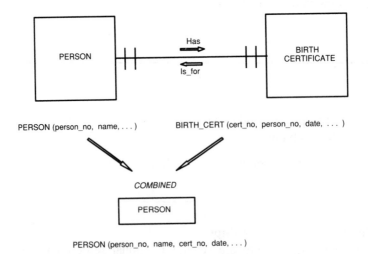

Fig. 4.9   Representing a 1:1 doubly mandatory relationship.

Another alternative sometimes chosen, particularly when the one-to-one relationship is mandatory both ways, is to combine the attributes of both tables into one entity type. In the example of Fig. 4.8, this would not be satisfactory since the resulting table EMPLOYEE would have null values for all the driving licence attributes for non-driving employees. (Naturally we would not consider placing all the employee attributes in LICENCE since then it would only be possible to store data about employees who had driving licences.) In Fig. 4.9 we do have the choice of combining the tables since the relationship is mandatory in both directions. Everyone has a birth certificate and every birth certificate is for someone. The attributes of both tables can be combined without introducing any null attributes.

There are two reasons that might legitimately be given for not combining two entity types linked solely by a one-to-one doubly mandatory relationship. The first is that the two database tables are subject to very different sets of processing activities. If PERSON records were frequently queried and updated independently of the birth certificate details then the tables would probably best be kept separate. The second is that the two entity types take part in different relationship types. See Fig. 4.10. When considering the sporting achievements of the person, the first two or three entity types would be considered together using a join. Similarly the latter three entity types may be joined for birth-related queries. It is unlikely that all four tables would ever be used together.

Entity types related by a 1:1 relationship type are sometimes combined into one entity type.

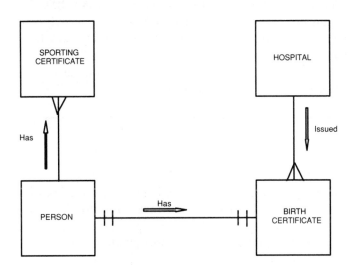

Fig. 4.10   1:1 entity types are not always combined.

Exercise 4.5

1. Think of an example of a one-to-one relationship that is mandatory in both directions and in which merging of the entity types and hence the relations, is not appropriate, giving reasons. Show the relational representation.

2. Think of an example of a one-to-one doubly mandatory relationship in which you would merge the entity types.

3. Think of an example of a unary one-to-one relationship that is mandatory in both directions and show its relational representation.

4. Think of an example of a unary one-to-one relationship that is optional in both directions and show its relational representation.

5. Produce illustrative extensions of each of the relational intensions in questions 1 to 4.

6. Produce a graph of each of the extensions in 5. (This is a very worthwhile and interesting exercise.)

Foreign keys from more than one table

In Fig. 4.11, which is a part of an election database, the CANDIDATE entity type is related by one-to-many relationships to both CONSTITUEN-CY and PARTY. There are thus two foreign keys in CANDIDATE. CONS_NO is a foreign key from CONSTITUENCY showing which constituency the candidate is standing in and PARTY_NO is a foreign key from PARTY showing which political party the candidate is standing for.

In general, a database table will contain a foreign key from each table (entity type) which has a one-to-many relationship type to it.

Exercise 4.6

1. Produce an outline relational representation for each of the entity-relationship diagrams in Fig. 3.8 apart from 3.8(a). Choose a primary key for each entity type (Lecturer_no, Course_no, and Text_no or ISBN will do) and then go through each of Figs. 3.8(b) to 3.8(f), producing a relational design for each. Check that only your design corresponding to Fig. 3.8(f) can answer all relevant queries.

2. Think of another example in which each of several entity types has a one-to-many relationship to the same entity type. Draw the entity-relationship model and produce a relational representation. Do not forget to underline the primary keys with a solid line and the foreign keys with a dotted line.

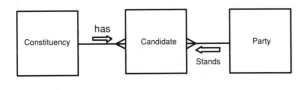

Constituency(Cons_no,Name,Town_hall_addr)

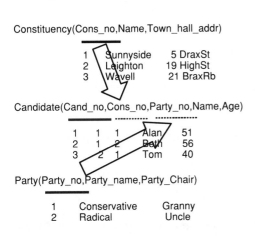

1	Sunnyside	5 DraxSt
2	Leighton	19 HighSt
3	Wavell	21 BraxRb

Candidate(Cand_no,Cons_no,Party_no,Name,Age)

1	1	1	Alan	51
2	1	2	Beth	56
3	2	1	Tom	40

Party(Party_no,Party_name,Party_Chair)

| 1 | Conservative | Granny |
| 2 | Radical | Uncle |

Fig. 4.11   Foreign keys from more than one table.

The effect of optionality on foreign keys

Figure 4.12 considers two cases. In Fig. 4.12(a) the relationship r is optional and its inverse r' is not. Because every B tuple is related to an A tuple (by r'), the foreign key A_no will never be null. The fact that r is optional simply means that there will be some values of A_no that do not appear as foreign key values in B.

In Fig. 4.12(b) however, a nullable foreign key is unavoidable. In this case, some B tuples are not related to an A tuple and consequently those B tuples will have a null value for the foreign key A_no. So if there is an optionality at the 'one' end of a one-to-many relationship type, the entity type at the 'many' end will have a nullable foreign key. 'Nullable' in this context means that it is possible that some values will be null. 'Null' in this context means: 'denoting nothing'.

Exercise 4.7

1. Check that your answers to all previous exercises involving optionality conform to this rule.

2. In a binary relationship type which is optional in both directions, is it necessary to have nullable foreign keys at both ends?

3. In a unary relationship type which is optional in both directions, is it ever possible (or necessary) to have a nullable primary key?

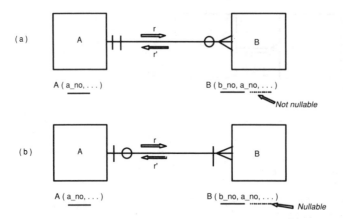

Fig. 4.12   Null values for the foreign key cannot be avoided in (b).

Entity integrity

The entity integrity rule should at this point come as no surprise. It states that:

> No component of the primary key of a base relation is allowed to accept nulls.

A base relation is a relation actually represented on the database, not something derived from it by a query or a view.

It is possible to speculate about what a null actually represents. Date (1990) does so for several pages and comes to no conclusion other than that it can mean 'property does not apply' or 'unknown' (p.279) or 'something else again' (p.281) and that it is 'still not properly understood' (p.385), and that the number of meanings might be 'theoretically infinite' (p.388).

Given these various usages, Date wishes to find out instead what null actually means, independent of context, and of course is at a loss. There is not much evidence to go on, just a blank field. He then attempts instead to legislate on what it should mean, and this is equally fruitless since one of the meanings already established for it is that it 'denotes nothing'. This can be confirmed in a dictionary.

Why NULL is necessary.

If it denotes nothing, why use it at all? The use of null can arise in a relational databases, as it does in paper form filling, as a consequence of attempting to force knowledge into a fixed number of columns. In such circumstances, any value is inapplicable (e.g. maternity leave date for a male employee). You might leave a field blank because you do not have the knowledge at that time, or for reasons of privacy. The 'meaning' of null must be related to its context. In a relational database this might be deduced from attribute names, but it is better if the meaning is explicitly stated in a data dictionary.

It would be a problem if null were allowed as a legitimate value for a primary key, because if more than one tuple had this value, then one of the tenets of relational databases, that each tuple is distinguishable by at least its primary key value, would be broken. Incidentally, the idea that each tuple in a relation must be distinguishable from all the others derives from the definition of a set, and a relation is a kind of set (Chapter 2). The uniqueness of each item in a set (i.e. its non-duplication) in turn derives from the belief that each entity in the world has a separate and continuing existence, a separate 'identity'. Duplicates must consequently be abandoned (according to Relational theory), because they cannot exist. In practice of course duplicates do exist and special measures must be taken in a relational database to 'remove' them. One common measure is to add an extra attribute, such as customer number, which does distinguish the tuples, if not the entities they model. For all practical purposes, two mass-produced transistors on a production line are identical. If it is necessary for some purpose to distinguish each transistor uniquely, an artificial attribute, such as a serial number, is placed on it.

Entity integrity is tied up with the notion of identity and the primary key idea is the mechanism for establishing an entity's identity, that is, its uniqueness. Paradoxically, we allow (not in relational databases and set theory but in other areas), two distinct objects to be 'identical'. They have all the same attribute values and yet they have a different identity. Identical entities have different identities. Identity thus has two meanings. On the one hand it means what a thing is, on the other hand what properties 'it' displays.

Exercise 4.8

1. If two distinct objects display the same attributes (of the set of attributes you are perceiving or modelling) are they identical? Do they have the same identity?

2. Think of a situation in which you might want to store attribute values of two identical entities. How would you do it on a relational database? (Remember each tuple has to be 'distinct', i.e. different in at least one way: different in at least the value of the primary key.)

The qualities necessary for an attribute or set of attributes to together qualify for being a primary key are illustrated in Fig. 4.13. There is a set of entities that we wish to store data about and a set of key values. Each entity should have one key value and each key value should refer to one entity. The 'relationship' (usually unnamed) between the entities and the keys is one-to-one mandatory in both directions. If the first set is a set of customers

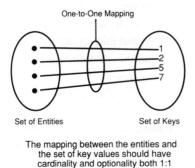

The mapping between the entities and
the set of key values should have
cardinality and optionality both 1:1

Fig. 4.13 Primary keys are 1:1 mandatory to the entity type they identify.

and the second set is a set of customer numbers, then each customer should
have one customer number (and not zero or more than one) customer number, and each key value on the database extension should be allocated to one
(and not zero or more than one) customer.

It is often said that the key value is 'unique' or is 'unique to the entity'.
Unfortunately this is ambiguous. Take the following statement:

'Every customer has a unique Customer Number.'

It is possible to interpret this statement in such a way that the following are
allowable:

(a) Jones and Co. have a Customer Number that nobody else has. It is
     unique. They also have some other Customer Numbers which they
     share with other customers. (Many–many.)
(b) Every customer has only one Customer Number. It is impossible to
     have two or more. Customers may share a Customer number.
     (many–one.)
(c) Every customer has the same customer number. (Many–one.)

It would have been better to say:

'Every customer has one Customer Number.'

Here (b) and (c) are still possible. The statement is still ambiguous.

The following is, one hopes, unambiguous and a true representation of
what was intended:

'Every customer has one customer number and every customer number is
given to one customer.'

This is similar to the discussion in Chapter 2 where it was necessary to make a separate statement about each direction of the relationship to be perfectly clear about it.

It is important for a systems analyst to be able to spot ambiguities in English statements because problem specifications are often given verbally or in writing. Since interpretation depends on the individual, there is a constant struggle in database design to be sure that the designer and the analyst and the user are understanding each other. Many seeming differences of opinion turn on ambiguity. Worse than a difference of opinion is the situation in which the parties seem to agree but have different things in their minds because the statements they are agreeing to are ambiguous. In this situation, the notion of 'common sense' as a substitute for precision is seen to be potentially dangerous not least because it can lead to inappropriate system design.

Cultivate an ability to recognize ambiguities in English statements.

Exercise 4.9

1. See if you can spot the ambiguities in the following statements. The first appeared in a national newspaper and the second in an examination question:

   (a) 'The contract can be ended, if 98% of prisoners do not reach court on time each month.'
   (b) 'A worker may not yet be allocated to a particular job.'

2. How can you be precise and unambiguous without seeming pedantic? Do diagrams and skill in English help? What should be meant by 'good communication skills' when recruiting a systems analyst? List the qualifications and personal qualities you consider most important when recruiting a trainee systems analyst.

Figure 4.14 shows in diagrammatic form (an entity-relationship diagram), using the customer example, what is expected of a primary key. Every customer should have one customer number; not more than one (right-hand cardinality) and not less than one (right-hand optionality). Every customer number currently in use should have been given to one customer; not more than one (left-hand cardinality) and not less than one (left-hand optionality). The mapping between customers and their primary key values is one-to-one and mandatory in both directions.

The entity integrity rule is saying that no part of the primary key can be null. If null were allowed, then in Fig. 4.14 the cardinality at the left-hand end of the relationship would be 'many', since more than one customer may have this null value. For a compound or a composite key (a primary key consisting of more than one attribute), the same would apply, since all components of compound and composite keys are required to ensure 'uniqueness';

The entity integrity rule says that no part of a primary key can be null.

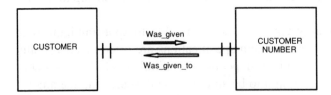

Fig. 4.14 Primary keys are 1:1 mandatory to the entity type.

more than one entity may have the same value for the non-null part of the key, since otherwise that would be a satisfactory key by itself.

Compound and composite primary keys

Although definitions vary, the distinction between compound and composite keys made in this book is as follows. A compound primary key is a primary key which consists of more than one attribute and every attribute in the key is a primary key in some other relation. Suppose there is a relation:

```
ORDER_LINE(Order_No, Product_No, Quantity_Required ...
```

and further suppose that Order_No is a primary key in an ORDER relation, and Product_No is a primary key in a PRODUCT relation.

Then the underlined primary key is a compound key since both of its attributes is a primary key in another relation.

However, if the definition of the ORDER_LINE relation were as follows:

```
ORDER_LINE(Order_No, Line_No, Product_No, Quantity_Required...
```

then the underlined attributes constitute a composite primary key since although Order_No is a primary key in the ORDER relation, Line_No is not a primary key anywhere.

Referential integrity

The referential integrity rule states that:

The database must not contain any unmatched foreign key values.

This means that a non-null foreign key value must have its counterpart in the tuple to which it refers. That is, this value of the foreign key must appear as one of the values of a primary key. In Fig. 4.15, the first INV tuple obeys the rule; its C_NO value of 1 appears in CUS as a primary key value. This is also true of the fourth tuple, invoice 40. The second INV tuple obeys the referential integrity rule because this rule refers to non-null foreign keys

Every foreign key value must be a primary key value in the table to which it is linked by a relationship.

only. The third tuple disobeys the referential integrity rule since its foreign key value C_NO = 3 is not to be found as a value of C_NO in the CUS relation.

The utility of the referential integrity rule is clear enough, as this example shows. There is a contradiction on the database, a lack of consistency and therefore a lack of database integrity. The third tuple in INV is stating that a customer number 3 exists and that he or she was sent this invoice. The CUS relation on the other hand is stating that no customer 3 exists. Referential integrity has been broken.

Having an invoice with no 'owning' customer, i.e. nobody to whom the invoice was sent (null foreign key), probably makes no sense, but does not break the referential integrity rule. The rule (if it is a rule in this particular organization's operations) that every invoice should have an 'owning' customer is best expressed technically by saying that the foreign key C_NO in INV is (or should be) non-null.

In Fig. 4.16, the particular extension of the database that is shown does not break the referential integrity rule. The fact that a toy might legitimately not be owned by any baby does not break the rule. It merely means that the optionality of the 'belongs-to' rule is zero, that is, it is an optional relationship. This means that B_NO (baby number) in TOY can legitimately be null. We say that it is nullable.

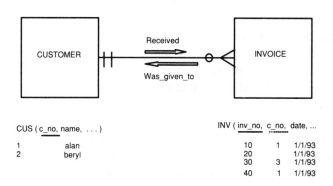

Fig. 4.15 The third INV tuple disobeys the referential integrity rule.

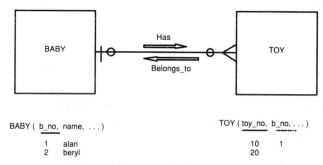

Fig. 4.16 A toy with no baby does not break the referential integrity rule.

Exercise 4.10

Is it possible to show referential integrity via relationship degree on an entity-relationship diagram?

Referential integrity should be maintained on relational databases by ensuring that all processes that update the database (insertions, deletions and modifications) take the necessary steps to check foreign key relationships.

If any invoice tuple were to be deleted from the INV table, the referential integrity rule would not be broken. Consequently it would not be necessary for the program to check the CUS table. (There may be other reasons of course, such as modifying the customer's outstanding balance.) If however a customer tuple in CUS were to be deleted, it would be necessary to check that there were no invoices for that customer. If, for example, the row for customer number 1 in Fig. 4.15 were to be deleted, then invoice numbers 10 and 40 would break the referential integrity rule since they would then refer to a customer who did not exist in the CUS table.

If a CUS row were to be inserted with no invoices being associated with it, the referential integrity rule would not be broken. If however an INV tuple were to be inserted then it would not be breaking the referential integrity rule for that invoice not to have an 'owning' CUS tuple. The foreign key INV.C_NO (i.e. the C_NO attribute in the INV table) could be set to null. The referential integrity rule would be broken if an INV tuple were inserted with a non-null value of C_NO and that value did not correspond to any value of C_NO in CUS.

If the value of CUS.C_NO were to be modified then there is one potential referential integrity problem. (This would incidentally be inadvisable because of the identity issues associated with entity integrity.) If the old value were associated with invoices, then those invoices would no longer have an 'owning' CUS tuple. That would break the referential integrity rule. If the value of INV.C_NO were changed, then care must be taken that the value to which it is changed corresponds to an existing CUS.C_NO value, otherwise the referential integrity rule would again be broken.

Exercise 4.11

1. What precautions involving considerations of entity and referential integrity should applications take if they were to be allowed to modify the value of INV.INV_NO? Assume INV is linked to another entity type PAYMENT via the foreign key PAYMENT.INV_NO.

2. In the database of Fig. 4.16, where both directions of the relationship are

optional, what entity and referential integrity constraints should be taken into account for updates of the type discussed in the previous section?

Enforcing integrity constraints in the DBMS

Maintaining database integrity is clearly an important issue. One method of ensuring the integrity (i.e. the correctness, consistency and completeness) of the database is to ensure that all of the applications that update the database themselves contain code which will perform the necessary checks. However this can lead to increased complexity of applications and coding time, increases in the communication time between applications and the DBMS, and a necessarily greater involvement of the DBA (Database Administrator) in detailed application code checking. This last can be implemented by management means. The use of standard libraries to perform various types of updates can be encouraged, if not enforced. When an application programmer wants his or her application to perform updates to a particular database table, the relevant installation-specific library routine is searched for and incorporated into the code. Privileges to update the tables directly can be withheld.

This approach has been formalized in some DBMSs, for example the later versions of INGRES, using database procedures and rules, which are stored in the database, are managed by the DBMS, and form part of the database definition. The traditional separation of data and process has thus been reduced. The DBA can use the grant statement to give a user permission to execute a procedure but withhold permission to access the tables directly. In this way the DBA controls exactly what operations a user can perform.

Rules are stored with the table in the database and consequently are applied continuously. Once the rule is defined, the DBMS invokes the rule's associated procedure whenever the rule's firing condition is met. In INGRES, the statement firing the rule can be a statement in an application program written in a host language with embedded SQL or it can be issued through ABF/4GL, or any of the INGRES user interfaces such as QBF (Query By Forms), and interactive query languages SQL and QUEL.

As an example, one of the referential integrity constraints mentioned above in connection with Fig. 4.15 can be enforced in the Knowledge Management Extension of INGRES using the code below. As we have seen, a referential integrity is an assertion of a relationship between two tables, Table1 and Table2, such that a column in Table1 must contain values that match those of the primary key in Table2 (or null). The column in Table1 containing the matching values is called a foreign key. The referential integrity constraint being enforced here is that when a new INV row is to be inserted, the C_NO in it (the foreign key from CUS) should exist in the CUS table:

The Knowledge Management Extension of INGRES can be used to enforce referential integrity.

```
1 CREATE PROCEDURE new_inv (cnum integer) AS
2 DECLARE
3    check_if_any INTEGER;
4    msg VARCHAR(80) NOT NULL;
5 BEGIN
6    SELECT COUNT(*) INTO :check_if_any
7    FROM cus
8    WHERE c_no = :cnum;
9    IF check_if_any = 0 then
10       msg = 'Error 1: Customer " + :cnum + '" not found.';
11       RAISE ERROR 1 :msg;
12       RETURN;
13    ENDIF;
14 END;


15 CREATE RULE new_inv AFTER INSERT INTO invoice
16       EXECUTE PROCEDURE new_inv (cnum = invoice.c_no);
```

It is worth looking at the main features of this code now. The line numbers are not part of the code; they just help in this explanation.

Lines 1 to 14 are the database procedure NEW_INV, which checks whether (lines 6 to 8) there is a customer with the C_NO input as the parameter CNUM in line 1. If there is not such a customer (lines 9 to 13), an error message is displayed and any changes that were caused to the database (here by INSERTing an INVOICE row) are rolled back, meaning that the database reverts to its previous state (in this example its state before the INSERTion of the INVOICE row).

Lines 15 to 16 are the database rule. Whenever any procedure, application program or interactive process INSERTs an invoice row, the procedure NEW_INV is called, the C_NO, which is the foreign key in INVOICE from CUS, is passed via the parameter CNUM, and as we have seen, if that value of C_NO cannot be found in the CUS table, the INSERT is aborted.

The definition of the rules and the database procedures originate with the DBA and are maintained by him or her. Rules and database procedures such as these can greatly enhance the integrity of the database and place its control more in the hands of the DBA and less in the hands of application designers and developers (systems analysts and programmers).

Normalization

Introduction

As with entity-relationship modelling, the purpose of normalization is to get the data into some simple or canonical form that truly reflects the separate entity types, their attributes, and the relationships between them.

Normalization is a somewhat more detailed and nondiagrammatical process which the data analyst or database designer carries out when designing the database schema. Rather than starting from the real world entities, it starts from predocumented sets of attributes and tries to group and regroup them in such a way that update, insertion and deletion anomalies are avoided. It does this by applying a number of normalization rules to initial groupings of data derived from an existing system. Examples of these anomalies and how normalization removes them are given in this section.

Historically, the origins of normalization (Codd, 1970) predate those of entity-relationship diagramming (Chen, 1976). In his seminal paper, Codd points out the dependence of program designs on the physical design of the database in existing systems. Codd describes several such dependencies, including ordering dependence (the program expecting to find the data in a particular order), indexing dependence (the program expecting to see the data in the order determined by an index and accessible via the index) and access path dependence (the program having to be aware of the pointers between record types). He points out that these physical characteristics of the database representation could be changed; if they were, the programs would no longer work.

The idea of normalization originated in Codd's 1970 paper.

Codd argues that there should be an intermediate level between the physical detail of the database and the user which made it unnecessary for the user to know these details in order to access the database and design programs to access the database. This principle is called program-data independence. Any reorganization of the physical data on the storage devices (in order to make accesses faster for example) should not make it necessary for the programs to change. The structure of this view of data was at Codd's suggestion based on an existing body of theory, that of mathematical relations.

An additional advantage in adopting a relational approach was that given the simple structure of such relations and the existing theory, many of the operations on data that programs would want to perform could be defined in terms of existing and well-known set operations, such as union, intersection, projection, permutation and composition. With the addition of join, the seeds of today's query languages had been sown.

In some circles, the two methods – entity modelling and normalization – may have been seen as being in competition, but in others, for example the SSADM method, they are seen as complementary (e.g. Ashworth and Goodland, 1990).

In SSADM, entity-relationship modelling and normalization are started entirely separately, their results being reconciled at a later stage. This forms a sort of self-checking mechanism. The entity-relationship model starts, as we have done in Chapter 3, from the position of asking the question;

'What real-world objects do we wish to store data about?'

Normalization starts, on the other hand, from collections of data attributes on data flows in data flow diagrams and associated forms, reports, etc.

An alternative approach, which can turn out to be quite effective, is to start with the production of an entity-relationship model, write down the collections of attributes in each entity type, identify the primary keys and the foreign keys, and then to apply the rules of normalization described below. In this way, normalization acts as a check on the data modelling of the entity-relationship diagram while adding more detail concerning the attributes. Normalization can result in considerable changes to the set of relations, most obviously in the form of relations being split into two or more parts. Since each relation corresponds to an entity type, the entity-relationship diagram should be redrawn after normalization has been performed.

Entity-relationship diagramming is said to be essentially top-down in its approach. It starts from 'high-level' (undetailed) concepts such as real-world entities and works towards detailed relations and their attributes.

Normalization is a 'bottom-up' procedure. Normalization is by this measure an essentially bottom-up method. It starts from detailed sets of attributes and works upwards towards a correctly structured set of relations, each of which represents a real-world entity type, and whose foreign keys represent relationships that also exist in the real world.

Of the two methods, normalization is perhaps the more precise, since there are well-defined normalization rules (described below) which virtually dictate the structure of the final database logical schema. Entity-relationship modelling depends rather heavily upon the analyst's impressions of the real-world situation he or she is modelling and these are inclined to differ somewhat from one person to another. Normalization, which starts from already existing groups of attributes, tends to be less subjective.

Entity-relationship modelling and normalization are complementary. If a new database is to be created for a new system, then entity-relationship modelling is recommended as the first step, to obtain an overall high-level view of the 'actors' (entity types) in the 'game' and their relationships. Attributes are then allocated to each entity type, primary keys are identified, and foreign keys to represent relationships. These groups of attributes are then normalized to check the design.

For an existing system, attributes will already be grouped in various ways in reports, files, indexes, etc. and so it is possible to start with normalization and 'build up' the entity-relationship model in parallel. Alternatively, design can proceed as with a new system. The only difference then would be that the identification of the attributes would be achieved not solely through asking questions such as:

'What data do we want to store about customers?'

but also by observing what data is currently stored.

As will be seen, each of the normal forms is associated with both a procedure that the designer carries out, and the state that is thereby achieved in the resulting relations. We might say:

'I shall apply First Normal Form to this relation so that the resulting relations will be in First Normal Form.'

Historically, each normal form was invented to deal with update, insert and deletion anomalies that were shown to exist in some relations that were in the currently highest normal form. Examples of these anomalies accompany the description of each of the normalization steps given in the following sections.

Applying 1NF (First Normal Form) to a relation will result in its being split into a number of relations which do pass the 1NF test if it is not itself already a 1NF relation. If the relation is already 'in' 1NF, then it will not have to be split when the 1NF test is applied; it can stay as it is. The same principle applies for all of the other normalization tests : 2NF, 3NF, 4NF, 5NF. Each normalization step applies a progressively more stringent test on the set of relations produced from the previous normalization step. This is illustrated in Fig. 4.17. Only first, second and third normal forms are shown.

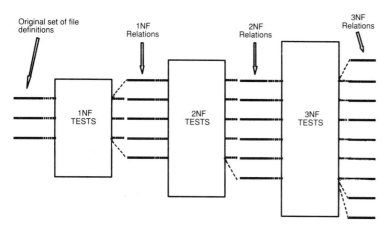

Fig. 4.17 Normalization progressively splits relations.

Notice that some of the original set of relations (which might have been derived from entity analysis or from documenting groups of data items from forms, reports, etc.), may remain completely unchanged by the normalization steps. The second of the original set for example, goes through all three steps unchanged. It was already in third normal form. Note also that the normalization constraints are cumulative. In order for a relation to qualify for being in third normal form, say, it must also pass the second normal form criterion. A 'fully normalized' relation is one which passes the criteria of the highest normal form you are considering. It will never be less than third normal form.

We are now in a position to describe the normalization tests in detail.

First normal form

A relation is in first normal form if and only if it contains no repeating attributes and no repeating groups of attributes.

Repeating attributes and repeating groups

The following relation contains a repeating attribute A4:

r1 (	A1,	A2,	A3,	(A4)*)		
	v1	v2	v3	v4	v4	v4
	v1	v2	v3	v4		
	v1	v2	v3	v4	v4	

A4 is a repeating attribute. Different rows contain different numbers of A4 values (v4's).

The top row shows the intension of the relation r1. A1, A2 and A3 are atomic attributes, so called because they cannot be broken down into smaller components. In the extension of r1, part of which is also shown, each tuple will only ever contain a single value of A1, a single value of A2, and a single value of A3. There will of course be different values of A1 in different tuples. 'v1' for example means 'a value of A1'. A4 is a repeating attribute, meaning that the attribute can occur a different number of times in different tuples. In the first tuple, there are three values of A4. A4 occurs three times. In the second tuple there is one value of A4 and in the third tuple there are two values of A4. A4 occurs twice. A1 is underlined here to show that it is the primary key.

The relation r1 is not in first normal form (1NF), because it contains a repeating attribute A4. This is shown by the round brackets and asterisk. In COBOL, r1 might be defined as:

```
FD R1-FILE.
01 R1.
    03 A1 PIC ...
    03 A2 PIC ...
    03 A3 PIC ...
    03 I PIC 99.
    03 A4-GROUP OCCURS 1 TO 10 DEPENDING ON I.
       05 A4 PIC ...
```

A repeating attribute in a COBOL file definition.

I is the count of how many times the A4 field occurs in each record. This is necessary for the software to know where one record ends and the next begins, since clearly records will have different lengths, depending on the number of A4's they contain. Most other general-purpose languages such as PASCAL, C, BASIC, FORTRAN and PL/I also allow repeating attributes and groups and they have been used frequently in the past to represent one-to-many relationships all in one record type. In COBOL, this is known as an

OCCURS group. COBOL is used in the following description rather than a database language because relational databases do not support repeating group structures.

Of the high-level data processing oriented languages, COBOL is probably the most widely known. Note that in COBOL the notion of primary key is unfortunately bound up with indexing. For a file whose ORGANIZATION IS INDEXED, it is possible to nominate a RECORD KEY whose values must remain unique. In a file whose ORGANIZATION IS SEQUENTIAL, completely duplicated records are permitted. Other breaches of the relational philosophy are also permitted. It is possible for example to have different record types within the same file. For example a customer order file could contain customer records, order records and order line records all held together in the same file.

In relational databases, repeating groups are not possible; every tuple contains the same number and set of attributes. All relations in relational databases therefore have to be in at least first normal form. It is advisable of course that they should be fully normalized. Relational databases do not allow mixed record types; all tuples are of the same 'type'; they all have the same attributes.

> In a relational database repeating attributes and groups of attributes are not possible.

The following relation r2 contains a repeating group (A4, A5):

```
r2 (    A1,     A2,     A3,     (A4, A5)* )
        v1      v2      v3      v4      v5      v4      v5
        v1      v2      v3      v4      v5
        v1      v2      v3      v4      v5      v4      v5      v4      v5
```

> r2 contains a repeating group (A4, A5).
> In the third row of r2, the group occurs 3 times.

Here, instead of a single attribute repeating, the group of attributes A4 with A5 repeats. Here, the repeating group consists of two attributes. A COBOL representation might be:

```
FD R2-FILE.
01 R2.
    03 A1 PIC ...
    03 A2 PIC ...
    03 A3 PIC ...
    03 I PIC 99.
    03 A4-GROUP OCCURS 0 TO 10 DEPENDING ON I.
        05 A4 PIC ...
        05 A5 PIC ...
```

> COBOL representation of a repeating group.
> I counts the number of occurrences of the group.

There can be more than one repeating group in a relation, as the following example shows:

```
r3 (    A1,     (A2,    A3,     A4)*, (A5)*)
        v1      v2      v3      v4      v2      v3      v4      v5      v5
        v1      v2      v3      v4      v5      v5      v5
        v1      v5      v5
```

> r3 contains two repeating groups.
> In row 3, the first group occurs zero times, and the second group twice.

In the first tuple, the first repeating group (A2, A3, A4) occurs twice and the second (A5) twice. In the second tuple, the first repeating group occurs once and the second occurs three times. In the third tuple, the first repeating group occurs zero times and the second occurs twice. A COBOL representation might be:

COBOL representation of r3.

```
FD R3-FILE.
01 R3.
    03 A1 PIC ...
    03 G1-COUNT PIC 99.
    03 GROUP-1 OCCURS 0 TO 20 DEPENDING ON G1-COUNT.
        05 A2 PIC ...
        05 A3 PIC ...
        05 A4 PIC ...
    03 G2-COUNT PIC 99.
    03 GROUP-2 OCCURS 1 TO 10 DEPENDING ON G2-COUNT.
        05 A5 PIC ...
```

The optionality of the relationship between the entity represented by the R3 record and the entity represented by each of the repeating group can be clearly seen. It is optional in the first group (0 to 20) and mandatory in the second group (1 to 10). Notice also that the names of the relationships do not appear anywhere in the record type definition.

Exercise 4.12

In addition to allowing the record length to be determined, G1-COUNT and G2-COUNT serve another important purpose. What is it?

It is also possible for repeating groups to contain other repeating groups.

r4 contains one repeating group within another.

r4 (	A1,	(A2,	A3,	(A4,	A5)*	)*,	A6)
	v1	v2	v3	v4	v5	v4	v5	v6
	v1	v6					
	v1	v2	v3	v2	v3	v4	v5	v6

Exercise 4.13

Produce the COBOL file definition statement corresponding to relation r4. Is it possible for the outer group to be optional and the inner group mandatory?

Fig. 4.18 is a data structure diagram for r4. The repeating groups are represented by a box containing an asterisk. If known, the minimum and maximum number of occurrences can be written above the asterisk, and the name of the group can be written in the box. It is also possible to draw an entity-relationship diagram corresponding to r4 (Fig. 4.19). Note that the E-R diagram is capable of showing much more detail than any of the other representations. This accounts for the question marks on this particular diagram.

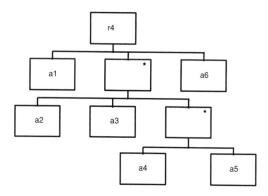

Fig. 4.18   A data structure diagram for r4.

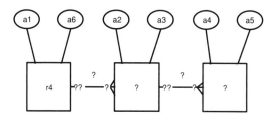

Fig. 4.19   An entity-relationship diagram for r4.

The following relation r5 does not contain a repeating group.

r5 (	A1,	A2,	A3,	A2,	A3,	A4)
	v1	v2	v3	v2	v3	v4
	v1	v2	v3	v2	v3	v4
	v1	v2	v3	v2	v3	v4

In practice, the two occurrences of A2 and A3 would be given different names on a relationship database.

Although the group of attributes A2 with A3 occurs twice, it occurs exactly twice in every tuple. The record length (measured in numbers of attributes) is always the same. A COBOL representation is:

```
FD R5-FILE.
01 R5.
  03 A1 PIC ...
  03 GROUP-1 OCCURS 2 TIMES.
    05 A2 PIC ...
    05 A3 PIC ...
  03 A4 PIC ...
```

In Fig. 4.20, the curly brackets show a repeating group.

Let us now consider a more realistic example. Suppose we had found in an existing system a file with the record data structure shown in Fig. 4.20. The fields in this record type indicate the data structure of Fig. 4.21.

Order(Ord_no,Date,Acc_no,Name,Addr,{Prod_no, Descr,Qty,Price,Row_tot},Ord_tot)

Fig. 4.20   Original ORDER file definition.

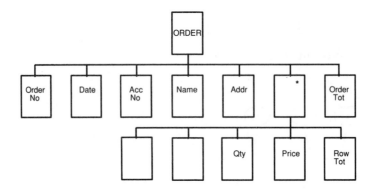

Fig. 4.21   A data structure diagram for the ORDER file.

A COBOL definition of the file might look like this:

```
FD CUS-ORDER-FILE.
01 CUS-ORDER-REC.
    03 ORD-NO PIC 9(5).
    03 ORD-DATE PIC 9(6).
    03 ACC-NO PIC 9(6).
    03 NAME PIC X(20).
    03 ADDRESS PIC X(80).
    03 ORDER-LINE-COUNT PIC 99.
    03 ORDER-LINE OCCURS 1 TO 20 DEPENDING ON ORDER-LINE-COUNT.
      05 PROD-NO PIC 9(5).
```

```
      05 DESCR PIC X(20).
      05 PRICE PIC 9(4)V99.
      05 QTY PIC 999.
      05 ROW-TOT PIC 9(6)V99.
   03 ORD-TOT PIC 9(7)V99.
```

Fig. 4.22 COBOL file definition of customer order.

This is a very convenient data structure for containing the data input from the customer order form shown in Fig. 4.23. (Let us assume that all of our company's customers use our standard order form so that the format will always be the same.) ORDER-LINE is a repeating group showing the details of each of our products that the customer has ordered. ORDER-LINE-COUNT contains the number of different products the customer has ordered.

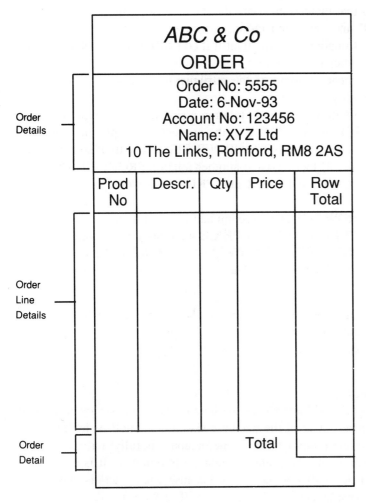

Fig. 4.23 The customer order form.

Exercise 4.14

Suppose ADDRESS in Fig. 4.22 were to be replaced by the structure:

```
03 ADDRESS.
  05 ADDR-LINE-CT PIC 99.
  05 ADDRESS-LINE PIC X(27)
     OCCURS 1 TO 3 DEPENDING ON ADDR-LINE-CT.
```

Does this constitute a repeating group?

Data redundancy

One problem with the data structure shown in Fig. 4.22 that will justify our normalizing it to 1NF (as a start), is that such a structure fosters data redundancy. It is not that there is any data there that is not required, but some of the data 'facts' may be stated more than once. In Codd's 1970 paper, he says that a set of relations is redundant if it contains data in a relation that is derivable from other relations by simple repetition (repeating whole rows) or projection (repeating some of the attributes) or joins (combinations of attributes from other relations).

Non-1NF files may contain data redundancy. Here we have within this single relation a simple case of repetition. The description DESCR and the PRICE of the product whose product number is PROD_NO will be stored in CUS-ORDER-REC every time someone purchases that product. If there existed another relation PRODUCT which also contained PROD-NO and DESCR and PRICE this would be further data redundancy.

The attribute ROW-TOT is also redundant because it can be derived from the product of PRICE and QTY. If PRICE were not contained in this relation but was in PRODUCT, then ROW-TOT would still be derivable and not necessary in CUS-ORDER-REC. There are three major objections to data redundancy:

- it wastes storage space and may consequently affect access time;
- it facilitates data inconsistency;
- it leads to update anomalies.

Data consistency

In the same paper, Codd introduces the idea of data consistency, a property of the instantaneous state of the database (i.e. its data not its definition), in which there are no contradictions. If the database is fully normalized, it is designed in such a way that data redundancy is removed. It is easy to see that inconsistencies will not then arise because each 'fact' is stated only once and no derivable facts (such as ROW-TOTAL) are stored.

Update anomalies

Suppose that the only source of information about the descriptions and prices of the products we sold were the DESCR and PRICE attributes in the customer order file CUS-ORD-FILE of Fig. 4.22. Then it would be impossible to insert these details for a new product into the database if no customer had yet purchased the product. Remember that the entity integrity rule of the relational model does not allow any component of the primary key to be null; in relation CUS-ORDER-REC, the primary key is ORD-NO. The order would not exist, there would be no ORD-NO, consequently no CUS-ORD-REC, and therefore nowhere to insert the attributes PROD-NO, DESCR and PRICE for the new product. This is known as an insertion anomaly.

Conversely, if during normal data processing operations, orders which have been fulfilled are deleted, deletion of the last order containing information (description and price) about a particular product would remove that information from the database. This is called a deletion anomaly.

Suppose the price of product number 23 were to change from £10 to £11. It would then be necessary to find every occurrence of product number 23 in CUS-ORDER-FILE and alter it. One price has changed and an unknown number of records must be updated. If any is missed, data inconsistency will result. This is called an update anomaly. (These three anomalies are also collectively called 'update anomalies' but that is just a minor terminological problem.)

Normalization aims to remove all of these anomalies and ensure data consistency by removing data redundancy.

Un-normalized data results in insertion, deletion and update anomalies.

Comment

It is worth noting that normalization is not the only way of removing data redundancy and removal of data redundancy is not the only way of ensuring data consistency. Other methods of achieving the latter include the complete control of all updates to the database by strictly unifying all programs (hard to achieve in practice) and the incorporation of rules and procedures into the database definition to disallow updates that would lead to inconsistency and to automatically perform 'knock-on-effect' updates (such as changes to all the CUS-ORDER-REC.PRICE fields affected by a change in price of a product). This depends on a complete understanding of all dependencies and redundancies on the database, as does the requirement for complete normalization.

See page 95 for details of rules and procedures.

Exercise 4.15

1. What other methods are there for removing data redundancy?

2. What other methods are there for ensuring data consistency?

Performing first normal form

We first repeat the definition of first normal form:

> A relation is in first normal form if and only if it contains no repeating attributes and no repeating groups of attributes.

The relation is split or rearranged so that the repeating attributes and repeating groups no longer repeat. Let us take relation r1 for example, and assume that A1 is the primary key.

The repeating attribute A4 can be removed in one of the ways shown in Fig. 4.24. Primary keys are underlined. The left-most column shows the original record number (not contained in the record but used for explanation purposes only).

Before 1NF

r1 (	A1,	A2,	A3,	(A4)*)		
1	v1	v2	v3	v4	v4	v4
2	v1	v2	v3	v4		
3	v1	v2	v3	v4	v4	

After 1NF (method 1)

	r1 (	A1,	A2,	A3,	A4)
Row 1 has been	1	v1	v2	v3	v4(1)
replaced by 3 rows	1	v1	v2	v3	v4(2)
with one value v4 of A4	1	v1	v2	v3	v4(3)
in each.	2	v1	v2	v3	v4
	3	v1	v2	v3	v4(1)
	3	v1	v2	v3	v4(2)

After 1NF (method 2)

	r1.1(	A1,	A2,	A3)
An alternative method	1	v1	v2	v3
of achieving 1NF (two	2	v1	v2	v3
tables).	3	v1	v2	v3

r1.2(	A1,	A4)
1	v1	v4(1)
1	v1	v4(2)

1	v1	v4(3)
2	v1	v4
3	v1	v4(1)
3	v1	v4(2)

Fig. 4.24 Alternative methods of achieving 1NF with rl.

Assume that A1 is the primary key for rl. Remember that in this diagram 'v1' means 'a value of A1', 'v2' means 'a value of A2', etc. If we take rl.1 for example, each value of v1 would be different since A1 is the primary key.

In method 1, the brackets and asterisk are simply removed and A4 becomes an atomic attribute. A tuple is created for each value of the repeating attribute. The first tuple of the non-1NF relation, which contains three values for A4, is thus replaced by three tuples, each containing one of the A4 values and the original value of A1, the key. Consequently there are three tuples in rl containing the same value of A1, which can therefore no longer qualify as a primary key. The primary key must be extended to include A4. A1 together with A4 form a satisfactory composite or compound key since the combination must be unique in the relation (assuming each value of v4 was unique in the tuple).

In method 2, two separate relations result. The original relation rl is replaced by the relations rl.1 and rl.2. Attribute A4 is excised from rl. Thus the repeating group has been 'split off'. To maintain the relationship showing which value of A1 is related to which values of A4, the second relation rl.2 must be added. Both attributes must be key attributes by the same argument as above.

In COBOL terms, 1NF applied to rl appears as in Fig. 4.25.

Before 1NF

```
FD R1-FILE.
01 R1.
   03 A1 PIC ...
   03 A2 PIC ...
   03 A3 PIC ...
   03 I PIC 99.
   03 A4-GROUP OCCURS 1 TO 10 DEPENDING ON I.
     05 A4 PIC ...
```

After 1NF (method 1)

```
FD R1-FILE.
01 R1.
```

```
03 A1 PIC ...
03 A2 PIC ...
03 A3 PIC ...
03 A4 PIC ...
```

After 1NF (method 2)

```
FD R1-1-FILE.
01 R1-1.
   03 A1 PIC ...
   03 A2 PIC ...
   03 A3 PIC ...


FD R1-2-FILE.
01 R1-2.
   03 A1 PIC ...
   03 A4 PIC ...
```

Fig. 4.25 COBOL version of Fig. 4.24.

Note that the primary key is not shown as such in the FD statement, and that the count 'I' has been lost. It might be enquired as to which method of achieving 1NF is better in this example. Certainly method 1 is simpler: simply remove the round brackets! Method 2 is better in that (in this example) both relations r1.1 and r1.2 are also in 2NF, whereas the r1 resulting from method 1 is not. In practice, it does not matter which method is chosen, since later normalization steps will ensure a convergence to the same ultimate fully normalized solution.

Exercise 4.16

Perform 1NF on relations r2 and r3, and show the corresponding COBOL representations.

The 1NF normalization of r4 is now discussed. This is the example with one repeating group inside another. See Fig. 4.26.

Before 1NF

1NF applied to r4 which has one repeating group within another.

r4 (	A1,	(A2,	A3,	(A4,	A5)*	)*,	A6)	
1	v1	v2	v3	v4	v5	v4	v5	v6
2	v1	v6						
3	v1	v2	v3	v2	v3	v4	v5	v6

After 1NF (method 1)

r4 (	A1,	A2,	A3,	A4,	A5,	A6)
1	v1	v2(1)	v3(1)	v4(1,1)	v5(1,1)	v6
1	v1	v2(1)	v3(1)	v4(1,2)	v5(1,2)	v6
2	v1	v6				
3	v1	v2(1)	v3(1)	v4(1,1)	v5(1,1)	v6
3	v1	v2(2)	v3(2)	v4(1,1)	v5(1,1)	v6

After 1NF (method 2)

r4.1(A1,	A6)	
1	v1	v6
2	v1	v6
3	v1	v6

r4.2(A1,	A2,	A3)
1	v1	v2	v3
3	v1	v2(1)	v3(1)
3	v1	v2(2)	v3(2)

r4.3(A1,	A2,	A4,	A5)
1	v1	v2	v4(1,1) v5(1,1)
1	v1	v2	v4(1,2) v5(1,2)
3	v1	v2	v4(2,1) v5(2,2)

Fig. 4.26 1NF applied to relation r4.

Notice that in method 1, additional duplication of data has resulted from the normalization step. In the first and second rows for example, which derive from the original tuple 1, the association of v1, v2(1), v3(1), v6 is repeated. Notice also that the primary key has also had to be extended to make it 'unique'. v4(1,2) is the second occurrence of the inner repeating group within the first occurrence of the outer repeating group.

If the second method of removing the repeating groups under 1NF is used, the three relations r4.1, r4.2 and r4.3 result. r4.2 contains the information deriving from the outer repeating group of the original relation and r4.3 contains the information from the inner repeating group. In order to preserve the relationship between original relation and the outer repeating group, A1 has had to be included in r4.2 as a foreign key.

In this example, A2 is the identifier for the outer repeating group data and with A1 forms a composite or compound key. (Remember that in a compound key, all components are a primary key in another relation; a system-wide identifier and that in a composite key not all of the components are. If the subtuples in the outer repeating group had obtained their identity only by a combination of A2 and A1 values, then the primary key in r4.2 would be a composite key rather than a compound key.)

In a similar way, r4.3 contains A1 with A2 as attributes to retain the relationship with r4.2. The three relations r4.1, r4.2, and r4.3 may form a hierarchy. Each level of the hierarchy has to be linked to its 'owning' level via a foreign key. The corresponding evolution of the entity-relationship diagram for this set of data is illustrated in Fig. 4.27. The relations might not form a hierarchy however, as this diagram shows. The question marks immediately to the right of entity type r4 indicate that the degree of the relationship at this end cannot be ascertained. The only way to do this is to know about the relationships between the entity types in the real world.

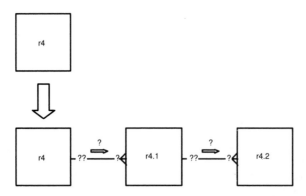

Fig. 4.27   The evolution of the entity-relationship model for r4 after INF.

There might not appear to be any duplication of data in r4.1, r4.2 and r4.3, but looking at r4.3 it can be seen that the association of a particular pair of values of A1 and A2 is duplicated and occurs once for each occurrence of the original inner repeating group.

Let us return now to the more concrete example of Fig. 4.22, the CUS-ORDER-FILE and perform 1NF on it.

Before 1NF
FD CUS-ORDER-FILE.
01 CUS-ORDER-REC.
   03 ORD-NO PIC 9(5).
   03 ORD-DATE PIC 9(6).
   03 ACC-NO PIC 9(6).
   03 NAME PIC X(20).

03 ADDRESS PIC X(80).
03 ORDER-LINE-COUNT PIC 99.
03 ORDER-LINE OCCURS 1 TO 20 DEPENDING ON ORDER-LINE-
COUNT.
    05 PROD-NO PIC 9(5).
    05 DESCR PIC X(20).
    05 PRICE PIC 9(4)V99.
    05 QTY PIC 999.
    05 ROW-TOT PIC 9(6)V99.
03 ORD-TOT PIC 9(7)V99.

After 1NF (method 1)
FD CUS-ORDER-FILE.
01 CUS-ORDER-REC.
  03 ORD-NO PIC 9(5).
  03 ORD-DATE PIC 9(6).
  03 ACC-NO PIC 9(6).
  03 NAME PIC X(20).
  03 ADDRESS PIC X(80).
  03 PROD-NO PIC 9(5).
  03 DESCR PIC X(20).
  03 PRICE PIC 9(4)V99.
  03 QTY PIC 999.
  03 ROW-TOT PIC 9(6)V99.
  03 ORD-TOT PIC 9(7)V99.

After 1NF (method 2)
FD CUS-ORDER-FILE.
01 CUS-ORDER-REC.
  03 ORD-NO PIC 9(5).
  03 ORD-DATE PIC 9(6).
  03 ACC-NO PIC 9(6).
  03 NAME PIC X(20).
  03 ADDRESS PIC X(80).
  03 ORD-TOT PIC 9(7)V99.

FD CUS-ORDER-LINE-FILE.
01 CUS-ORDER-LINE-REC.
  03 ORD-NO PIC 9(5).
  03 PROD-NO PIC 9(5).
  03 DESCR PIC X(20).
  03 PRICE PIC 9(4)V99.
  03 QTY PIC 999.
  03 ROW-TOT PIC 9(6)V99.

Using method 1, the repeating group is removed by simply having a separate record for each occurrence. If there had been two repeating groups, there would have had to be a separate record for each combination of attributes that occurred in the original record. One disadvantage of this approach is that all of the non-repeating attributes in the original record will now be repeated, once for each occurrence of the repeating group. This is demonstrated in Fig. 4.28.

Before 1NF

ORD-NO	ORD-DATE	ACC-NO	NAME	ADDRESS	ORD-L-CT	PROD-NO	DESCR	PRICE	QTY	ROW-TOT	ORD-TOT
1	1-jan-93	10	Alan	1 Nx St	3	100	Apple	1	5	5	17
						200	Ball	2	1	2	
						300	Cup	1	10	10	
2	2-jan-93	8	Kate	4 Ox St	2	200	Ball	2	5	10	13
						400	Dice	1	3	3	
3	5-jan-93	10	Alan	1 Nx St	1	300	Cup	1	1	1	1

After 1NF (method 1)

CUS-ORDER-REC

ORD-NO	ORD-DATE	ACC-NO	NAME	ADDRESS	PROD-NO	DESCR	PRICE	QTY	ROW-TOT	ORD-TOT
1	1-jan-93	10	Alan	1 Nx St	100	Apple	1	5	5	17
1	1-jan-93	10	Alan	1 Nx St	200	Ball	2	1	2	17
1	1-jan-93	10	Alan	1 Nx St	300	Cup	1	10	10	17
2	2-jan-93	8	Kate	4 Ox St	200	Ball	2	5	10	13
2	2-jan-93	8	Kate	4 Ox St	400	Dice	1	3	3	13
3	5-jan-93	10	Alan	1 Nx St	300	Cup	1	1	1	1

After 1NF (method 2)

CUS-ORDER-REC

ORD-NO	ORD-DATE	ACC-NO	NAME	ADDRESS	ORD-TOT
1	1-jan-93	10	Alan	1 Nx St	17
2	2-jan-93	8	Kate	4 Ox St	13
3	5-jan-93	10	Alan	1 Nx St	1

CUS-ORDER-LINE-REC

ORD-NO	PROD-NO	DESCR	PRICE	QTY	ROW-TOT
1	100	Apple	1	5	5
1	200	Ball	2	1	2
1	300	Cup	1	10	10
2	200	Ball	2	5	10
2	400	Dice	1	3	3
3	300	Cup	1	1	1

Fig. 4.28   1NF applied to CUS-ORDER-REC.

In the second method, the original file is split into two parts. Each of these relations should be given an appropriate name, such as (in COBOL parlance) CUS-ORDER-REC and CUS-ORDER-LINE-REC. Other names could be 'Customer Order' and 'Customer Order Line'.

There is less duplication of data here. The Order details only appear once and details of each of the order lines also appear only once. In entity-relationship diagram terms, the application of 1NF using the second method has produced the effect shown in Fig. 4.29. The names have to be invented by the analyst and the question mark illustrates the point that the relationship name will also need to be 'discovered'. Both this and the degree of the relationship, particularly at the CUS-ORDER end, will be identified by recourse to the real world situation. For example, is it true that an order line can only 'appear in' (relationship name) one order? Almost certainly. And this is assumed in Fig. 4.29.

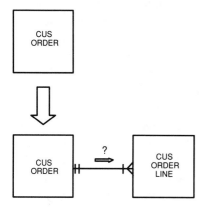

Fig. 4.29 The evolution of the entity relationship for CUS-ORDER after 1NF.

Close inspection of Fig. 4.28 reveals that duplication of data still exists in this example after 1NF even in the two-table variant.

Exercise 4.17

1. Show where duplication of data still exists in the 1NF normalized data of Fig. 4.28.
2. Suggest ways in which this duplication of data could be removed. Remember that you should not lose any data facts. Write out your new design and compare it with that of a colleague. Discuss the differences.

3. Assume all data about products is held in CUS-ORDER-LINE-REC. If there were a product that nobody had purchased, where could its details be stored?

4. Write down as many points as you can in favour of normalization.

There are further normalization steps to be performed on this set of relations because they still contain some duplication of data. It is possible that after 1NF, no data duplication exists. The set of relations will then be fully normalized and will require no further splitting. Many analysts find that after a bit of experience of drawing entity-relationship models, the set of tables they write out are already fully normalized. However, you will not know for sure that they are fully normalized until you perform all of the following normalization tests and each of your relations passes all these tests.

More often, one or more of your set of relations will need splitting at each normalization stage. It is interesting and informative to be able to show the evolution of the design for each of the final tables. Since normalization is basically a splitting process, (it is actually a splitting and merging process - see below), the evolution of a set of relations will have the form of a tree (Fig. 4.17). The question arises of how to lay out the normalization work that you do. The SSADM method recommends setting the relations out in columns as in Fig. 4.30 (Ashworth and Goodland, 1990). While neat, it is not always clear which relation is derived from which in this method, particularly where more than one relation is being normalized, and fitting in extra normal forms beyond the third can be inconvenient since there is a limit to the width of a page. The layout adopted in this book is exemplified in Fig. 4.31. The decision to split or not to split is often resolved by writing out sets of test data as we have shown in Fig. 4.28.

UNF	1NF	2NF	3NF
Ord_no	Ord_no		
Ord_date	Ord_date		
Acc_no	Acc_no		
Name	Name		
Address	Address		
Ord_l_ct	Ord_l_ct		
(Prod_no	Ord_tot		
Descr			
Price	Ord_no		
Qty	Prod_no		
Row_tot)	Descr		
Ord_tot	Price		
	Qty		
	Row_tot		

Fig. 4.30   SSADM performs normalization in columns.

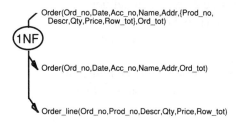

Order(Ord_no,Date,Acc_no,Name,Addr,{Prod_no,
Descr,Qty,Price,Row_tot},Ord_tot)

1NF

Order(Ord_no,Date,Acc_no,Name,Addr,Ord_tot)

Order_line(Ord_no,Prod_no,Descr,Qty,Price,Row_tot)

Fig. 4.31   Preferred method of showing normalization steps.

In practice, when a relation is split, you might discover that some of the collections of attributes are also contained in other relations. Hence all or part of a relation may be merged with another relation, or more precisely, all or part of a relation may be removed because the same association of attributes already appears in another relation. To merge in this way, it is not enough that the same two attributes appear together in two relations. For example the association of EMPLOYEE_NO and VEHICLE_REG_NO might appear in two different relations, in the one implying that the employee drives the vehicle and in the other that he or she services it. To qualify for removal, the meaning of the association between the attributes (in this book called a 'fact') must be the same in both relations. That is the true meaning of data duplication: the duplication (repetition) of a fact.

Merging of relations can be performed after each normalization step, or may be left to the end, after full normalization. In either case, merging ought to be followed by renormalization.

Second normal form

A relation is in second normal form if and only if it is in first normal form and every nonkey attribute is fully functionally dependent on the primary key.

Before demonstrating the meaning of this definition with examples, it is necessary to define functional dependency and full functional dependency.

Functional dependency

Here are two similar definitions of functional dependency:

Definition 1: Given a relation R, attribute Y of R is functionally dependent on attribute X of R if and only if each X-value in R has associated with it precisely one Y-value in R (at any one time). Attributes X and Y may be composite. (Date, 1990)

Definition 2: Given a relation R, attribute Y of R is functionally dependent on attribute X of R if and only if, whenever two tuples of R agree on their X-value, they must necessarily agree on their Y-value. (Date, 1990)

Note that there is no mention of keys here. A functional dependency may exist between any two sets of attributes. (It is however the purpose of normalization to limit the functional dependencies in a relation so that all dependencies are on the candidate keys only.)

Definitions 1 and 2 are not exactly equivalent. See Fig. 4.32.

If we represent this mapping in the definitions between attributes X and Y using a diagram, we get Fig. 4.32. The first definition is stronger in that it specifies that each value of X must have associated with it precisely one (meaning: one) value of Y. This is shown in Fig. 4.32(a) at the right-hand end of the (unnamed) relationship f that exists between X and Y. The cardinality and optionality are both one. Definition 2 is equivalent except for the fact that the optionality constraint is omitted. This is shown in Fig. 4.32(d).

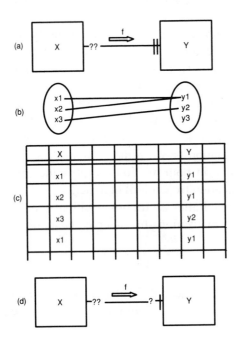

Fig. 4.32   The two definitions of functional dependency.

Fig. 4.32(b) gives some sample data in set-mapping form and Fig. 4.32(c) illustrates the same idea in an example table. Note that 'each X-value in R has associated with it precisely one Y-value' (definition 1) and 'whenever two tuples of R agree on their X-value, they must necessarily agree on their Y-value' (definition 2). So in the relation R as it stands, attribute Y is functionally dependent on attribute X. Note also that value x1 is associated with value y1 twice in relation R.

The extension of relation R can vary from minute to minute because of updates, but provided the constraints mentioned in the definitions always apply ('must necessarily apply'), Y remains functionally dependent on X.

It is worth repeating that neither X nor Y needs to be a candidate key. A functional dependency may exist between them without either of them being a candidate key. However, for the relation to be in third normal form (see below), X should be a candidate key. With the relation R as it appears in Fig. 4.32(c), X is clearly not a candidate key.

Exercise 4.18

Why is X 'clearly not a candidate key'?

Full functional dependency

As definition 1 states, either or both of the attributes X and Y may be composite, that is, a group of attributes. In Fig. 4.33, X is a composite attribute and let us suppose that Y is functionally dependent on X. The composite attribute X consists of atomic attributes A and B considered together. Y is said to be fully functionally dependent on X because it is functionally dependent on all of X, not just a part of it. Y is not functionally dependent on just A because, for example, value a1 is associated with both y1 (tuple 1) and y2 (tuple 6). Y is not functionally dependent on just B because, for example, value b2 is associated with both y1 (tuple 2) and y2 (tuple 3).

Y is 'fully functionally dependent' on X if it is functionally dependent on all of X, not any part of it.

If Y had turned out to be functionally dependent on just a part of X, then Y would be said to be partially dependent on X.

Exercise 4.19

1. State why the evidence of Fig. 4.33(a) points towards Y being functionally dependent on X.

2. Why is it that there is not sufficient evidence in Fig 4.33 to be able to say that Y is definitely functionally dependent on X?

3. In precise English, would the phrase 'fully dependent on' mean the same as 'dependent on all of'? Think of examples where it would not.

4. In precise English, would the phrase 'partially dependent on' mean the same as 'dependent on a part of'? Think of examples where it would not.

Notice that the particular instance of a composite attribute shown in Fig. 4.33(a) (attribute X), cannot be a candidate key because one of its values (a1, b1) is allowed to repeat (tuples 1 and 5).

In many relational DBMSs (e.g. ORACLE, INGRES, dBASE IV), it is not possible to give a collective name to subgroups of attributes, that is, it is

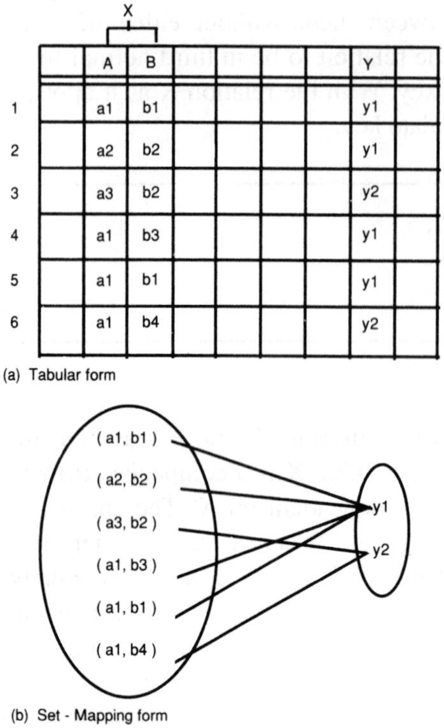

(a) Tabular form

(b) Set - Mapping form

Fig. 4.33 Functional dependencies on a composite attribute.

Group names are not possible in a relational database (apart from table names).

not possible to give a name to composite attributes. (It is possible in COBOL of course. In Fig. 4.22, ORDER-LINE, a group data item, is a collective name for the five data items below it.) This does not in general present any problem in practice.

Definition of 2NF revisited.

Having defined functional dependency and full functional dependency, we are now in a position to return to the definition of second normal form:

A relation is in second normal form if and only if it is in first normal form and every nonkey attribute is fully functionally dependent on the primary key.

On page 114, we had used 1NF to split the CUS-ORDER-FILE relation into the forms shown in Fig. 4.28. The results are reproduced here as Fig. 4.34.

After 1NF (method 1)

CUS-ORDER-REC

ORD-NO	ORD-DATE	ACC-NO	NAME	ADDRESS	PROD-NO	DESCR	PRICE	QTY	ROW-TOT	ORD-TOT
1	1-jan-93	10	Alan	1 Nx St	100	Apple	1	5	5	17
1	1-jan-93	10	Alan	1 Nx St	200	Ball	2	1	2	17
1	1-jan-93	10	Alan	1 Nx St	300	Cup	1	10	10	17
2	2-jan-93	8	Kate	4 Ox St	200	Ball	2	5	10	13
2	2-jan-93	8	Kate	4 Ox St	400	Dice	1	3	3	13
3	5-jan-93	10	Alan	1 Nx St	300	Cup	1	1	1	1

We apply 2NF to CUS-ORDER-REC. For completeness, we apply it to both of the versions that could have been produced by 1NF.

After 1NF (method 2)

CUS-ORDER-REC

ORD-NO	ORD-DATE	ACC-NO	NAME	ADDRESS	ORD-TOT
1	1-jan-93	10	Alan	1 Nx St	17
2	2-jan-93	8	Kate	4 Ox St	13
3	5-jan-93	10	Alan	1 Nx St	1

CUS-ORDER-LINE-REC

ORD-NO	PROD-NO	DESCR	PRICE	QTY	ROW-TOT
1	100	Apple	1	5	5
1	200	Ball	2	1	2
1	300	Cup	1	10	10
2	200	Ball	2	5	10
2	400	Dice	1	3	3
3	300	Cup	1	1	1

Fig. 4.34 INF applied to CUS-ORDER-REC.

Looking at the CUS-ORDER-REC relation resulting from method 1 of 1NF, we can see that the only candidate key is the composite attribute (ORD-NO with PROD-NO) which thus becomes the primary key. When the primary key contains two or more attributes like this, it is called a composite primary key. Neither attribute is a satisfactory key on its own as shown in this extension of CUS-ORDER-REC, where each repeats. The composite attribute will not repeat, since in a customer order, the same product would never be ordered more than once. If it was, we could simply add the values of the quantity attribute QTY for the two order lines.

The CUS-ORDER-REC relation resulting from method 1 can now be seen not to be in second normal form (2NF) and this is the cause of the duplication of data. First consider this duplication of data. As an example, we are told three times that order number 1 was sent in on the first of January 1993 and that the sending account number was 10 and the owner of this account is Alan and he lives at 1, Nx Street. Similarly, we are told twice that product number 200 is a ball and 300 a cup.

CUS-ORDER-REC is not in 2NF.

The relation is not in second normal form because some of the nonkey attributes are not 'fully functionally dependent on the primary key'. That is, some of the nonkey attributes are functionally dependent on a part of the composite primary key. They should, to be in 2NF, only be dependent on the whole key, not just a part of it. For example, attribute ORD-DATE is functionally dependent on ORD-NO because each value of ORD-NO will have just one value of ORD-DATE. ORD-NO functionally determines ORD-DATE and ORD-NO is only a part of the primary key. ORD-DATE is 'partially dependent' on the composite primary key (ORD-NO with PROD-NO). Second normal form has thus been broken in this relation.

Exercise 4.20

1. List out all the other partial dependencies in this relation.

2. Why do partial dependencies cause data duplication?

In the second version of 1NF (i.e. that shown as 'After 1NF – method 2'), the relation CUS-ORDER-REC is in 2NF. Its primary key is atomic (i.e. it consists of a single attribute). The key is ORD-NO. There is no possibility of a partial dependency, and so this relation is clearly in 2NF.

CUS-ORDER-LINE-REC is not in 2NF.

With the CUS-ORDER-LINE-REC relation however, the primary key is again the composite key (ORD-NO with PROD-NO) and there are partial dependencies from PROD-NO to DESCR and PROD-NO to PRICE. So CUS-ORD-LINE-REC is not in 2NF.

To put these non-2NF relations into 2NF, we must split the relations. In the case of the first version of CUS-ORDER-REC, all of the attributes that are functionally dependent on just ORD-NO can stay in CUS-ORDER-REC (ORD-DATE, ACC-NO, NAME, ADDRESS, ORD-TOT). Each of these has just one value for a given value of ORD-NO, so they are functionally dependent on it and belong with it. DESCR and PRICE are functionally dependent on PROD-NO. These attributes are all 'about' a product, so a new relation PRODUCT is created with these attributes. The remaining attributes QTY and ROW-TOT are functionally dependent on the whole composite key (ORD-NO with PROD-NO). They are attributes of an order line, for which we have created a relation CUS-ORDER-LINE-REC. Notice that 2NF has 'automatically' created this relation and in so doing, has corrected one of the major differences between the two versions of the schema that we produced after 1NF. In this sense, normalization can be said to contain a measure of intelligence, since it clearly has a view of its own as to how data should be organized and classified to produce a model of a part of the world. In practice of course, we would have produced only one version of the 1NF relations. The comforting fact is, that no matter which version we had produced (provided it was correct), at the end of complete normalization, the resulting set of relations would be the same.

We now apply 2NF to the second version of the set of relations that we produced in the 1NF normalization step. The primary key ORD-NO of CUS-ORDER-REC is atomic and so the relations must already be in 2NF. CUS-ORDER-LINE-REC has a composite key (ORD-NO with PROD-NO). DESCR and PRICE are functionally dependent on just PROD-NO, a part of the key. They must therefore be removed from the relation and placed into a new relation which we have called PRODUCT. QTY and ROW-TOT remain since they are dependent on the composite (ORD-NO with PROD-NO).

The results of the 2NF normalization stage are shown in Fig. 4.35.

After 2NF

CUS-ORDER-REC

ORD-NO	ORD-DATE	ACC-NO	NAME	ADDRESS	ORD-TOT
1	1-jan-93	10	Alan	1 Nx St	17
2	2-jan-93	8	Kate	4 Ox St	13
3	5-jan-93	10	Alan	1 Nx St	1

CUS-ORDER-LINE-REC

ORD-NO	PROD-NO	QTY	ROW-TOT
1	100	5	5
1	200	1	2
1	300	10	10
2	200	5	10
2	400	3	3
3	300	1	1

PRODUCT

PROD-NO	DESCR	PRICE
100	Apple	1
200	Ball	2
300	Cup	1
400	Dice	1

Fig. 4.35 2NF applied to the order processing schema.

Exercise 4.21

Show where data duplication still exists in the post-2NF version of the schema.

Third normal form

There is still some data duplication in the schema as it stands. The fact that the name and address associated with account number 10 is 'Alan, 1 Nx St' is stated twice in CUS-ORDER-REC. In fact it would appear every time that customer placed an order. If this were the only place that a customer's name and address appeared, removal from the database of the last order for a customer would remove access to his or her name and address.

Exercise 4.22

State the insertion, update and deletion anomalies that exist in the CUS-ORDER-REC relation.

The way to remove this type of duplication is to apply third normal form.

Four near-equivalent definitions of 3NF.

Definition 1: A relation is in third normal form if and only if it is in 2NF and every nonkey attribute is nontransitively dependent on the primary key. (Date, 1990)

Definition 2: A relation is in third normal form if and only if the nonkey attributes are:

(a) mutually independent, and;
(b) fully dependent on the primary key. (Date, 1990)

We adopt Definition 3 for 3NF in this text. See below.

Definition 3: A relation is in third normal form if and only if it is in second normal form and there are no functional dependencies between nonkey attributes.

Definition 4: A relation R is in third normal form if it is in first normal form and, for every attribute collection C of R, if any attribute not in C is functionally dependent on C, then all attributes in R are functionally dependent on C. (Codd, 1974)

Definitions 1, 2 and 3 are intended to be equivalent. Definition 4, due to Codd and Boyce, has become known as BCNF (Boyce–Codd Normal Form) and is intended to overcome certain deficiencies in the other definitions. BCNF is dealt with on page 128. In this section, we deal with the first three definitions. In practice, and for the purposes of examinations, any of the first three definitions is satisfactory.

The meanings of the definitions depend of course on the meanings ascribed to the individual terms. For definition 1, we need to describe the accepted meaning for the term transitive dependence. The term is borrowed from the theory of relations.

Transitive dependence

Let us first get the accepted definition of a transitive relation:

A binary relation R on a set A is transitive if for all elements x, y, z of A

x R y & y R z –> x R z (Daintith and Nelson, 1989)

where '&' means 'and' and '–>' means 'implies'. Remember that binary relations only (i.e. relations between pairs of elements) are being referred to here, not their generalization into *n*-ary relations that we are using in relational database theory. In the latter, as we have said before, the binary relations between pairs of attributes are not in general named. This fact is ignored in the definition of transitive dependence used in relational database theory. We shall return to this shortly, but first, let us consider a couple of examples of transitive and nontransitive binary relations.

Consider the binary relation 'lives next door to', defined on the set of suburban house-dwellers. Is it transitive? Three people x, y and z live in the same street. Person x lives next door to person y. And person y lives next door to person z. Is it true that person x necessarily lives next door to person z? If the answer is no (and it certainly is on this planet), then the relation 'lives next door to' is nontransitive.

Now consider the binary relation 'is older than', defined on the same set of suburban house-dwellers. If x is older than y and y is older than z, is x necessarily older than z? The answer is yes. So the relation 'is older than' is transitive.

Exercise 4.23

1. This exercise is not entirely essential to our study of normalization, but it may interest some students. In what pattern of housing arrangement would the relation 'lives next door to' be transitive?

2. Think of some more examples of transitive and non-transitive relations and swap them with a colleague for discussion.

Now consider our *n*-ary relation CUS-ORDER-REC which we are about to claim is not in third normal form. We have already noted the duplication of data in this relation (page 121). Definition 1 of 3NF requires that every nonkey attribute of the relation is nontransitively dependent on the primary key. The primary key in CUS-ORDER-REC is clearly ORD-NO.

The attribute NAME is transitively dependent on ORD-NO. ORD-NO functionally determines ACC-NO (there is only one ACC-NO for an ORD-NO) and ACC-NO functionally determines NAME (there is only one NAME for an ACC-NO). Consequently, ORD-NO functionally determines NAME (there is only one NAME for an ORD-NO).

NAME is transitively dependent on ORD-NO.

Notice however that this transitive dependency is not quite as strong as the mathematical transitive relation defined above. First of all, the dependency is not named. Secondly, the relation from ORD-NO to ACC-NO (we might call it 'was sent in by') is not the same relation as that between ACC-NO and NAME (we might call it 'is owned by'). There is consequently a problem with calling what is happening between ORD-NO, ACC-NO and NAME 'a transitive dependency' since the two dependency relations are qualitatively different. However this is the term that is used.

What is important here, and this is what is responsible for the data duplication, is simply that ACC-NO functionally determines NAME, or to use even less jargon, each ACC-NO is associated with only one NAME. Since ACC-NO is not the primary key, it may appear more than once, and every time ACC-NO 10 appears, so will the name Alan (and the ADDRESS 1 Nx St). The real problem is that there are functional dependencies between nonkey attributes. We are heading in the direction of arguing that definition 3 is the one we should adopt for third normal form.

Going back now to definition 2, we see that in addition to requiring no functional dependencies between nonkey attributes [clause (a)], it requires [clause (b)] that all nonkey attributes must be fully dependent on the primary key. The 'fully' part has already been dealt with by 2NF. If a nonkey attribute were not functionally dependent at all on the primary key, this would mean that for a given value of the primary key, there could be several different values (in different tuples because of 1NF) of this nonkey attribute. Consequently, the primary key would have to be extended to include the attribute and the 2NF test applied. Consequently, clause (b) is equivalent to saying that the relation must be in 2NF.

Exercise 4.24

Is it possible for a relation to be non-2NF and at the same time to comply with definition 2, clause (a)?

The answer to this exercise is clearly 'yes'. In the relation:

R(<u>A</u>, <u>B</u>, C)

there is no chance of attribute C being dependent on any other nonkey attribute since there are no other nonkey attributes. However there still may be a partial dependency; C might be dependent on attribute B on its own, in which case relation R would be non-2NF.

The conclusion is that in definition 2, clause (b) specifies the 2NF constraint, and clause (a) specifies the new constraint for 3NF. A second conclusion is that definition 2 and definition 3 are equivalent. We shall adopt the form of words of Definition 3 because it is simpler. If we also adopt the convention that each normal form includes the constraints of all lower normal forms, we could drop the explicit statement of the clause 'it is in second normal form and' from definition 3, making it even simpler.

We return now to the task of normalizing the CUS-ORDER-REC relation of Fig. 4.35. Since NAME and ADDRESS are both functionally dependent on ACC-NO, and ACC-NO is not the primary key, the relation is not in 3NF and it must be split. Figure 4.36 shows the resulting relations. Note that a new relation ACCOUNT has had to be created. If that relation had already been in existence, then the attributes NAME and ADDRESS could simply have been removed from CUS-ORDER-REC.

3NF applied to CUS-ORDER-REC.

After 3NF

CUS-ORDER-REC

ORD-NO	ORD-DATE	ACC-NO	ORD-TOT
1	1-jan-93	10	17
2	2-jan-93	8	13
3	5-jan-93	10	1

CUS-ACCOUNT-REC

ACC-NO	NAME	ADDRESS
8	Kate	4 Ox St
10	Alan	1 Nx St

CUS-ORDER-LINE-REC

ORD-NO	PROD-NO	QTY	ROW-TOT
1	100	5	5
1	200	1	2
1	300	10	10
2	200	5	10
2	400	3	3
3	300	1	1

PRODUCT

PROD-NO	DESCR	PRICE
100	Apple	1
200	Ball	2
300	Cup	1
400	Dice	1

Fig. 4.36 3NF applied to the order processing schema.

The complete 1NF, 2NF and 3NF processing applied to CUS-ORDER-REC is shown in Fig. 4.37.

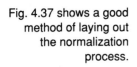

Fig. 4.37 shows a good
method of laying out
the normalization
process.

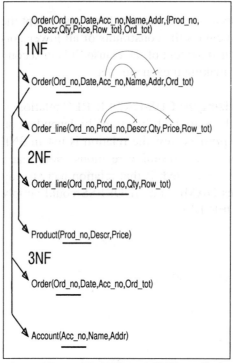

Fig. 4.37   1NF, 2NF and 3NF applied to the CUS-ORDER-REC.

Boyce–Codd normal form (BCNF)

BCNF is essentially a clearer formulation of Codd's 3NF definition which also caters for two additional cases:

- Relations with more than one candidate key, and;
- relations with overlapping candidate keys.

Let us start with the definition of BCNF:

A simple definition of
BCNF.

A relation is in Boyce–Codd normal form (BCNF) if and only if every determinant is a candidate key.

Originally, definition 4 of 3NF on page 124 was used to clear up known deficiencies in 3NF. This definition was then respecified in the terms given here and renamed BCNF.

Notice that there are two simplifications in this definition compared to the definitions of 3NF given above. Firstly, it is shorter and therefore easier to remember (useful in exams!). Secondly, as with definition 4 of 3NF, there is no mention of second normal form. The definition does not first state that the relation must first be in second normal form and then state an additional condition. To check whether a relation is in BCNF, we simply identify all determinants and ascertain whether they are candidate keys (identifiers for the entity type). If they are, the relation is in BCNF; otherwise, it is not.

A determinant is an attribute (possibly composite) that functionally determines one or more other attributes. For example, in the following relation:

CUS-ORDER-REC

ORD-NO	ORD-DATE	ACC-NO	ORD-TOT
1	1-jan-93	10	17
2	2-jan-93	8	13
3	5-jan-93	10	1

ORD-NO is a determinant of all of the other attributes, because it functionally determines each one; that is, a given value of ORD-NO in this relation will have only one value of each of the other attributes. Because ORD-NO is a candidate key for CUS-ORDER-REC (in fact it is the only candidate key and it has thus been chosen as the primary key), and because ORD_NO is the only candidate key, the relation is in BCNF.

Exercise 4.25

Show that all of the other relations in Fig. 4.36 are in BCNF.

It is also worthwhile to show that the BCNF test can be used instead of using the 3NF wording. In fact, because the BCNF test does not depend on the relation complying with lower normal forms, we should be able to go right back to un-normalized form and apply BCNF and ultimately achieve the same effect as before. Take for example the 1NF but not 2NF relation CUS-ORDER-LINE-REC from Fig. 4.34:

BCNF can be used instead of earlier 3NF definitions.

CUS-ORDER-LINE-REC

<u>ORD NO</u>	<u>PROD NO</u>	DESCR	PRICE	QTY	ROW-TOT
1	100	Apple	1	5	5
1	200	Ball	2	1	2
1	300	Cup	1	10	10
2	200	Ball	2	5	10
2	400	Dice	1	3	3
3	300	Cup	1	1	1

The composite primary key has been underlined. This relation is not in 2NF. Let us apply the BCNF test immediately. First we must find all the determinants:

1. PROD-NO is a determinant; it functionally determines DESCR and PRICE, because given a PROD-NO, there is only one DESCR and only one PRICE.

2. ORD-NO with PROD-NO is a determinant. It functionally determines DESCR (because there is only one DESCR for a given ORD-NO/PROD-NO combination) and it is also a determinant of every other nonkey attribute.

CUS-ORDER-LINE-REC is not in BCNF because of 1. PROD-NO is a determinant but it is not a candidate key. The fact that it is not a candidate key can be seen from the fact that in the above sample extension, the values 200 and 300 repeat.

More than one candidate key

BCNF clarifies the situation when normalizing relations with more than one candidate key.

Where the BCNF definition of 3NF is really superior to the old version however, is the situation in which there is more than one candidate key. The old definition of 3NF is not entirely clear on this point. In the following relation, there are three candidate keys.

DEPARTMENT

DEPT NO	DEPT_NAME	NO_OF_EMPS	MANAGER_EMP_NO	MANAGER_NAME
1	Accounts	20	100	Alan
2	Billing	15	300	Betty
3	Despatch	30	200	Carl

This relation shows which departments exist in an organization and details of the manager. There is one manager in each department, and a manager manages only one department. To see whether the DEPARTMENT relation is in BCNF, we list all of the determinants and then see if each one is a candidate key. The determinants are:

1. DEPT_NO. This is a determinant of every other attribute. It is also a candidate key since each department has one DEPT_NO and each DEPT_NO is for only one department.
2. DEPT_NAME is a determinant in this organization, since the company ensures (quite sensibly) that no two departments have the same name. Because of this, there will be only one value for NO_OF_EMPS and all the other attributes, and hence DEPT_NAME is a determinant and a candidate key for DEPARTMENT.
3. MANAGER_EMP_NO determines MANAGER_NAME (and all the other attributes) and is thus a determinant. It is also a candidate key, because each department has one manager and a manager manages only one department.

Each of the determinants is thus a candidate key. The relation is therefore in BCNF. DEPT_NO has been selected as the primary key as that seems more sensible for a relation called DEPARTMENT. Notice that there will always be a 1:1 both-ways mandatory relationship between alternative candidate keys. This corresponds to a 1:1 both-ways mandatory relationship between the entity types DEPARTMENT and MANAGER as shown in Fig. 4.38.

Fig. 4.38 BCNF clarifies normalization with 1:1 mandatory relationships.

We noted in Chapter 3 that when a 1:1 two-way mandatory relationship arises in the entity-relationship model, one option is to combine the entity types, as has happened in the DEPARTMENT relation above. Refer to Chapter 3 for a discussion of how to decide whether to combine or leave distinct entity types in this situation.

If we had used the standard 3NF test with the DEPARTMENT (i.e. 2NF plus no functional dependencies between nonkey attributes), we might have argued that this relation is not in 3NF because there is for example a functional dependency from MANAGER_EMP_NO to MANAGER_NAME, and MANAGER_EMP_NO is 'nonkey'. The question turns on what is meant by 'nonkey'. If it means 'noncandidate key' then that makes 3NF equivalent in this sense to BCNF. If we adopt BCNF instead of the old 3NF definition, we do not have to answer this question.

Overlapping candidate keys
Suppose we have the following relation:

EMPLOYEE

NAME	DEPT	ROOM_NO	GRADE	SALARY
Alan	1	1000	A	20000
Alan	2	1050	A	15000
Betty	1	1000	B	10000
Carol	1	1010	A	17000

Assume that each employee works in just one department. Each room is in one department. NAME is not a satisfactory candidate key on its own, but assume that NAME with DEPT is a satisfactory candidate key because there will never be two employees with the same name in the same department. Also assume that employees are allocated to just one ROOM_NO (although employees can share rooms as Betty does with one of the Alan's) but there will never be two employees with the same name allocated to the same room. There are thus two composite candidate keys for EMPLOYEE, namely NAME with DEPT, and NAME with ROOM_NO.

NAME with DEPT and NAME with ROOM-NO are both candidate keys. They overlap.

The functional dependencies are as follows:

NAME, DEPT –> ROOM_NO, GRADE, SALARY
NAME, ROOM_NO –> DEPT, GRADE, SALARY
ROOM_NO –> DEPT

where −> here means 'functionally determines', i.e. 'is a determinant of'. The last functional dependency here simply indicates the fact that a room is in just one department.

Notice that there is duplication of data here. For example, we are told twice in this particular extension (set of tuples) that room number 1000 is in department 1.

If we select NAME with ROOM_NO as the primary key, then the relation is not in 2NF, since DEPT is then functionally dependent on just part of the primary key, namely ROOM_NO.

If however we select NAME with DEPT as the primary key, then the relation is in third normal form. There are no functional dependencies among nonkey attributes (DEPT is part of the primary key), and in fact all nonkey attributes are functionally dependent on the whole key. We have a relation that is in third normal form but which contains duplication of data!

The relation is not in BCNF. This is because we have the attribute ROOM_NO which is a determinant (of DEPT) but not a candidate key. BCNF is thus a superior normal form than the older 3NF because it can detect data duplication that 3NF misses.

We now split up EMPLOYEE in order to remove that data duplication:

EMPLOYEE

NAME	ROOM NO	GRADE	SALARY
Alan	1000	A	20000
Alan	1050	A	15000
Betty	1000	B	10000
Carol	1010	A	17000

ROOM

ROOM NO	DEPT
1000	1
1010	1
1050	2

The relations are now in BCNF and we have removed all data duplication that was present in the merely 3NF version.

There is however one disadvantage with this split. The functional dependency:

NAME, DEPT −> ROOM_NO, GRADE, SALARY

has been dispersed. It is still a functional dependency, but it is between attributes that do not appear in the same relation. If we were to make the query:

'What is the salary of Alan in department 1?'

the query would involve accessing both tables.

To ensure that a department never had two employees with the same name would also be more involved than in the non-BCNF version. In the days before built-in database integrity rules and procedures (page 95), maintaining this functional dependency would have made the validation routines of many processes which updated these tables that much more complex than in the non-BCNF version.

Summary of 'overlapping candidate keys'
The real problem with this example can be stated more clearly (even though with more words) without using the term 'overlapping candidate keys'. The real problem is that:

> There was a functional dependency from a nonkey attribute to part of a composite key.

If there exists a nonkey attribute which functionally determines a part of the composite primary key, then it can replace that part in the primary key and maintain uniqueness. The replaced attribute will now have to be removed because it would infringe 2NF. It and the replacing attribute will now have to be removed to another relation.

This overlapping candidate keys situation in BCNF is in one sense the opposite of 2NF, where we look out for a functional dependency from part of a composite key to a nonkey attribute.

Cases such as this pass the old 3NF test because that test only tests for functional dependencies between nonkey attributes ('nonkey' here means 'not the primary key').

Figure 4.39 is a simple diagram that summarizes each new type of unwanted functional dependency that 2NF, 3NF and BCNF can detect. BCNF can of course detect all three types.

Fig. 4.39 summarizes 2NF, 3NF & BCNF.

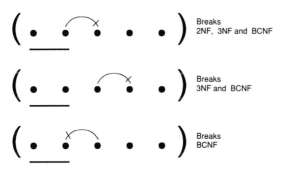

Fig. 4.39 The unwanted functional dependencies detected by 2NF, 3NF and BCNF.

Exercise 4.26

Find an example of a relation with overlapping candidate keys that is in BCNF. *Hint:* Make sure that there is not a functional dependency between the attributes that are not common to the two overlapping candidate keys, e.g. if in R(a,b,c,d), (a,b) and (a,c) are both candidate keys, make sure that neither b –> c nor c –> b.

Chapter 5

Higher normalization

In this chapter you will learn:

- □ to define multivalued dependencies;
- □ to use fourth normal form;
- □ to define nonloss decomposition;
- □ to understand join dependencies;
- □ to define fifth normal form;
- □ to define domain key normal form (DKNF);
- □ to demonstrate the need for further optimization of the relational design in some cases;
- □ to explain the advantages and disadvantages of limited denormalization and where it is appropriate;
- □ to use Codd's 12 rules for relational databases.

Fourth normal form

A relation R is in fourth normal form (4NF) if and only if, whenever there exists an MVD (multivalued dependency) in R, say A —>—> B, then all attributes of R are also functionally dependent on A. Equivalently: R is in 4NF if it is in BCNF and all MVDs in R are also FDs. (Date, 1990)

The new terminology in this definition is described below.

Multivalued dependencies

Up until this point, we have been saying that a functional dependency (A —> B) allowed us to predict the value of B given the value of A because each A 'had' only one value of B. Given a value of attribute A, there would only ever be one value of B that could be found in the tuples of the database. Every time a given value a of A occurred in a tuple of the relation, the same value b of B would occur in the tuple. For example, given a customer account number CUS_ACC_NO, there would only ever be one value of customer name CUS_NAME for that account number in the CUSTOMER relation.

But functional dependencies are not the only type of dependency that you could imagine. Why should there be only one predictable value B given a value A? Consider Fig. 5.1.

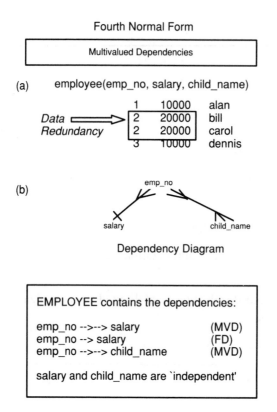

Fourth Normal Form

Multivalued Dependencies

(a)   employee(emp_no, salary, child_name)

Data ⟹ | 1 | 10000 | alan |
Redundancy | 2 | 20000 | bill |
| 2 | 20000 | carol |
| 3 | 10000 | dennis |

(b)

emp_no

salary   child_name

Dependency Diagram

EMPLOYEE contains the dependencies:

emp_no -->--> salary   (MVD)
emp_no --> salary   (FD)
emp_no -->--> child_name   (MVD)

salary and child_name are 'independent'

Fig. 5.1   EMPLOYEE is non-4NF (and non-2NF).

A multivalued dependency is a generalization of a functional dependency.

Given a value of EMP_NO, we can obtain a fixed set of values for CHILD_NAME. To show that this EMP_NO is associated with each of these CHILD_NAMEs, the same EMP_NO is shown against each CHILD_NAME. For example, emp_no 2 has two children Bill and Carol, and thus appears twice. This is the normal way of showing a 1:N or M:N relationship in a relational database. This is not a functional dependency, since a value in the domain EMP_NO can map to more than one value in the co-domain CHILD_NAME. But it is a dependency. Notice that the fact that emp_no 2 receives a salary of 20 000 also occurs twice, one for each child! Fagin (1977) introduces the term multivalued dependency for this situation and says that EMP_NO multidetermines CHILD_NAME, written:

EMP_NO —>—> CHILD_NAME

Multivalued dependencies are important for database design because they cause data duplication and update anomalies, just as non-1NF, non-2NF, non-3NF and non-BCNF relations do.

Date (1990) defines nontrivial MVDs this way:

Given a relation R with attributes A, B, and C, the MVD
R.A —>—> R.B

holds in R iff the set of B-values matching a given (A-value, C-value) pair in R depends only on the A-value and is independent of the C-value. A, B, and C may be composite (i.e. they may consist of more than one attribute)

Note that 'iff' means 'if and only if'. It is also taken to mean, equivalently, 'implies and is implied by'. In Fig. 5.1, The set of CHILD_NAME (B) values matching a given (EMP_NO, SALARY) (A–C) pair depends only on the EMP_NO (A) value and is independent of the SALARY (C). Here, A, B and C are atomic (not composite). Consequently, there is an MVD between EMP_NO (A) and CHILD_NAME (B). EMP_NO —>—> CHILD_NAME. For example, the set of CHILD_NAME values matching (EMP_NO, SALARY) = (2, 20 000) is { bill, carol } and this set depends only on the EMP_NO (2) and is independent of the SALARY (20 000).

Note also that there is also an MVD between EMP_NO and SALARY. The set of SALARY (B) values matching a given (EMP_NO, CHILD_NAME) (A–C) pair depends only on the EMP_NO (A) value and is independent of the CHILD_NAME (C). For example, the set of SALARY values matching (EMP_NO, CHILD_NAME) = (2, bill) is { 20 000 } and this set depends only on the EMP_NO (2) and is independent of the CHILD_NAME (bill).

MVDs generally go together in pairs like this. The two MVDs here are:

EMP_NO —>—> SALARY
EMP_NO —>—> CHILD_NAME

The way MVDs are defined in Fagin (1977), a functional dependency (FD) is a special case of a multivalued dependency (MVD). In the example of Fig. 5.1 in fact, the MVD from EMP_NO to SALARY is also an FD, since in this relation, only one salary, the current salary, will ever be shown for a given EMP_NO. Because of this, we may summarize the dependencies in the EMPLOYEE relation of Fig. 5.1 as follows:

An FD is a special case of an MVD.

EMP_NO —>—> SALARY   (MVD)
EMP_NO —> SALARY   (FD)
EMP_NO —>—> CHILD_NAME   (MVD)

One of the MVDs is an FD and one is not. In Fig. 5.1(b), the dependencies are shown in a dependency diagram. We can see quite clearly on this diagram that EMP_NO functionally determines SALARY (because there is only one value of SALARY for each EMP_NO) and that EMP_NO multi-determines CHILD_NAME (because there can be several values of CHILD_NAME for a given EMP_NO).

The relation EMPLOYEE of Fig. 5.1(a) contains some redundancy. The 'fact' that EMP_NO 2 receives a salary of 20 000 is stated twice; once for each CHILD_NAME related to EMP_NO 2. This redundancy will occur for every employee with more than one child.

Dependency diagram indicates EMPLOYEE (Fig. 5.1) is non-4NF
The dependency diagram of Fig. 5.1(b) indicates a simple interpretation of how a non-4NF relation can be produced. There are two dependencies here, one from EMP_NO to SALARY and one from EMP_NO to CHILD_NAME. If both dependencies were FDs, that is if SALARY and CHILD_NAME were both functionally dependent on EMP_NO, then there would be no problem of redundancy; both nonkey attributes would be functionally dependent on EMP_NO which could then serve as the primary key. The problem here is that one of the dependencies (EMP_NO —>—> CHILD_NAME) is not functional and the three attributes and two dependencies have been crammed into one relation. CHILD_NAME and SALARY are independent.

Dependency diagrams aid the detection of non-4NF relations.

One way therefore of detecting a non-4NF relation containing three attributes is to:

(a) draw a dependency diagram;
(b) look for a 'tree' configuration (two dependencies; no loops);
(c) check that the dependencies are functional (N:1 or 1:1) from the 'root' of the tree; if not, the relation is not in 4NF.

In terms of the definition given above for 4NF, the reason EMPLOYEE is not in 4NF is that the MVD EMP_NO —>-—> CHILD_NAME is not also an FD.

Putting EMPLOYEE (Fig. 5.1) into 4NF
The EMPLOYEE relation of Fig. 5.1 can be put into 4NF by splitting it into the following relations:

EMPLOYEE (emp_no, salary)
EMP_CHILD(emp_no, child_name)

EMPLOYEE has been replaced by two projections EMPLOYEE and EMP_CHILD (which might be better named PARENTHOOD). This is a nonloss decomposition because the original relation can be regenerated by joining the new EMPLOYEE relation with EMP_CHILD on the attribute EMP_NO. As we shall see on page 150, fifth normal form (5NF) is defined in terms of nonloss decomposition. The important point here is that by splitting the relation this way, we have lost no data, and the redundancy has been removed. The question of how to split EMPLOYEE, that is what projections to take, is easily answered by looking at the dependency diagram. The two 'independent' dependencies, corresponding to the two lines on the dependency diagram, are placed in separate relations.

A nonloss decomposition splits a relation without losing data.

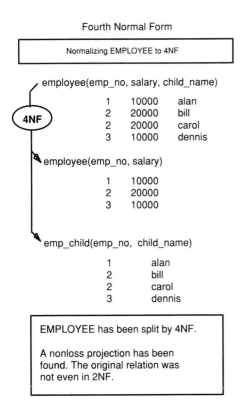

Fig. 5.2 Splitting EMPLOYEE (Fig. 5.1) to get it into 4NF.

Exercise 5.1

1. Is the EMPLOYEE relation of Fig. 5.1 in 2NF?
2. (a) Think of an example where there are three dependencies from a

common attribute (possibly composite), some of which are not functional.

(b) Normalize the relation to 4NF.

3. Create other non-4NF relations by starting with an entity-relationship diagram with three entity types and cramming all the attributes into one relation. Show where the multivalued dependencies are.

Trivial and nontrivial MVDs

We should now distinguish between **trivial** and **nontrivial** MVDs. Nontrivial MVDs always involve at least three attributes A, B and C and a multivalued dependency between A and B requires that for each set of related values of A and C, all the B values related to the A value have to be repeated. Trivial MVDs are just binary relations; the relation has just two attributes A and B and does not require any duplication of data. In the example of Fig. 5.1, if there were just two attributes EMP_NO and CHILD_NAME, the MVD EMP_NO —>—> CHILD_NAME would still exist but it would be a 'trivial' MVD. This is the situation with the new EMP_CHILD relation of Fig. 5.2.

If in Fig. 5.1 we assume no employee has two or more children with the same name, and that only one salary is shown for each employee, there is a composite candidate key in EMPLOYEE consisting of EMP_NO with CHILD_NAME. The relation is consequently not in second normal form since the functional dependency from EMP_NO to CHILD_NAME is a partial dependency. This non-2NF relation has a nontrivial MVD and is thus not in 4NF. In Fagin (1977) it is demonstrated that if a relation fails any of the lower normal forms then it will fail 4NF.

BCNF but not 4NF (Fig. 5.3)

We now consider an example relation that is in all lower normal forms (and is thus in BCNF, the next one down), but is not in 4NF. We need to find such an example of course, to show that 4NF is necessary!

EMPLOYEE in Fig. 5.3 is all-key and is in BCNF. However, it still contains data redundancy.

In Fig. 5.3 a different EMPLOYEE relation now shows a salary history for each employee, as well as the employee's children. There is considerable data redundancy. We are told twice that employee 1 has a child called Alan, once for each salary-year. Employee 2 has two salary-year items and two children, and this results in $2 \times 2 = 4$ rows of data for this employee. If employee 2 had five salary-year items and three children, he or she would have $5 \times 3 = 15$ rows to show these eight facts! As with the example of Fig. 5.1, the redundancy has been caused by cramming unrelated data facts (salary data and child data) into one relation.

Unlike Fig. 5.3 however, this EMPLOYEE relation is in BCNF (and consequently in all lower normal forms). The reason is that all normal forms lower than 4NF are defined in terms of functional dependencies, and there

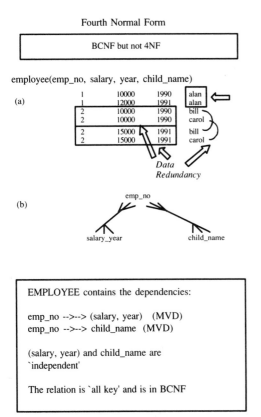

Fourth Normal Form

BCNF but not 4NF

employee(emp_no, salary, year, child_name)

EMPLOYEE contains the dependencies:

emp_no -->--> (salary, year) (MVD)
emp_no -->--> child_name (MVD)

(salary, year) and child_name are
'independent'

The relation is 'all key' and is in BCNF

Fig. 5.3 EMPLOYEE is in BCNF but not in 4NF.

are no FDs in this relation, as the dependency diagram of Fig. 5.3(b) indicates. Also, all lower normal forms involve noncandidate key attributes, and EMPLOYEE is all-key.

Figure 5.3(b) shows that, unlike Fig. 5.1(b), both dependencies are merely multivalued; neither is functional. The composite salary history item (SALARY, YEAR) is 'independent' of CHILD_NAME, as shown by the fact that there is no direct relationship (dependency) between (SALARY, YEAR) and CHILD_NAME on the dependency diagram.

Putting EMPLOYEE (Fig. 5.3) into 4NF

The question of how to split EMPLOYEE to get it into 4NF, that is, what projections to take, is easily decided by inspection of the dependency diagram. There is one relation for each of the 'independent' dependencies, as shown in Fig. 5.4.

That this decomposition is nonloss can be demonstrated by rejoining the new EMPLOYEE and EMP_CHILD relations on EMP_NO, wherein the original EMPLOYEE relation is produced.

EMPLOYEE in Fig. 5.3 can be split to get Fig. 5.4, which is in 4NF.

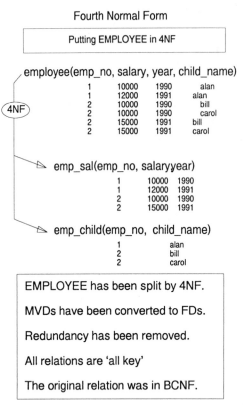

Fourth Normal Form

Putting EMPLOYEE in 4NF

employee(emp_no, salary, year, child_name)

1	10000	1990	alan
1	12000	1991	alan
2	10000	1990	bill
2	10000	1990	carol
2	15000	1991	bill
2	15000	1991	carol

4NF

emp_sal(emp_no, salaryyear)

1	10000	1990
1	12000	1991
2	10000	1990
2	15000	1991

emp_child(emp_no, child_name)

1	alan
2	bill
2	carol

EMPLOYEE has been split by 4NF.

MVDs have been converted to FDs.

Redundancy has been removed.

All relations are 'all key'

The original relation was in BCNF.

Fig. 5.4   Splitting EMPLOYEE (Fig. 5.3) to get it into 4NF.

What 'dependency' actually means

Date's definition of MVD might be criticized because it uses the phrase 'depends on' without being absolutely precise about what this means. We use the phrase 'depends on' in the sense that if in a relation R, attribute B depends on attribute A (both possibly composite), then the set of values appearing under the B attribute must always be the same for a given A value, whatever the values of the other attributes. For a multivalued dependency, the 'set of values' will be one or more part-tuples $b_1,...,b_n$ appearing under the B columns. For the particular case of a functional dependency, there is only one value of B ($b_1,...b_n$) for a given A. Note that in this situation where A, B and C are composite (the most general case), what we mean by 'B value' is one value for each B attribute, i.e. $b_1,...,b_n$. Similarly for 'an A value' and 'a C value' in what follows. One merit of Fagin's definition (which is equivalent to Date's) is that it does not require the phrase 'depends on'; it replaces it with simple equality, as here.

A being 'composite' means 'A' is a group of attributes.

Fagin's definition of MVD

Fagin's definition of MVD is expressed mathematically.

Fagin's definition of multivalued dependencies (Fagin, 1977) is expressed in a more mathematical form which, as we have said, is precise because it does not require us to know what the phrase 'depends only on' means. It uses the notion of set equality instead, which is probably clearer to most people.

Suppose we have a relation R:

$$R(A_1,...A_m, B_1,...B_n, ... C_1,...C_r)$$

Let $A_1,...A_m$ be called A, $B_1,...B_n$ be called B and $C_1,...C_r$ be called C.

Define B_{AC} to be the set of all the $b_1,...b_n$ part-tuples that appear for a given combination of A value and C value.

The multivalued dependency A —>—> B is said to occur in R if B_{AC} is the same for each value of C.

In Fagin's description, the last sentence is expressed as:

The MVD A —>—> B holds if:

$$B_{AC} = B_{AC'} \text{ for each } _{A}, _C \text{ and } _{C''}.$$

Note that in this situation where A, B and C are composite (the most general case), what we mean by 'B value' is one value for each B attribute, i.e. $b_1,...b_n$. Similarly for 'an A value' and 'a C value'.

Let us illustrate this by showing an example:

$$R1(A_1, A_2, B_1, B_2, B_3, C_1, C_2)$$

```
1   2   10   20   30   3   4
1   2   40   50   60   3   4
1   2   10   20   30   5   6
1   2   40   50   60   5   6
```

There is a multivalued dependency in R1 between A and B and this causes the two B_{AC}'s $B_{A1=1,A2=2,C1=3,C2=4}$ and $B_{A1=1,A2=2,C1=5,C2=6}$ to be identical, that is:

$$B_{A1=1,A2=2,C1=3,C2=4} = \{(10,20,30),(40,50,60)\} \text{ and}$$

$$B_{A1=1,A2=2,C1=5,C2=6} = \{(10,20,30),(40,50,60)\}.$$

The set of B_{AC} values is the same for a given A and each value of C. This represents duplication of data. For every value of C, the set of B values associated with a given A has to be repeated. If there were more data in the table, then for a given A, B_{AC} would be repeated for each occurrence of C. If this rule were not maintained in R1, then the implication would be that the set of B values for a given A depended in some way on the C value, which is not true here.

Notice that there is also a multivalued dependency in R1 between A and C because the two C_{AB}'s, $C_{A1=1,A2=2,B1=10,B2=20,B3=30}$ and $C_{A1=1,A2=2,B1=40,B2=50,B3=60}$, are identical. That is:

$$C_{A1=1,A2=2,B1=10,B2=20,B3=30} = \{(3,4),(5,6)\}, \text{ and}$$

$$C_{A1=1,A2=2,B1=40,B2=50,B3=60} = \{(3,4),(5,6)\}.$$

The set of C_{AB} values is the same for a given A and each value of B. This again represents duplication of data. For every value of B, the set of C values associated with a given A has to be repeated. If there were more data in the table, then for a given A, C_{AB} would be repeated for each occurrence of B. If this rule were not maintained in R1, then the implication would be that the set of C values for a given A depended in some way on the B value, which is not true here.

The duplication has occurred in R1 because for a given A, there are several Bs and for a given A there are also several Cs and A, B and C have been placed in one relation R1. Placing the two MVDs:

$$A \longrightarrow \longrightarrow B$$
$$A \longrightarrow \longrightarrow C$$

in one relation R1 has resulted in data redundancy.

Putting R1 into 4NF
As shown in the EMPLOYEE examples above, R1 can be put into 4NF by placing the two MVDs in different relations:

$R1(A_1, A_2, B_1, B_2, B_3, C_1, C_2)$

1	2	10	20	30	3	4
1	2	40	50	60	3	4
1	2	10	20	30	5	6
1	2	40	50	60	5	6

is replaced by:

$R2(A_1, A_2, B_1, B_2, B_3)$

| 1 | 2 | 10 | 20 | 30 |
| 1 | 2 | 40 | 50 | 60 |

and:

$R3(A_1, A_2, C_1, C_2)$

| 1 | 2 | 3 | 4 |
| 1 | 2 | 5 | 6 |

To ensure familiarity with the Fagin notation, we return briefly to the EMPLOYEE relation of Fig. 5.3, which we reproduce here:

Showing the MVD of Fig. 5.3 in Fagin's notation.

EMPLOYEE	(EMP_NO,	SALARY,	YEAR,	CHILD_NAME)
	1	10000	1990	alan
	1	12000	1991	alan
	2	10000	1990	bill
	2	10000	1990	carol
	2	15000	1991	bill
	2	15000	1991	carol

As in the dependency diagram of Fig. 5.3(b), we consider three groups of attributes:

EMP_NO   (SALARY, YEAR)   CHILD_NAME

There is, in Fagin's symbolism, an MVD:

EMP_NO —>—> (SALARY, YEAR)

because given any value of EMP_NO,

$(SALARY, YEAR)_{EMP\_NO,CHILD\_NAME}$ is the same for each value of CHILD_NAME

For example:

$(SALARY, YEAR)_{EMP\_NO=2, CHILD\_NAME=bill} =$
$\{ (10000, 1990), (15000, 1991) \}$

which is the same as:

$(SALARY, YEAR)_{EMP\_NO=2, CHILD\_NAME=carol} =$
$\{ (10000, 1990), (15000, 1991) \}$

The salary history depends only on the employee number and is independent of the child name.

Similarly, the other MVD:

EMP_NO —>—> CHILD_NAME

is illustrated by the fact that:

$CHILD\_NAME_{EMP\_NO,(SALARY, YEAR)}$ is the same for each value of the composite $_{(SALARY, YEAR)}$

For example:

CHILD_NAME$_{EMP\_NO=2, (SALARY, YEAR)=(10000, 1990)}$ =
{ bill, carol }

which is the same as:

CHILD_NAME$_{EMP\_NO=2, (SALARY, YEAR)=(15000, 1991)}$ =
{ bill, carol }

The set of children depends only on the employee number and is independent of the salary-year.

We return now to relation R1 to investigate its update anomalies.

Update anomalies caused by R1 not being in 4NF

$R1(A_1, A_2, B_1, B_2, B_3, C_1, C_2)$

1	2	10	20	30	3	4
1	2	40	50	60	3	4
1	2	10	20	30	5	6
1	2	40	50	60	5	6

If we were to retain the non-4NF R1 instead of its two 4NF projections R2 and R3, there would be update anomalies exemplified by the following:

Insertion anomaly

If we wanted to associate (1, 2) with (70, 80, 90), then *two* tuples would have to be inserted: one for each (C_1, C_2) combination associated with $(A_1, A_2) = (1, 2)$.

If the tuple:

1   2   70   80   90   3   4

were to be inserted, then the tuple:

1   2   70   80   90   5   6

would also have to be inserted.

Update anomaly
If the tuple:

1   2   10   20   30   3   4

were to be altered to:

1   2   10   21   30   3   4

then the tuple:

1   2   10   20   30   5   6

would also have to be altered to:

1   2   10   21   30   5   6

Deletion anomaly
If the tuple:

1   2   10   20   30   3   4

were to be deleted, then the tuple:

1   2   10   20   30   3   4

would also have to be deleted.

Similar update anomalies occur with the EMPLOYEE relations of Fig. 5.1 and Fig. 5.3.

Fourth Normal Form

Course - Teacher - Text Exercise

ctx(course_no, teacher_no, text_no)

1	1	1
1	1	2
1	2	1
1	2	2
2	1	1
2	1	3
2	1	4

Fig. 5.5   See Exercise 5.2(3).

Exercise 5.2

1. Produce a dependency diagram for relation R1 and hence verify that R2 and R3 are the appropriate 4NF projections.

2. Illustrate the update anomalies associated with the non-4NF relations of Fig. 5.1 and Fig. 5.3.

3. Suppose that the CTX relation of Fig. 5.5 means that on the course COURSE_NO, teacher TEACHER_NO uses text TEXT_NO, that all

the teachers and texts for a course are shown in CTX, and that the set of texts used is fixed for a given course, as is the set of teachers. That is, each COURSE_NO completely determines the set of TEACHER_NOs, and it similarly completely determines the set of TEXT_NOs.

(a) Using Fagin's symbolism (B_{AC}, etc.), show that there are MVDs in CTX.
(b) Point out the data redundancy in CTX.
(c) Give examples of insertion, update and deletion anomalies in CTX.
(d) Draw the dependency diagram for CTX.
(e) Put CTX into 4NF by replacing it with suitable projections and show that the data redundancy and the update anomalies have been removed.

Definitions of 4NF

We are now in a position to restate the definition of 4NF. Three equivalent formulations are given.

A relation R is in 4NF iff:

1. Whenever there exists an MVD in R, say A—>—> B, then all attributes of R are also functionally dependent on A.
2. The only dependencies from a candidate key to other attributes are FDs.
3. R is in BCNF and all MVDs are FDs.

Detecting non-4NF relations using a dependency diagram

These definitions make it clear that the dependency diagram method of detecting a non-4NF relation given above is generally applicable. It can also be used to indicate the required 4NF projections.

How to detect a non-4NF relation.

A non-4NF relation can be detected by the following method:

(a) draw a dependency diagram;
(b) look for a 'tree' configuration (no loops);
(c) check that the dependencies are functional from the 'root'; if not, the relation is not in 4NF.

How to correct a non-4NF relation.

A non-4NF relation can be put in 4NF by replacing it using the following method:

(d) create a new relation containing the 'root' and any functionally determined attributes (FDs);
(e) create a new relation for each non-functionally determined attribute (MVD). Each of these relations will contain the 'root' and one non-functionally determined attribute.

This process is shown in Fig. 5.6.

Fourth Normal Form

Detecting & Correcting non-4NF Relations

employee(emp_no, salary, year, child_name, emp_name)

(a) Dependency Diagram:

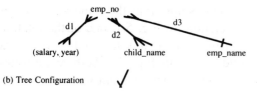

emp_no

d1   d2   d3

(salary, year)   child_name   emp_name

(b) Tree Configuration   ✓

(c) Two dependencies (d1, d2) are non-functional
    so relation is not 4NF

(d) employee(emp_no, emp_name)

(e) emp_salary(emp_no, salary, year)

emp_child(emp_no, child_name)

Fig. 5.6 Detecting and correcting non-4NF relations by dependency diagram.

Exercise 5.3

If we consider just two (both-ways mandatory) relationships (dependencies) r1 and r2 within a relation, it is apparent that, in terms of the cardinalities of these two relationships, there are ten cases to consider:

case	r1	r2
1	1:1	1:1
2	1:1	1:N
3	1:1	N:1
4	1:1	M:N
5	1:N	1:N
6	1:N	N:1
7	1:N	M:N
8	N:1	N:1
9	N:1	M:N
10	M:N	M:N

1. Draw a dependency diagram for each of these cases.

2. Assume all three groups of attributes start out in one relation. State where possible which normal forms (if any) are being infringed in each case.

Summary

A relation (consisting of at least three attributes) infringes 4NF if a mixture of functional and nonfunctional relationships from the same attribute (the 'root') have been joined into one relation. In Fig. 5.1, one of the relationships was functional (many—one) from emp_no to salary and the other was multivalued from emp_no to child_name. In Fig. 5.3, both relationships were multivalued. In each case, the dependency diagram was a tree shape, and the attributes at the ends of the angle were 'independent', i.e. 'orthogonal'. The problem was that the attributes from the root and branches of the tree had been combined into one relation, whereas there should have been two separate relations, one for each branch. This caused data redundancy.

Fifth normal form

A relation is in fifth normal form iff every join dependency is a consequence of its candidate keys.

Nonloss decomposition and join dependencies

Relation SPJ has several possible interpretations.

Consider the following relation:

SPJ(s_no, p_no, pr_no)

s_no is a supplier number
p_no is a part number
pr_no is a project number

Given the noncommittal name of the relation SPJ, it might have been set up to have one of several different meanings. We discuss several (but by no means all) possible interpretations of SPJ. Only one of these interpretations would be in force at a company using this relation. For some of the interpretations, a nonloss decomposition is possible which removes data redundancy but retains the same information.

In some interpretations, a two-way decomposition is possible and indicated by 4NF. There follows an interpretation of SPJ where it is not 'two-decomposable' but is 'three-decomposable'. Fifth normal form promotes this decomposition. We conclude with an interpretation of SPJ where it is not possible to find a nonloss decomposition because SPJ is already in 5NF.

We assume here that the only things a supplier supplies are parts.

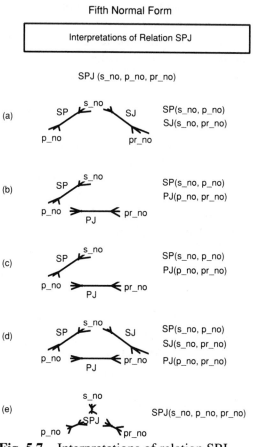

Fifth Normal Form

Interpretations of Relation SPJ

SPJ (s_no, p_no, pr_no)

(a) SP — s_no — SJ   SP(s_no, p_no)
    p_no   pr_no   SJ(s_no, pr_no)

(b) SP — s_no   SP(s_no, p_no)
    p_no — PJ — pr_no PJ(p_no, pr_no)

(c) SP — s_no   SP(s_no, p_no)
    p_no — PJ — pr_no PJ(p_no, pr_no)

(d) SP — s_no — SJ   SP(s_no, p_no)
    p_no — PJ — pr_no SJ(s_no, pr_no)
                      PJ(p_no, pr_no)

(e) s_no   SPJ(s_no, p_no, pr_no)
    p_no — SPJ — pr_no

Fig. 5.7   Interpretations of relation SPJ.

Interpretation (a)

SPJ is intended to show only that a supplier S_NO supplies P_NO and is a recognized supplier for PR_NO. The dependency diagram shown in Fig. 5.7(a) applies. P_NO and PR_NO are under this interpretation independent, and the two MVDs are nonfunctional since a supplier may supply many parts and a supplier may be a recognized supplier for many projects.

SPJ is therefore not in 4NF because of the two MVDs:

S_NO —>—> P_NO
S_NO —>—> PR_NO

and it could be replaced without loss of data by its two projections:

SP(s_no, p_no)
SJ(s_no, pr_no)

Since under these conditions no data would be lost by this decomposition, this is called a nonloss decomposition of SPJ. The original SPJ can be reconstituted by joining SP and SJ. We say that SPJ has a join dependency since it can be reconstructed from a join of some of its projections. Because it has this join dependency, SPJ is not in 5NF.

In this interpretation of SPJ, there is no conceivable reason why SPJ would be reconstituted. SPJ would be an enormous relation, because every combination of P_NO that a supplier supplies and PR_NO that the supplier is a recognized supplier for is shown.

Notice that S_NO being a recognized supplier for PR_NO and supplying P_NO does not imply anything else. For example, if we were to suppose (incorrectly) that we could find out which parts were used in which projects by joining SP and SJ and projecting onto (P_NO, PR_NO) we would be led to the erroneous conclusion that a supplier supplying a part and being a recognized supplier for a project implied that that part was used on that project.

The fact that SPJ is nonloss decomposable indicates that it has a join dependency and thus is not in 5NF. In this example it is not even in 4NF. The projections SP and SJ are in 5NF; they cannot be further decomposed without loss of data.

Interpretation (b)

SPJ is intended to show only that part P_NO is supplied by S_NO and that P_NO is used in PR_NO. The dependency diagram shown in Fig. 5.7(b) applies. S_NO and PR_NO are under this interpretation independent, and the two MVDs are nonfunctional since a part may be supplied by many suppliers and a part may be used in many projects.

SPJ is therefore not in 4NF because of the two MVDs:

P_NO —>—> S_NO
P_NO —>—> PR_NO

and it could be replaced without loss of data by its two projections:

SP(s_no, p_no)
PJ(p_no, pr_no)

Since under these conditions no data would be lost by this decomposition, this is a nonloss decomposition of SPJ. The original SPJ can be reconstituted by joining SP and PJ. Thus SPJ has a join dependency and is not in 5NF.

In this interpretation of SPJ, there is no conceivable reason why SPJ would be reconstituted. SPJ would be an unnecessarily large relation, because for each part, every combination of S_NO supplying that part and PR_NO in which the part is used, is shown.

Notice that P_NO being supplied by S_NO and being used in PR_NO does not imply anything else. For example, if we were to suppose (incorrectly) that we could find out for which projects a supplier was a recognized supplier by joining SP and PJ and projecting onto (S_NO, PR_NO), we would be led to the erroneous conclusion that a supplier supplying a part and a part being used in a project implied that that supplier was a recognized supplier for that project. Or equally erroneously, we might suppose that the supplier supplied that part for that project.

The fact that SPJ is nonloss decomposable indicates that it has a join dependency and so is not in 5NF. In this example it is not even in 4NF.

Interpretation (c)

Suppose that it happens to be true that a supplier supplying a part and a part being used on a project implied that a supplier supplied that part to that project. That is what we intend our SPJ relation to mean. This is the most liberal buying policy we could have. We use any supplier for a part and it does not matter for which project. This can be expressed in the following rule:

Rule c
    if s_no supplies p_no
    and p_no is used in pr_no
    then s_no supplies p_no for pr_no

> Rule c expresses the 'liberal' buying policy.

The two projections SP and PJ would be satisfactory and constitute the nonloss decomposition:

SP(s_no, p_no)
PJ(p_no, pr_no)

The dependency diagram of Fig. 5.7(c) applies here.

Again the original SPJ relation would not have been in 4NF because of the redundancy brought about by the two MVDs:

P_NO —>—> S_NO
P_NO —>—> PR_NO

This is the same decomposition of SPJ but we have assigned a different meaning to the relation SPJ. There is no concept of 'recognized supplier' and the result of joining SP and PJ on P_NO and projecting onto (S_NO, PR_NO) would be interpreted as 'This supplier is a potential supplier for this project (because he or she supplies a part that this project uses)'.

Interpretation (d)

With each of the interpretations (a), (b) and (c), SPJ was two-decomposable, and 4NF did the job of indicating the possibility of such a decomposition. Here, we are seeking an interpretation of SPJ in which SPJ is three-decomposable only, not two-decomposable.

Suppose the meaning of SPJ is such that the following rule applies:

A slightly less liberal
buying policy is
indicated in Rule (d).

Rule d
   if s_no supplies p_no
   and p_no is used in pr_no
   and s_no is a recognized supplier for pr_no
   then s_no supplies p_no for pr_no

Unlike rule c, which applies to interpretation (c) above, this is not a particularly liberal buying policy. In order for a supplier to be able to supply a part for a project, he must of course be able to supply the part, and the part must of course be needed in the project but, in addition, the supplier must be a recognized supplier for the project.

Under these circumstances, it is necessary, but also sufficient, to store data in the following three relations, in order to ascertain whether a supplier supplies a particular part for a particular project:

SP(s_no, p_no)   s_no supplies p_no
PJ(p_no, pr_no)   p_no is used in pr_no
SJ(s_no, pr_no)   s_no is a recognized supplier for pr_no

The dependency diagram of Fig. 5.7(d) applies here.

SPJ is now in 4NF but
not in 5NF.

The SPJ relation is thus 3-decomposable but not 2-decomposable. SPJ is in 4NF since there are no MVDs. It is however not in 5NF since it can be non-loss decomposed as shown and consequently contains a join dependency.

Interpretation (e)

Under Interpretation
(e), SPJ is already in
5NF since any set of
projections would lose
information.

Under what circumstances would the original SPJ be non-decomposable? [Corresponding dependency diagram in Fig. 5.7(e).]

If rule d did not apply and the fact that a supplier was recognized for a project, a project needed a part, and the supplier could supply the part, did not necessarily indicate that he supplied that part to that project, then SPJ would have to stay as it is. This scenario is, incidentally, realistic. A particular supplier of a part may be in the habit of supplying out-of-tolerance components of a particular type. They are satisfactory for some projects but not others.

In this situation, SPJ is not nonloss decomposable, has no join dependencies, and is thus in 5NF.

Update anomalies with non-5NF relations

The original SPJ relation under the conditions of interpretation (d) and rule d, contains a join dependency, since SPJ is equal to the join of its projections SP, PJ and SJ. We focus on Interpretation (d) since we wish to show an update anomaly occurring with a relation that is in 4NF but not in 5NF. (See Fig. 5.8.)

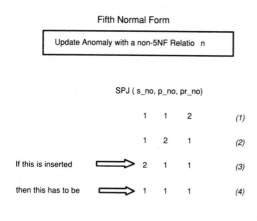

Fig. 5.8 Update anomalies with a non-5NF relation SPJ.

When inserting the new tuple (3), the new tuple (4) also has to be inserted. This is an example of an insertion anomaly that SPJ possesses under interpretation (d):

1. We know that s_no 1 supplies p_no 1 (tuple (1));
2. We now know that p_no 1 is used in pr_no 1 (tuple (3));
3. We know that s_no 1 is a supplier for pr_no 1 (tuple (2));

and by rule 1, we can infer that:

4. s_no 1 supplies p_no 1 for pr_no 1.

To preserve the integrity of the relation, i.e. its adherence to rule d, we must add the extra tuple.

The point is that since we have this rule, and are aware of its universal applicability in this particular situation (for this company, say), the relation SPJ is not necessary and can be nonloss decomposed into SP, PJ and SJ. If it is so decomposed, no data redundancy and consequent update anomalies will result.

The original relation SPJ was not in 5NF since it could be nonloss decomposed into the three projections shown. It should be emphasized that, as we have seen, whether a relation is in 5NF or not depends on knowledge we have about the application area, that is, the rules obtaining in the particular situation being modelled. Join dependencies (5NF) arise because of a rule such as rule d. Multivalued dependencies (4NF) arise because of knowledge about the independence of groups of attributes. Functional dependencies (BCNF, 3NF, 2NF) arise because of knowledge about the M:1 or 1:1 mapping between attributes.

Exercise 5.4

Show the equivalent updates that would occur in the 5NF version, i.e. SP, SJ and PJ.

Fifth normal form

Let us revisit the definition of 5NF:

> A relation is in 5NF iff every join dependency is a consequence of its candidate keys.

This can also be expressed as:

> A relation R is in 5NF iff the only nonloss decompositions all have a candidate key of R as a candidate key.

Except for the cases below, we could say, very roughly, that a 5NF relation is one which has no nonloss decompositions and thus should stay 'all together'. That is, if it were split (vertically), data would be lost.

SPJ under rule d was not in 5NF because there was a nonloss decomposition (into SP PJ and SJ) whose candidate keys were not the candidate key of SPJ.

The reason the more precise definitions above are necessary is to guard against someone saying that even a relation such as:

cus(c_no, name, street, city, postcode)

could be split into, for example:

cus1(c_no, name
cus2(c_no, street
cus3(c_no, city)
cus4(c_no, postc)

Clearly this split is not necessary, and the definition makes it clear why by saying that the original CUS relation is already in 5NF since its only nonloss decompositions all have to contain a candidate key (here c_no) from the original relation.

How to check whether a relation is in 5NF

The most practical method of ensuring a relation is in 5NF is usually to first draw an entity-relationship diagram, perform 1NF, 2NF, BCNF, and 4NF on the resulting relations, and then to ask, in the case of all-key relations containing more than two attributes, whether it is possible to perform projections without loss of data. If not, the relations are all in 5NF. In Ricardo (1990), an algorithm is given for testing whether a given decomposition is lossless, but the above procedure will almost always produce 5NF relations.

In Fig. 5.9, an attempt is made to produce a quick-reference summary of what to look out for with each normal form.

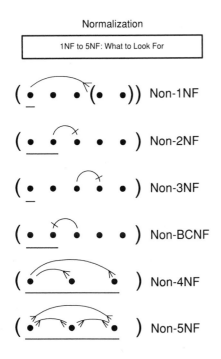

Fig. 5.9   What to look for in 1NF to 5NF.

Exercise 5.5

1. Students enrol on courses, each student enrolling on just one course. Courses contain modules, and a module can appear on several different courses. Produce a set of 5NF relations for each of the following situations:

(a) there is a fixed number of modules on each course and students must take them all;

(b) there is a set of modules on each course from which students can take a selection.

2. Consider the following relation:

person (<u>person no</u>, spouse_no, person_name)

Where every spouse_no must also appear as a person_no in another tuple so that his or her name can be established.

(a) Is the relation in 5NF?

(b) Is data redundancy possible?

Chapter 6

Relational algebra

In this chapter you will learn:

- □ to specify the purpose of the relational algebra;

- □ to use the relational algebraic operators;

- □ to show how relational algebraic operators can be combined to produce a compact representation of database queries;

- □ to indicate the connection between relational algebra and SQL.

The purpose of relational algebra

In Chapters 3, 4 and 5, we described how entity-relationship modelling and normalization are used to design the database schema into which the data will be stored. In this chapter, we move from data representation to database querying. We want to define a basic set of operators which will allow us to retrieve the data we want from the database. It is interesting to find that there is a small set of relational algebraic operators which when combined in various ways will allow us to retrieve the answer to any query that the database is capable of answering.

Relational algebra gives us a basis for specifying and evaluating practical relational query languages such as SQL, QUEL, etc. The query languages should be capable of implementing any relational algebraic expression.

It should be noted that relational algebra is, in a sense, a paper-based language. While it would be possible for an interpreter for the relational algebra itself to be written, in practice query languages present to the user a more 'user-friendly' appearance, a language that is more like English.

There are two main advantages to being able to specify queries in relational algebra. Firstly, relational algebra is a relatively standard implementation-independent form in which to express a query, although (just like pseudo-code) the syntax is not completely standardized. What is standard is the set of relational algebraic operators and the way they operate on data held in relational form.

The second reason why you should know relational algebra is that it is a compact way of specifying a query on paper. In this chapter we present two

> Relational algebra is, like pseudo-code, an implementation-independent way of concisely specifying queries.

ways in which to write down relational algebraic expressions. We call these two forms Greek and English respectively. The Greek form is so called because it uses Greek letters to represent the relational algebraic operators. This makes the relational algebraic (RA) operators appear rather mathematical. Its advantage is that it is compact. The English form is more immediately readable.

Codd cites relational algebra usage as an advantage of the relational approach.

In Codd (1970), there are essentially two arguments for adopting a relational approach to database. The first, as we have seen in previous chapters, is that data can be represented in a simple tabular form without data redundancy. The second is that data can be manipulated using a simple set of set-oriented commands, the relational algebra.

To perform a query, the basic RA operators and the relations they operate on are combined into an RA expression. The order in which these operators are performed can in many cases be changed while still performing the same logical function and producing the same data output from the query. In Chapter 9, we discuss query optimization, which considers the question of which order the RA operators should be performed in, in order to produce the output in the most 'efficient' (fastest and/or minimum intermediate storage usage) way possible. It is shown there that the best sequence is often dependent on the nature of the data. When writing an SQL query, the user does not need to consider this question. The query interpreter/optimizer decides, on the basis of its knowledge of the data on the database, in which order to implement the RA operators contained in the query. In other words, it decides what RA to produce from the SQL query.

We now introduce the RA operators.

The relational algebraic operators

Figure 6.1 shows in simple diagrammatic form the operation of each of the relational algebraic operators. RA operators work on one or more input tables (relations) to produce an output table. They can be combined in various ways to produce an output table. Each individual operator produces its own output which is then fed on to the next operator in an RA expression.

SELECT (RESTRICT)

'SELECT' is also known as 'RESTRICT'. The RA operation 'SELECT' should not be confused with the SQL SELECT.

The purpose of SELECT is to retrieve a subset of the rows (tuples) of a table (relation). Figure 6.1(a) shows the effect of a SELECT. The shaded rows are the ones retrieved. A condition is specified to decide for each row in the table whether or not it should be retrieved, that is, sent to the output. The condition can be called a predicate. A predicate is a condition that evaluates to 'true' or 'false'. In a SELECT, the values of attributes in each row are checked to see if they obey the predicate. If so, the row is delivered to the output; if not, it is not.

Relational Algebra

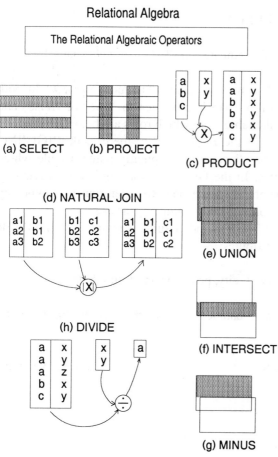

Fig. 6.1 Relational algebraic operators.

Note that in SQL there is also a SELECT statement. It is different from an RA SELECT. The RA SELECT just has this specific purpose, to retrieve a subset of rows. The SQL SELECT can combine many RA commands. It is the main SQL command for retrieving data and has a quite highly developed syntax with lots of optional clauses. To distinguish it from the SQL SELECT, the RA SELECT is sometimes called RESTRICT. The output is 'RESTRICTed' to a subset of the input rows.

> SELECT retrieves a subset of rows.

As we said, we can write an RA expression in Greek or English.

Greek way of writing a SELECT

$\sigma_{\text{predicate}}(\text{table-name})$

σ is the Greek letter sigma, equivalent to our 's' and it is used here to stand for the SELECT RA operator.

English way of writing a SELECT

SELECT table-name WHERE predicate [GIVING new-table-name]

As you can see, the English form is clearer but more verbose. In both forms, 'predicate' is a condition which evaluates to 'true' or 'false' and 'table name' is the name of the table from which rows are being selected.

GIVING shows where the result should go.

Another difference is that in the English form, there is the '[GIVING new-table-name]' option. This allows us to explicitly name a table which will contain the output tuples. In the Greek version, this is not necessary since we show the passage of data from one RA operation to another by nesting the operations. Examples of this nesting appear later.

As an example of a SELECT command, assume we have a CUSTOMER relation with the following attributes:

CUSTOMER(c_no, name, street, city, postcode, cred_lim, balance)

A list of all customers whose balance exceeds their credit limit can be expressed in RA form as:

$$\sigma_{\text{balance} > \text{cred\_lim}} (\text{CUSTOMER}) \qquad\qquad \text{(Greek version)}$$

or

SELECT CUSTOMER
WHERE balance > cred_lim
GIVING TEMP   (English version)

In the second version, a table called TEMP contains the output results.

To list all customers who do not live in London and who are within their credit limit, we can write:

$$\sigma_{\text{city} \neq \text{'London' and balance} \leq \text{cred\_lim}} (\text{CUSTOMER})$$

or

SELECT CUSTOMER
WHERE city ≠ 'London'
AND balance ≤ cred_lim

To list all customers who are not overdrawn Londoners, we could write:

$$\sigma_{\text{not(city = 'London' and balance > cred\_lim)}} (\text{CUSTOMER})$$

or

SELECT CUSTOMER
WHERE NOT (city = 'London' AND balance > cred_lim)

PROJECT

An RA PROJECT operation retrieves a subset of the columns of a table, and eliminates duplicates from the output. The basic idea of PROJECT is shown in Fig. 6.1(b).

PROJECT retrieves a subset of columns, removing duplicates.

The symbolic or Greek version of the PROJECT operator is given using a π ('pi') symbol, which is the Greek letter 'p', for 'PROJECT'. The syntax is:

$$\pi_{\text{col-name, ... , col-name}} \text{(table-name)}$$

The list of column names shows the columns that will appear at the output.

The English version is:

PROJECT table-name
OVER (col-name, ... , col-name)
[GIVING new-table-name]

As an example, suppose we wanted to list all of the cities that our customers live in. This can be performed by:

$$\pi_{\text{city}}(\text{CUSTOMER})$$

or

There may be several customers in the same city. PROJECT ensures each city is listed once only.

PROJECT CUSTOMER
OVER city
GIVING TEMP

Every city will be listed just once, despite the fact that there may be many rows for each city in the CUSTOMER table. The reason is that the PROJECT operator eliminates duplicates from its output.

Combining SELECT and PROJECT

It is often necessary to combine RA operators. For example, suppose we wished to produce an RA expression to perform the following English query:

'List the name, balance and credit limit of all London customers.'

The Greek version is:

The RA operations
start from the most
deeply-nested
brackets.
$\pi_{name, cred\_lim, balance}(\sigma_{city = 'London'}(CUSTOMER))$

while the English version is:

SELECT CUSTOMER
WHERE city = 'London'
GIVING TEMP

PROJECT TEMP
OVER (name, cred_lim, balance)

Notice that in the Greek version, no temporary table is required; the output
of the SELECT is passed to the PROJECT by nesting. Any number of steps
can be nested in this way. In the English version, an intermediate table
TEMP is required to pass the output from the SELECT to the PROJECT.

Exercise 6.1

1. Write the RA expression, in both forms, for the English query:

'List the names and postcodes of all customers who live in neither
London nor Birmingham.'

2. Does it matter whether you do the SELECT or the PROJECT first?

JOIN

There are several variants of the JOIN RA operator. What they all have in
common is that rows of one table are joined (sideways) to rows of another
table.

If there are two tables:

$A(a_1, a_2, a_3)$
$B(b_1, b_2)$

Then rows of A will be 'joined' to rows of B to give rows of the form:

$(a_1, a_2, a_3, b_1, b_2)$

Just which rows from the two tables are joined depends on the type of
JOIN in use; each has its specific purpose.

Cartesian product join (PRODUCT)

The Cartesian Product Join, sometimes just called the PRODUCT, is the
simplest join of all. Every row of the first table is joined to every row of the

second table. We show the product of two tables A and B using the symbol
×:

A × B

or

A TIMES B

The product outputs every combination of the rows of tables A and B. The
idea of PRODUCT is shown in Fig. 6.1(c).

Exercise 6.2

Think of an example where the Cartesian product join would be useful.

Suppose we had two relations CUSTOMER and INVOICE defined as
follows:

CUSTOMER(c_no, name, street, city, postcode, cred_limit, balance)

INVOICE(inv_no, c_no, date, amount)

If we performed the product of these tables:

CUSTOMER × INVOICE

then every row in CUSTOMER would be joined to every row in INVOICE.
Each CUSTOMER would be joined to all the INVOICEs, not only those
which had been sent to him or her, but all the others as well! If there were
100 customers and 200 invoices, the product CUSTOMER × INVOICE
would contain $100 \times 200 = 20\,000$ rows. Most of those rows would be non-
sensical because they joined nonmatching data.

Cartesian Project Join
joins all rows from two
tables. This is often
inappropriate.

Theta join
Clearly we will often want to perform a SELECT after the PRODUCT in
order to output only those rows which 'match' in some way. The theta join
is a general kind of join in which a SELECT follows the PRODUCT. The
theta join of two tables A and B is written:

A |×|$_\theta$ B

or

A TIMES B WHERE Θ

Theta (Θ) is a Greek letter used here to mean 'any predicate'. Any join involving a PRODUCT followed by a SELECT is a theta join. Consequently, this example could be rewritten as:

$$\sigma_{\Theta}(A \times B)$$

which means: do the PRODUCT (×) first, then perform the SELECT using the predicate (Θ).

For example, using the CUSTOMER and INVOICE tables, we might perform the theta join:

$$\text{CUSTOMER} \mid \times \mid_{c\_no < 23} \text{INVOICE}$$

This would join every CUSTOMER to every INVOICE and then restrict the output to those rows where the predicate

$$\Theta = \text{`c\_no} < 23\text{'}$$

was true.

Exercise 6.3

Rewrite this query in the 'English' form.

Equijoin

A particular, and useful, case of the theta join is the EQUIJOIN. Here, the two tables are joined on equality of common columns. The rows which are joined and passed to the output are those which have the same values for their 'common' columns, that is the column names they both have.

In our CUSTOMER and INVOICE tables, there is one column name they both have: the attribute c_no, which is the primary key in CUSTOMER and the foreign key in INVOICE. Foreign keys are put in precisely so that the equijoin can be performed. They show the links between rows in (usually) different tables. To combine the data from matching rows in different tables, you perform the EQUIJOIN.

The EQUIJOIN of CUSTOMER and INVOICE is written:

$$\text{CUSTOMER} \mid \times \mid_{\text{CUSTOMER.c\_no} = \text{INVOICE.c\_no}} \text{INVOICE}$$

or

CUSTOMER EQUIJOIN INVOICE

Notice that the equijoin does not have its own Greek symbol. Note also that it depends for its operation (theoretically) on having identically named columns in the tables to be joined. This is certainly true in the English version, where column names are not explicitly named. In the Greek version, since there is no special symbol, you have to name the columns.

We have so far discussed only equality in our joins. We could equally well define GREATERTHANJOIN, LESSTHANJOIN, NOTEQUALJOIN, NOTLESSTHANJOIN, etc.

Natural join

With the EQUIJOIN, there is the slight inconvenience that the output contains both copies of the identically named columns. In the NATURAL JOIN, the duplicate column name or names are removed. The basic idea of NATURAL JOIN is shown in Fig. 6.1(d). This is the most common form of join, and is often written as just | × | or JOIN.

Natural Join is the most commonly used join.

Thus if we wished to perform the natural join of CUSTOMER with INVOICE, we would simply write:

CUSTOMER | × | INVOICE

or

CUSTOMER JOIN INVOICE

Just to repeat, if you see the | × | symbol without any predicate, or the word JOIN on its own, it is a NATURAL JOIN.

Assuming we had the following data in CUSTOMER and INVOICE:

CUSTOMER

c_no	name	street	city	postcode	balance	cred_lim
1	Alan	Fax St	London	W1	1000	2000
2	Bill	Cax St	Bristol	BS8 9EE	2000	1500
3	Carl	Max St	Lee	LS3 1JJ	1000	1000

INVOICE

inv_no	c_no	date	amount
10	1	1/1/93	500
20	1	2/2/93	500
30	2	5/1/93	2000

Then CUSTOMER | × | INVOICE would be:

c_no	name	street	city	postcode	balance	cred_lim	inv_no	date	amount
1	Alan	Fax St	London	W1	1000	2000	10	1/1/93	500
1	Alan	Fax St	London	W1	1000	2000	20	2/2/93	500
2	Bill	Cax St	Bristol	BS8 9EE	2000	1500	30	5/1/93	2000

Customer 1 is joined to two invoices and customer 2 is joined to one invoice. Customer 3 has no invoices. Notice INVOICE.c_no has been removed in the natural join.

In the natural join it is not strictly necessary that the column names on which the join is being performed are identically named. All that is required is that the domains (value sets) of the attributes be the same.

Suppose we had two tables:

EMPLOYEE

emp_no	name	salary
1	Alan	10 000
2	Beryl	20 000
3	Carol	15 000

MANAGER

mgr_no	department
1	Accounts
3	Stores

and emp_no and mgr_no have the same domain. Then we could join EMPLOYEE and MANAGER over emp_no and mgr_no as follows:

It is a good idea to always show the join criteria to make the meaning of the join clear.

$$\text{EMPLOYEE} \mid \times \mid_{emp\_no, mgr\_no} \text{MANAGER}$$

or

JOIN EMPLOYEE, MANAGER
OVER emp_no, mgr_no

(making it clear what the 'common' attributes are), with the result:

emp_no	name	salary	department
1	Alan	10 000	Accounts
3	Carol	15 000	Stores

Semijoin

The SEMIJOIN of A with B is the natural join of A with B followed by projecting the result back onto A. This gives the effect of listing all A rows that match a row in B. Only the A attributes are shown. The semijoin of A with B is written as:

A | × | B

or

A SEMIJOIN B

As an example, the semijoin of EMPLOYEE and MANAGER shows the EMPLOYEE attributes of all employees who are also managers:

EMPLOYEE | × | MANAGER

is:

emp_no	name	salary
1	Alan	10 000
3	Carol	15 000

From the definition of semijoin, we could have written this RA expression equivalently using an EQUIJOIN and a PROJECT as:

$$\pi_{\text{emp\_no, name, salary}}(\text{EMPLOYEE} \mid \times \mid_{\text{emp\_no = mgr\_no}} \text{MANAGER})$$

Exercise 6.4

1. Write the RA expression above in English form.

2. Write down the result of performing:

MANAGER | × | EMPLOYEE

and explain the result.

Outer join

In all of the joins covered so far (apart from PRODUCT), the rows that appeared at the output were those in which a match occurred between the two tables. Sometimes we may wish nonmatching rows also to occur. For example, suppose we wanted to produce a table suitable for producing customer Statements of Account or 'Statements'. (You receive a Statement from a company which shows all the invoices they sent you with all the payments you have made against those invoices.) The INVOICE and PAYMENT data we need would be contained in tables like:

INVOICE(inv_no, cus_no, i_date, i_amount)
         10   1   1/1/93   100
         20   1   5/1/93   200

PAYMENT(inv_no, pmt_no, p_date, p_amount)
         10   1   20/1/93   50
         10   2   20/2/93   50

In the Statement, we must show not only those invoices for which there have been payments, but also those for which there have not been payments. Otherwise customers would not be reminded of the bills they have not paid!

We thus require the output from the join to appear as follows:

The nulls show unpaid
invoices.

(inv_no cus_no i_date i_amount pmt_no p_date p_amount)
         10   1   1/1/93   100   1   20/1/93   50
         10   1   1/1/93   100   2   20/2/93   50
         20   1   5/1/93   200

with nulls under the last three columns in the last row, signifying nonpayment.

This is precisely what the following LEFT OUTER EQUIJOIN would do in this case:

INVOICE LEFT OUTER EQUIJOIN PAYMENT

In the general case, A LEFT OUTER EQUIJOIN B outputs all the matching rows together with all rows of A which do not match any row in B. A RIGHT OUTER EQUIJOIN B outputs all the matching rows together with all rows of B which do not match any row in A.

If we required both nonmatchers from A and nonmatchers from B in the output, we simply perform an OUTER EQUIJOIN:

A OUTER EQUIJOIN B

We have mentioned only the OUTER EQUIJOIN here. The meaning of such joins as OUTER NATURALJOIN, OUTER GREATERTHANJOIN, etc. should be readily apparent.

Exercise 6.5

1. Write down the results of:

   (a) EMPLOYEE LEFT OUTER EQUIJOIN MANAGER

   (b) EMPLOYEE RIGHT OUTER EQUIJOIN MANAGER
   (c) EMPLOYEE OUTER EQUIJOIN MANAGER

2. Produce a pair of tables and a situation which would justify the use of a LEFT OUTER GREATERTHANJOIN.

Self join

Sometimes it is necessary to join a table to itself to answer a query. Suppose we have the following table:

EMP(emp_no, name, dept_no)

1	Alan	10
2	Bruce	20
3	Carole	10
4	Denise	10

and we wish to find all the employees who work in the same department as employee 1.

The query we require is:

$$\pi_{name}(\text{EMP} \mid \times_{dept\_no} (\sigma_{emp\_no = 1}(\text{EMP})))$$

In its 'English' version it is easier to see the steps:

1. SELECT EMPLOYEE WHERE emp_no = 1 GIVING TEMP1
2. EMP SEMIJOIN TEMP1 OVER dept_no GIVING TEMP2
3. PROJECT TEMP2 OVER name GIVING RESULT

Step 1: TEMP1 table
TEMP1(emp_no, name, dept_no)

1	Alan	10

The effect of the SELECT has been to retrieve the row for employee number 1. Now the computer knows (we don't) which department he or she is in – department 10.

Step 2: TEMP2 table
TEMP2(emp_no, name, dept_no)

1	Alan	10
3	Carole	10
4	Denise	10

The SEMIJOIN joins all rows of EMP with the TEMP1 table on dept_no 10 and projects out the EMP attributes. This aspect of the semijoin is useful

A self-join joins a table to itself.

here since otherwise there would have been confusion between identically named columns in EMP and TEMP2.

Step 3: RESULT table
RESULT(name)

      Alan
      Carole
      Denise

Note that Alan is quite naturally in the same department as himself!

This query was a SELF JOIN because it involved joining some rows of EMP to other rows of EMP.

Exercise 6.6

Think of other examples where self joins are appropriate. In each case:

1. Write the query in ordinary English.

2. Define the appropriate table you would wish to appear on the database.

3. Write the RA expression in Greek and English forms.

Union

Duplicate rows are removed in a UNION.

The UNION of two tables A and B is formed by simply appending the rows of B to those of A and removing any duplicate rows. Figure 6.1(e) gives the basic idea. The tables A and B must be union compatible (also known as column homogeneous), which means A and B must have the same number of columns, the columns must be from the same domains (not necessarily the same names but the values must be from the same value set), and be in the same order.

Assume we have the following three tables on the database:

VIOLIN(stud_no,	name,	age)
1	Fred	10
2	Sally	11
4	David	10

PIANO(st_no,	name,	age)
2	Sally	11
4	David	10
5	Zena	11

CELLO(st_no,	age,	name)
4	10	David
6	11	Josey

Then VIOLIN and PIANO are union compatible since their three columns are of the same type and in the same order. It would not be possible to form the union of either of them with CELLO because it has the columns in a different order.

The UNION symbol is U. The union of tables A and B is thus written as:

A U B

or

A UNION B

VIOLIN U PIANO is:

(stud_no,	name,	age)
1	Fred	10
2	Sally	11
4	David	10
5	Zena	11

Note that duplicate rows have been removed. We decided arbitrarily to call the first column 'stud_no' rather than 'st_no'.

Intersection

The INTERSECTION of two tables contains the rows which are in both tables. That is, a row appears at the output if it appears identically in both tables. Figure 6.1(f) illustrates INTERSECTION.

The symbol for INTERSECTION is ∩.

The INTERSECTION of VIOLIN with PIANO is written:

VIOLIN ∩ PIANO

or

VIOLIN INTERSECTION PIANO

and with the tables above, is:

(stud_no,	name,	age)
2	Sally	11
4	David	10

because these two students play both violin and cello; they appear in both tables.

MINUS is also known
as COMPLEMENT and
DIFFERENCE.

MINUS (complement, difference)

A MINUS B, where A and B are column homogeneous tables, also written
A – B, is the set of all rows in A that do not appear in B. Notice that A – B
is not the same as B – A. Figure 6.1(g) illustrates MINUS.

In our example, VIOLIN – PIANO is:

(stud_no,	name,	age)
1	Fred	10

and PIANO – VIOLIN is:

(stud_no,	name,	age)
5	Zena	11

because Fred plays violin but not piano and Zena plays piano but not violin.
MINUS is sometimes called DIFFERENCE because its output shows the
'difference' between one table and the other. But notice that with our definition of difference, the difference between A and B is never the same as the
difference between B and A! The only exception would be if A and B were
identical.

DIVISION

It might seem surprising that one table can be divided by another! However,
there is a RA operation that we have not yet described which does have a
very useful function. The basic idea of tabular division is shown in Fig.
6.1(h). We define R1 DIVIDEBY R2 (also written R1 ÷ R2) by first giving
an example.

Suppose the tables R1 and R2 have the following attributes and data:

R1(	A,	B,	C,	D)
	1	2	3	4
	1	2	5	6
	1	2	7	8
	2	3	3	4
	2	3	5	5

R2(C,	D)
3	4
5	6

Then R1 ÷ R2 is:

(	A,	B)
	1	2

(A=1, B=2) is the only combination of A with B which in R1 'has the full set' of values of C with D in R2. There is a tuple in R1 for all tuple values in R2.

Using the terminology of conventional arithmetic division, R1 is the dividend, R2 is the divisor, and the result is the quotient.

All columns in the divisor must be column homogeneous (same type and value set) with a corresponding set of columns in the dividend. In our example the two columns C and D in the divisor also appear in the dividend. The output is the other columns in the dividend, and only those rows which have the full set of divisor row values. In our example, the divisor is {(3,4), (5,6)}. In the dividend, (1,2,3,4) and (1,2,5,6) both exist, so (1,2) is output. It is matched in R1 with the 'full set' of rows in the divisor R2.

While it might sound unnecessarily involved, DIVIDEBY does have useful applications. Suppose we had two tables:

PURCHASE(c_no, prod_no, qty, ord_no)

PRODUCT(prod_no, qty_in_stock, price)

and we wished to perform the following query:

'List customers who have purchased all products.'

The steps would be as follows:

1. PROJECT PRODUCT OVER prod_no GIVING ALL_PRODS
   This step is performed to form a suitable divisor. We intend to divide PURCHASE by PRODUCT but to perform a DIVIDE operation, the divisor must only contain attributes that appear in the dividend.
2. PROJECT PURCHASE OVER (c_no, prod_no) GIVING ALL_PURCHS
   This step is necessary to remove qty and ord_no from PURCHASE before the divide. See Exercise 6.7.
3. DIVIDE ALL_PURCHS BY ALL_PRODS GIVING RESULT
   That is all that is required. If in ALL_PURCHS any c_no is found against every prod_no, then that c_no is output.

The query can be written symbolically as:

$$(\pi_{c\_no,\ prod\_no}(\text{PURCHASE})) \div (\pi_{prod\_no}(\text{PRODUCT}))$$

Exercise 6.7

1. Why was it necessary to remove ord_no from PURCHASE by projection before the divide?

2. If we had not done so, what would the English interpretation of the query then be?

3. Write an RA expression which outputs any products which have been purchased by all customers. Specify any additional database tables you may need.

Relational algebra and SQL

We have seen how the relational algebra can be used to express a range of queries that one might want to make of a relational database. It consists of a number of RA operators which can be combined in different ways to perform the queries. In some cases, the order in which the RA operations are performed can be changed while producing the same output result. If we wanted to perform the query:

'List all invoices that were sent to Smith & Co.'

we might perform the natural join CUSTOMER JOIN INVOICE followed by the SELECT and then a PROJECT:

1. JOIN CUSTOMER, INVOICE GIVING CUS_INV
2. SELECT CUS_INV WHERE name = 'Smith & Co.' GIVING SMITH_CUS_INV
3. PROJECT SMITH_CUS_INV OVER (inv_no, date, amount) GIVING SMITH_INV

See page 284 for a discussion of query optimization.

Here, in Step 1, all matching customers and invoices are joined. Given that we are only interested in the invoices of Smith & Co., it might have been more efficient (faster; less space) to perform a SELECT on CUSTOMER first:

1. SELECT CUSTOMER WHERE name = 'Smith & Co.' GIVING SMITH_CUS
2. JOIN SMITH_CUS, INVOICE GIVING SMITH_CUS_INV
3. PROJECT SMITH_CUS_INV OVER (inv_no, date, amount) GIVING SMITH_INV

Here, only the relevant CUSTOMER row needs to be joined to its matching INVOICE rows. This is likely to produce a faster result and to use less intermediate space. (SMITH_CUS_INV will be smaller than CUS_INV).

Other relational algebraic sequences are possible.

In SQL, the programmer is freed from the responsibility of specifying the order in which the RA operations will be performed. Any RA expression can be realized in SQL but the SQL programmer has only to specify what must be output, not exactly how. In this sense, relational algebra is characterized as procedural while SQL is called declarative.

In practice, one may argue with this distinction. When you are writing SQL, it often feels as if you are specifying how an output is to be produced – which tables need to be accessed, which columns, which SQL clauses, etc. Perhaps we can say that the real advantages of SQL over relational algebra include these:

1. The sequence in which the various selects, projects, joins, unions, etc. are performed is determined by the query interpreter, the program that translates an SQL query into machine code and executes it. The query interpreter is likely to 'know' and use more information about the database (number of rows in tables, which indexes could profitably be used, likely hit-rates) than the user.

2. To many people, SQL queries are more readable than RA expressions, particularly those in 'Greek' form.

3. SQL has a standard syntax which many people know.

'Hit rate' is the proportion of rows in a table relevant to a particular query or update.

We shall return to the relational algebra in Chapter 9 on Query Optimization (page 284).

Chapter 7

Introduction to SQL

In this chapter you will learn:

- □ to use SQL;

- □ to CREATE, DROP and ALTER tables in SQL;

- □ to show how the database schema can be tested against typical queries;

- □ to explore the features of the SQL SELECT, INSERT, UPDATE and DELETE statements.

Introduction

SQL (Structured Query Language) is the almost universally used language for accessing databases. There are several aspects to relational database schema that are implemented using SQL. These include:

Table creation (this chapter)
Indexing (Chapter 8)
Security (Chapter 9)

In Chapters 3 to 5 we showed how to create the logical database design and in Chapter 6 we discussed relational algebra, a language for describing database queries. In this chapter we describe how to create database tables using SQL and to perform a rich variety of queries using the SQL SELECT statement.

Creating database tables

The SQL CREATE TABLE command
At this stage we have a fully normalized paper database design which we can now proceed to implement using the SQL CREATE command. The basic syntax forms of the CREATE command are as follows:

```
CREATE TABLE table-name
 (column-name data-type [NULL | NOT NULL], ... )
CREAT TABLE table-name
 (column-name [NOT NULL], ... )
 AS query
```

Fig. 7.1 Basic syntax of CREATE TABLE.

The ellipsis (...) indicates that the preceding items can be repeated. The NOT NULL option specifies that when data is being INSERTed into that column, or when its value is being UPDATEd, the NULL value is not allowed. This forces the user or application program to specify a value for the field. One column at least must not be null, that is, the column used as the primary key since, as discussed, it will be used as a foreign key to link the row to other rows in the database and it also serves as the row's identifier. So always specify NOT NULL for primary keys and any other columns which you want to ensure will always have an 'actual' value. The uniqueness property of primary keys is often enforced using CREATE INDEX (Chapter 8). In the ISO 9075 and ANSI-86 SQL standards it is enforced in CREATE TABLE with CREATE TABLE UNIQUE.

In the second form of the command, the AS clause allows the new table to be defined in terms of columns from tables that already exist on the database. The columns' types and sizes are copied from the result of the AS query. If all the columns in the query have well-defined and unique names, then (column, ...) may be omitted. The major difference between this form and the first form however is that here the CREATE TABLE actually writes rows into the new table. The main use we have found for this second form of the command is to produce temporary tables during the execution of complex queries.

Example 1

```
1 CREATE TABLE CUS
2 (C_NO NUMBER(2) NOT NULL,
3 TITLE  CHAR(5),
4 SNAME  CHAR(10),
5 INITS  CHAR(4),
6 STREET CHAR(10),
7 CITY CHAR(6),
8 POSTC  CHAR(7),
9 CRED_LIM NUMBER(5,0),
10 BALANCE NUMBER(7,2) ) ;
```

The first form of
CREATE TABLE

This is how the CUS table, which is shown in the Appendix, was created. Since C_NO is the primary key it has been defined as NOT NULL. Any

The default NULL means the attribute is allowed to be NULL.

combination of the other columns may be null. The default is NULL. CRED_LIM is a five-digit integer. BALANCE can have maximum value 9999.99 since the number 7 in the column data type description shows the maximum total width including the decimal point. Check the data types that are allowed on your database. The line numbers are not included in the CREATE TABLE command and are shown here merely for clarity of exposition.

Example 2

The second form of CREATE TABLE

```
1 CREATE TABLE TEMP2 AS
2 SELECT SUM(NO_OF_VOTES) T
3 FROM CANDIDATE ;
```

Here, in line 1, the AS indicates that the second form of the CREATE TABLE command is being used. Lines 2 and 3 constitute an SQL SELECT command, the description of which follows in the next section. In this very simple example, a single-column, single-row table called TEMP2 is being created which will contain the sum of the votes from table CANDIDATE.

Inserting rows into tables with INSERT

Having defined the columns in a table, rows containing data can be inserted using the SQL INSERT command. The syntax is:

INSERT INTO table
[(col_name,...)]
VALUES (value,...) ;

INSERT INTO table
[(col_name,...)]
query ;

The first form inserts just one row, whereas the second form inserts rows derived from the query.

Example 1

The first form of INSERT

```
1 INSERT INTO INVOICE
2 INV_NO, C_NO, INV_DATE, AMOUNT
3 VALUES (1018, NULL, '25-jan-94', 100) ;
```

Note that a NULL is being placed in C_NO, possibly because it is not yet known. The same effect is obtained with:

```
1 INSERT INTO INVOICE
2 INV_NO, INV_DATE, AMOUNT
3 VALUES (1018, '25-jan-94', 100) ;
```

Example 2

```
1 CREATE TABLE TEMP
2 (C_NO        NUMBER(5),
3 BALANCE      NUMBER(6,2)) ;
1 INSERT INTO TEMP
2 SELECT C_NO, BALANCE
3 FROM CUS
4 WHERE BALANCE > CRED_LIM ;
```

The second form of INSERT

Exercise 7.1

1. Create all the tables shown in Appendix A on your database.

2. Populate the tables with the data shown in Appendix A.

All of the following examples use the table definitions and contents shown in the Appendix.

Deleting rows from tables with DELETE

The SQL DELETE command is used to delete specified rows from a table. The syntax is:

DELETE FROM table
[WHERE condition]

Example 1

```
1 DELETE FROM INVOICE
2 WHERE C_NO = 1 ;
```

This deletes all rows for C_NO 1.

Example 2

```
1 DELETE FROM INVOICE A
2 WHERE AMOUNT <=
3 (SELECT SUM(AMOUNT)
4 FROM PAYMENT B
5 WHERE B.INV_NO = A.INV_NO) ;
```

This deletes all invoices where the total payment is greater than or equal to the invoice amount. Lines 3 to 5 are a subquery used to define which rows of INVOICE are to be deleted. SUM(AMOUNT) is an aggregate function which adds up all the payment amounts for the invoice. Note the use of table aliases A and B. Subqueries and aggregate functions are defined below.

Subqueries are covered on page 208.

Updating rows with UPDATE

This is used for updating (changing) one or more values in the rows of a table. There are two forms:

UPDATE table
SET col_name = expr [col_name = expr,...]
[WHERE condition]
UPDATE table
SET (col_name,...) = (subquery)
[WHERE condition]   ·

Example 1

The first form of
UPDATE

```
1 UPDATE PRODUCT
2 SET PRICE = PRICE * 1.1
3 WHERE DESCR = `Bat' ;
```

This increases the value of bats by 10%.

Example 2

The second form of
UPDATE

```
1 UPDATE CUS
2 SET BALANCE =
3 (SELECT CUS.BALANCE + SUM(AMOUNT)
4 FROM INVOICE
5 WHERE CUS.C_NO = INVOICE.C_NO
6 AND INV_DATE BETWEEN `1-jan-94' AND
`31-jan-94')
7 AND CITY = `London' ;
```

Exercise 7.2

Explain the above UPDATE command in English. You will have to read ahead to do this.

Dropping tables

Tables can be removed from the database (provided the user has the appropriate database privileges – Chapter 9) using the simple syntax:

DROP TABLE table ;

For example we could remove all the CUS table data and its definition in the data dictionary from the database by:

```
1 DROP TABLE CUS ;
```

The data dictionary is a set of tables, maintained by the DBMS, which contains details of the definitions of all tables, views, indexes and other data about the database.

Altering table definitions

The descriptions of columns in a table can be modified, and extra columns can be added to a table in ORACLE using the ALTER TABLE command. The methods used in INGRES and dBASE IV are shown later. The syntax forms of the ALTER TABLE command are:

ORACLE has a simple way of changing table definitions.

ALTER TABLE table
ADD (column-name data-type [NULL|NOT NULL], ...)
ALTER TABLE table
MODIFY (column-name [data-type] [NULL|NOT NULL],   ...)

Square brackets show optional items.

Both these forms can be used without any interference with the data already in the table. The first form adds one or more new columns which can be entered in the same way as the CREATE TABLE command above. In the second form of the command either the data type, or the 'nullability' of the column, or both can be altered for one or more columns.

A column (attribute) is 'nullable' if it is allowed to contain NULL.

Example 1
```
1 ALTER TABLE CUS
2 ADD (COMPANY_NAME CHAR(30) );
```

This ALTER TABLE command adds a new column COMPANY_NAME to the CUS table and places NULL in it throughout. NULL is the default value for ADD. A NOT NULL column can be added only to a table that has no rows since if you attempted to add a NOT NULL column to a table with existing rows, the system would not know what values to put in the column (clearly NULL would be no good). If you want to add a NOT NULL column, first add it as the default, then fill in values for every existing row, then use the MODIFY form of ALTER TABLE to make it NOT NULL.

Example 2
```
1 ALTER TABLE CUS
2 MODIFY
3 (INITS CHAR(6),
4 STREET NOT NULL) ;
```

This command modifies two things in the table. First, the INITS column is expanded to 6 characters (it was 4). This is presumably so that longer initial strings, such as 'A.J.P.' can be accommodated. Second, the STREET column of CUS is now specified as NOT NULL. You had better ensure that no existing STREET values do contain the value NULL before you execute this command.

Adding extra columns in other DBMSs such as INGRES is slightly more involved. First it is necessary to create the definition of a temporary table containing the new column:

Adding an extra column in INGRES is more involved.

```
1 CREATE TABLE TEMP <-- New Temporary Table
2 (C_NO SMALLINT NOT NULL,
3 TITLE  VCHAR(5),
4 SNAME  VCHAR(10),
5 INITS  VCHAR(4),
6 STREET VCHAR(10),
7 CITY VCHAR(6),
8 POSTC  VCHAR(7),
9 CRED_LIM MONEY,
10 BALANCE MONEY,
11 COMPANY_NAME VCHAR(30) ) ; <-- New Column
```

This step can be performed in SQL itself using this CREATE TABLE command or more quickly outside of SQL using the INGRES CREATE NEW TABLE menu option and then the GetTableDef option to save having to retype existing column names. Having created the new table definition, the rows in the existing CUS table are copied into it using the SQL INSERT command:

```
1 INSERT INTO TEMP
2 SELECT *
3 FROM CUS ;
```

The new COMPANY_NAME column will of course remain NULL. The next step is to DROP the old CUS table and CREATE the new from TEMP:

```
1 DROP TABLE CUS ; <-- 'DROP CUS' for INGRES V 5.0
1 CREATE TABLE CUS AS
2 SELECT *
3 FROM TEMP ;
```

Finally DROP the temporary table:

```
1 DROP TABLE TEMP ;
```

A similar procedure has to be performed in dBASE IV when altering a table definition.

The SQL SELECT statement

The SELECT
statement is used to
perform queries.

The purpose of the SQL SELECT statement is to retrieve and display data gathered from one or more database tables. SELECT is the most frequently used SQL command and can be used interactively to obtain immediate answers to queries, or embedded in a program written in a host language such as C or COBOL for more complex data retrieval and reporting. Interactive use of SELECT is where the power of SQL is most readily demonstrated, with many complex data retrieval operations often requiring just a few well-chosen lines of SQL.

SELECT with a single table

Descriptions of all of the tables used in the following examples are given in Appendix A.

The basic syntax of the SELECT statement for a single table is shown in Fig. 7.2.

```
SELECT       [DISTINCT] {*|col_exp [,col_exp, ...]}
FROM             table_name [table_alias]
[WHERE      condition
[AND/OR     condition, [AND/OR condition, ...]])
[GROUP BY   col_name [,col_name, ...]
[HAVING     condition]]
[ORDER BY   {col, [,col, ...]}]
```

Fig. 7.2 SELECT syntax for a single table.

Square brackets show nonmandatory items. Braces { } and bars show alternative items, and three dots ... mean the preceding item may be repeated. Additional clauses in the SELECT statement are covered in subsequent sections. The syntax may vary slightly from one implementation of SQL to another but all versions should contain at least this minimum set.

Square brackets mean
'optional'. Vertical bars
separate alternatives.
Three dots show
repetition.

Selecting columns

The simplest SELECT statement it is possible to enter will retrieve all columns from every row of a table. Remember that 'column' is SQL's name for what is commonly called a field or attribute and 'row' is the term used in SQL for what is often called a record. Similarly, the terms 'table' and 'file' are often used interchangeably. To list the entire CUS table the following SQL command would be entered:

Query 7.1 'List all details stored on every customer.'

```
1 SELECT *
2 FROM CUS ;
```

The semicolon at the end of the query informs the SQL interpreter that command input has finished and requests it to execute the command immediately.

Following the word SELECT in line 1 is the list of columns that are to be retrieved. Here, the asterisk means that all columns are required. In line 2, the FROM clause states the database tables the retrieved columns are to come from. In this SELECT, the table is the CUS table. So the command means 'Select all columns from the CUS table'. The output resulting from this SELECT command is:

C_NO	TITLE	SNAME	INITS	STREET	CITY	POSTC	CRED_LIM	BALANCE
1	Mr	Sallaway	G.R.	12 Fax Rd	London	WC1	1000	42.56
2	Mis	Lauri	P.	5 Dux St	London	N1	500	200
3	Mr	Jackson	R.	2 Lux Ave	Leeds	LE1 2AB	500	510
4	Mr	Dziduch	M.	31 Low St	Dover	DO2 9CD	100	149.23
5	Ms	Woods	S.Q.	17 Nax Rd	London	E18 4WW	1000	250.1
6	Mrs	Williams	C.	41 Cax St	Dover	DO2 8WD		412.21

The use of NULL

There is no value shown for CRED_LIM for C_NO 6. This field value is as yet unknown and contains NULL. NULL is a special value provided by SQL. You can use it to mean a variety of things. In the present example NULL means 'as yet unknown'. You might want to use it to mean 'not applicable' (this customer doesn't have a credit limit) or to have some other meaning. SQL treats NULL in a special way. The other properties of NULL are indicated in later examples.

Project

Query 7.2 contains a projection (Chapter 6) because only two of the columns in the table are required to be output.

Query 7.2 'List out the customer account numbers and the invoice amounts of all customers who have outstanding invoices.'

```
1 SELECT C_NO, AMOUNT
2 FROM INVOICE ;
```

Instead of listing all columns from INVOICE, only columns C_NO and AMOUNT are required. These column names are the usual form of the 'col_exp' (column expression) shown in Fig. 7.2. Column expressions can also contain arithmetic and various functions. The output from this command is:

C_NO AMOUNT

C_NO	AMOUNT
1	26.2
4	149.23
1	16.36
2	200
3	510
5	250.1
6	412.21

DISTINCT

DISTINCT removes duplicate output rows.

Duplicate output rows may arise when a project is used. An RA project operation removes those duplicates. In SQL you can choose to have the duplicates removed or leave them in.

Query 7.3 'List the account numbers of all customers with outstanding invoices.'
If we try:

```
1 SELECT C_NO
2 FROM INVOICE ;
```

the output is:

C_NO

C_NO
1
4
1
2
3
5
6

The C_NO 1 has appeared twice in the output because it appeared twice on the INVOICE table. Duplicate output rows can be removed using the DISTINCT option:

```
1 SELECT DISTINCT C_NO
2 FROM INVOICE ;
```

giving:

C_NO

C_NO
1

4
2
3
5
6

The only effect of DISTINCT is to prevent duplicate rows appearing in the output.

Column expressions
Column expressions may be more than simply column names:

Query 7.4 'For each product, list out the percentage by which the current stock level exceeds minimum stock level.'

An output 'column' may be an expression.
```
1 SELECT PROD_NO, DESCR, 100 * (QIS - MINQ)/ MINQ
2 FROM PRODUCT ;
```

The third column expression is an arithmetic expression involving two column names QIS and MINQ (quantity in stock and minimum stock level respectively) and the constant 100. The output is:

PROD_NO	DESCR	100*(QIS-MINQ)/MINQ
1	Bat	100
2	Ball	0
3	Hoop	−40
4	Net	−60
5	Rope	−90

Columns may be given aliases so that we could use the command:

'EXCESS' is a column alias
```
1 SELECT PROD_NO, DESCR, 100*(QIS-MINQ)/MINQ EXCESS
2 FROM PRODUCT ;
```

This command uses the column alias EXCESS for the arithmetic expression preceding it. The output is now:

PROD_NO	DESCR	EXCESS
1	Bat	100
2	Ball	0
3	Hoop	−40
4	Net	−60
5	Rope	−90

The command is the same for INGRES version 6 except that the keyword AS precedes the column alias.

Selecting rows – the WHERE clause

The WHERE clause in the SQL SELECT statement syntax is used to specify a subset of rows that will be delivered to the output.

WHERE performs a RA 'select'. A subset of rows is output.

Query 7.5 'List the products whose price is greater than five pounds.'

```
1 SELECT PROD_NO, DESCR, PRICE
2 FROM PRODUCT
3 WHERE PRICE > 5 ;
```

Line 3 contains the simple condition 'PRICE > 5' which says that the only rows in the table PRODUCT that will be output are those where the value of the PRICE column in the row is greater than 5. The output is:

PROD_NO	DESCR	PRICE
1	Bat	12
4	Net	20
5	Rope	6

Exercise 7.3

1. Write the equivalent RA expression for Query 7.5.

2. Using the CANDIDATE table in the Appendix, write an SQL command to list the number of votes for each candidate. Include in the output CAND_NO, NAME, and NO_OF_VOTES only.

SQL uses the following simple comparison operators:

= equals
< is less than
> is greater than
<= is less than or equal to (i.e. not greater than)
>= is greater than or equal to (i.e. not less than)
<> is not equal to
!= can be used instead of '<>'.

All operators work with character and date as well as numeric data types. With inequality tests involving character data, the alphanumerical order of the data is used and for dates, chronological sequence is used, as in:

Query 7.6 'List details of all invoices sent out before 1st Jan 1993.'

```
1 SELECT *
2 FROM INVOICE
3 WHERE DATE < '1-jan-93' ;
```

Line 3 selects out all rows where the invoice date is before 1st Jan 1993.

Comparisons with NULL

Note that any of the comparison operators used to compare a value with a field containing the value NULL will fail. So if you used the WHERE clause:

WHERE CRED_LIM > 1000

and the customer had a NULL value for CRED_LIM, the row would not be output. The only test that will succeed with NULL is 'IS NULL'.

Exercise 7.4

Write SQL queries to answer the following English queries:

1. 'List details of all customers not living in London.'

2. 'List out the details of all customers who have exceeded their credit limit.' Pay particular attention here to C_NO 6.

3. 'List out the percentage shortfall in stock of all items that need to be reordered.'

The LIKE operator

Fuzzy matching characters.

LIKE works with character fields and allows 'fuzzy matching'. The query contains an approximation to the spelling of the required column contents and all rows where the corresponding characters match up are retrieved.

% matches with zero or more characters
_ (underscore) matches with just one character.

Query 7.7 'List the account details of all customers whose name starts with "Dz".'

```
1 SELECT *
2 FROM CUS
3 WHERE SNAME LIKE 'Dz%' ;
```

The % sign will match with any number of characters following the 'Dz'.

Exercise 7.5

Write SQL commands to implement the following English queries:

1. 'What's the address of that Czech customer? I can't remember the account number or how to spell the company name, but I think the second letter was a "z".'

2. The LIKE operator can sometimes be used to advantage with postcodes. 'List all customers living (a) in area MK2; (b) in area MK2 3DH.'

The BETWEEN operator
BETWEEN can be used in a WHERE clause to select rows where the value of a column is in a given range:

Query 7.8 'List out details of all invoices with an invoice date between 1st Dec 1993 and 13th Jan 1994.'

BETWEEN gives an inclusive comparison.

```
1 SELECT *
2 FROM INVOICE
3 WHERE INV_DATE BETWEEN '1-dec-93' AND '13-jan-94';
```

Note that the invoice rows with dates between 1st Dec 93 and 13th Jan 94 inclusive will be output.

The IN and NOT IN operators
In situations where it is required to test the value of some column against a given set of values, the IN operator can be used:

Query 7.9 'List the details of all deliveries of product numbers 1, 3 and 5.'

(1,3,5) is a set of values.

```
1 SELECT *
2 FROM DELIVERY
3 WHERE PROD_NO IN (1,3,5) ;
```

In line 3, each row in the DELIVERY table is checked to see if its PROD_NO value is in the list (1,3,5). If it is, the row is output, resulting in:

C_NO	PROD_NO	QTY	DEL_DATE
3	1	3	03-NOV-90
5	3	4	12-NOV-90
3	3	1	12_NOV_90

Query 7.10 'List the account numbers of customers who have purchased products other than product numbers 2, 4 and 5.'

```
1 SELECT DISTINCT C_NO
2 FROM DELIVERY
3 WHERE PROD_NO NOT IN (2,4,5) ;
```

The DISTINCT option is used here to prevent the repeated output of customer account numbers for customers who have purchased more than one product which is not in the list.

Watch out for ambiguities
Note that the query

Customers who have purchased products not in the list (2,4,5)'

is quite different from the query

'Customers who have not purchased products in the list (2,4,5)'.

Compound conditions using AND, OR and NOT
To perform two or more tests in a single WHERE clause, the AND and OR and NOT can be used to form a compound condition.

Query 7.11 'List details of all overdrawn London customers.'
To be output, customers must (condition 1) have a debt greater than their credit limit AND (condition 2) be based in London.
The SELECT command is:

```
1 SELECT *
2 FROM CUS
3 WHERE BALANCE > CRED_LIM
4 AND CITY = 'London' ;
```

Query 7.12 'List details of customers who are overdrawn or live in London.'
To be output, customers must (condition 1) have a debt greater than their credit limit OR (condition 2) be based in London.
The SELECT command is:

```
1 SELECT *
2 FROM CUS
3 WHERE BALANCE > CRED_LIM
4 OR CITY = 'London' ;
```

The output for this query is:

C_NO	TITLE	SNAME	INITS	STREET	CITY	POSTC	CRED_LIM	BALANCE
1	Mr	Sallaway	G.R.	12 Fax Rd	London	WC1	1000	42.56
2	Miss	Lauri	P.	5 Dux St	London	N1	500	200
3	Mr	Jackson	R.	2 Lux Ave	Leeds	LE1 2AB	500	510
4	Mr	Dziduch	M.	31 Low St	Dover	DO2 9CD	100	149.23
5	Ms	Woods	S.Q.	17 Nax Rd	London	E18 4WW	1000	250.1

The 'meaning' of NULL (again)

Note that the row for C_NO 6 (See Appendix A) is not present since the customer is neither a London customer nor is the BALANCE (= 412.21) greater than the CRED_LIM (= NULL). SQL has its own rules relating to NULL. This query illustrates one of those rules: when a number is compared with NULL, the result is NULL. 'OR' as defined in SQL is an 'inclusive' OR which means that in compound conditions such as the one shown in lines 3 and 4 above, the CUS row will be output if the line 3 condition alone is true, or if the line 4 condition alone is true, or if they are both true. An 'exclusive' OR does not produce output if both conditions are true, but does if one condition is true.

When a number is compared with NULL, the result is NULL.

Exercise 7.6

Write SQL commands to implement the following English queries.

1. 'List the details of those customers who are either overdrawn or London based but not both.'

2. 'List the details of all overdrawn and all London customers.'

3. 'List the details of customers who are overdrawn but not living in London.'

Query 7.13 'List out details of all non-overdrawn customers not living in Bradford, Leeds or London.'

```
1 SELECT *
2 FROM CUS
3 WHERE BALANCE <= CRED_LIM
4 AND CITY NOT IN ('Bradford', 'Leeds', 'London');
```

is a shorter equivalent of

```
1 SELECT *
2 FROM CUS
3 WHERE BALANCE <= CRED_LIM
4 AND CITY != 'Bradford'
```

```
5 AND CITY != 'Leeds'
6 AND CITY != 'London' ;
```

Compound conditions and NULL

The truth table below shows the result of compound conditions involving two conditions X and Y, where one or both evaluate to NULL.

X	Y	X AND Y	X OR Y	X	NOT X
NULL	NULL	NULL	NULL	NULL	NULL
NULL	TRUE	NULL	TRUE		
NULL	FALSE	FALSE	NULL		

Fig. 7.3 Truth table for compound additions with NULL values.

Query 7.14 'List customers who have a balance over \$400 or a credit limit over \$500.'

```
1 SELECT *
2 FROM CUS
3 WHERE BALANCE > 400
4 OR CRED_LIM > 500 ;
```

The output from this query is:

C_NO	TITLE	SNAME	INITS	STREET	CITY	POSTC	CRED_LIM	BALANCE
1	Mr	Sallaway	G.R.	12 Fax Rd	London	WC1	1000	42.56
3	Mr	Jackson	R.	2 Lux Ave	Leeds	LE1 2AB	500	510
5	Ms	Woods	S.Q.	17 Nax Rd	London	E18 4WW	1000	250.1
6	Mrs	Williams	C.	41 Cax St	Dover	DO2 8WD		412.21

For C_NO 6, the test in line 3 evaluates to TRUE and the test in line 4 evaluates to NULL since CRED_LIM is NULL. By line 2 of the main table of Fig. 7.3, the result is TRUE, so the row is output.

Aggregating data and groups

It is often necessary to obtain summary or aggregate results from database tables. With this idea goes the idea of a group. A number of rows in a table are considered as a group and some summary data extracted, such as the number of rows in the group or the maximum, minimum or average value of a column in the group. The group will be a group of rows which have a common value of some attribute, for example the same value in the 'department' column of an employee table.

The SQL GROUP BY clause

Groups are specified in the SQL SELECT command by the GROUP BY clause. After the groups have been formed there is the possibility of further filtering the results with the HAVING clause which acts on the group results. The following aggregate functions in SQL are used to produce summary results from groups of rows in database tables:

SQL aggregate functions.

AVG(X) Average value of numeric column X in the group of rows
COUNT(X) Number of rows where X is non-null in the group of rows
MAX(X) Maximum value in numeric column X in the group of rows
MIN(X) Minimum value in numeric column X in the group of rows
SUM(X) Sum of values in numeric column X in the group of rows

ORACLE SQL*PLUS also has the statistical functions:

VARIANCE(X) The variance (measure of spread) of numeric column X in the group of rows
STDDEV(X) The standard deviation (another measure of spread) of numeric column X in the group of rows

Note that in calculating the value of an aggregate function, all rows with a NULL value of X are ignored, so that for example the AVG of the set of numbers (2,4,null,6,8) is 5 since there are considered to be four numbers in the set, not five. The DISTINCT option can be used with all of these functions to ignore duplicates so that AVG(DISTINCT X) for the set of column X values (2,4,4,6,0) is (2+4+6+0)/4 = 3 whereas AVG(X) is (2+4+4+6+0)/5 = 3.2.

All NULLs are ignored by aggregate functions.

Query 7.15 'What is the total amount owed by our customers?'

```
1 SELECT SUM(BALANCE)     gives: SUM(BALANCE)
2 FROM CUS ;                     ---------
                                  1564.1
```

Here the aggregate function SUM ranges over the whole table (the 'group' is the whole table) to obtain the single value.

Next is an example of DISTINCT being used with COUNT. We have a database table called CITATION which is part of a database containing data about fossils. The CITATION table shows the species of living things (plant or animal) mentioned in various documents. The sequence number gives the order in which a given species is cited in a particular document. The structure of the table is:

DOCUMENT	SEQ_NO	GENUS	SPECIES	AGE	LOCATION
1	1	Felis	Tigris	10000	India
1	2	Vulpes	Vulpes	20000	Thailand
1	3	Felis	Tigris	20000	Thailand, etc.

Query 7.16 'How many different species are there in CITATION?'

'||' concatenates two
operands.

```
1 SELECT COUNT(DISTINCT GENUS || SPECIES)
2 FROM CITATION ;
```

Exercise 7.7

1. Write an SQL query to calculate the maximum, minimum, range and average credit limit of our customers. Use the CUS table.

2. Describe the effect the NULL credit limit of C_NO 6 has on the results of this query.

3. Explain the output of the following query:

Query 7.17 'Demonstrate how COUNT works with NULL values.'

```
1 SELECT COUNT(CRED_LIM), COUNT(BALANCE), COUNT(*)
2 FROM CUS ;
```

COUNT(CRED_LIM)	COUNT(BALANCE)	COUNT(*)
5	6	6

Forming groups with GROUP BY

'Groups' share some
common attribute
values.

So far, the 'group' on which the aggregate functions operated to obtain their numeric results was the whole table. In many queries the result of an aggregate function will be required on each of several groups. For example, if the SELECT command contains the code 'GROUP BY DEPARTMENT' then there will be one row output for each department.

Query 7.18 'List out the average age of employees in each department.'
Assuming an EMPLOYEE table of the form:

EMP_NO	NAME	AGE	DEPARTMENT
1	Judy	23	Billing
2	Madge	27	Accounts
4	Karen	9	Billing
3	Terence	42	Billing
5	Grace	25	Accounts

The query is:

```
1 SELECT DEPARTMENT, AVG(AGE)
2 FROM EMPLOYEE
3 GROUP BY DEPARTMENT ;
```

Find the average age
in each department.

The output will be:

DEPARTMENT	AVG(AGE)
Billing	28
Accounts	26

In line 3 of the query the GROUP BY clause forms intermediate groups of rows, one for each department. These groups of rows are said to be 'intermediate' because they do not last and are never displayed. They exist only temporarily for the purpose of calculating the results of the aggregate function. Since there are only two departments mentioned in the table, there will be two groups of intermediate rows formed.

EMP_NO	NAME	AGE	DEPARTMENT
The first group is:			
1	Judy	23	Billing
4	Karen	19	Billing
3	Terence	42	Billing
The second group is:			
2	Madge	27	Accounts
5	Grace	25	Accounts

There is one group of rows for each department. Now the SELECT in line 1 of the query asks for the department and the average age to be output for each group and the output is as shown above. It is possible to output a single department value for each group since every member of the group has the same value in the DEPARTMENT column. It is also possible to output a single value of average age for each group.

A single value is output
for each group.

It would not be possible to output a single value of EMP_NO for each group because there may be more than one employee number in each department. The following query would be incorrect because some of the columns in the SELECT line (line 1) could have more than one value per group:

```
1 SELECT EMP_NO, AVG(AGE)  <— Incorrect Query
2 FROM EMPLOYEE
3 GROUP BY DEPARTMENT ;
```

Query 7.19 'List out the number of employees and the maximum, minimum and average age of employees in each department.'

This query can be successfully accomplished because for each department there is a single value of each output item.

```
1 SELECT DEPARTMENT, COUNT(*), MAX(AGE), MIN(AGE),
2 AVG(AGE)
3 FROM EMPLOYEE
4 GROUP BY DEPARTMENT ;
```

The output is:

DEPARTMENT	COUNT(*),	MAX(AGE),	MIN(AGE),	AVG(AGE)
Accounts	2	27	25	26
Billing	3	42	19	28

Exercise 7.8

1. 'List out the average age of employees in each department. Only consider those whose age is over twenty.'

2. 'List out from the CUS table the total amount outstanding by city.'

In ORACLE SQL*PLUS (not in INGRES or dBASE), it is possible to nest the aggregate functions, so that the following query is possible:

Query 7.20 'What is the maximum total outstanding balance for a city?'
```
1 SELECT MAX(SUM(BALANCE))
2 FROM CUS
3 GROUP BY CITY ;
```

Grouping on more than one column
It is sometimes necessary to group on two or more columns at once. Consider the following table EMPLOYEE1:

DEPARTMENT	EMPLOYEE_NO	JOB_DESCRIPTION
1	12	Fitter
1	19	Turner
1	14	Fitter
1	20	Miller
2	6	Turner
2	17	Miller
2	21	Miller

Query 7.21 'List the number of employees in each job by department.'

```
1 SELECT DEPARTMENT, JOB_DESCRIPTION, COUNT(*)
2 FROM EMPLOYEE1
3 GROUP BY DEPARTMENT, JOB_DESCRIPTION ;
```

The output is:

DEPARTMENT	JOB_DESCRIPTION	COUNT(*)
1	Fitter	2
1	Miller	1
1	Turner	1
2	Miller	2
2	Turner	1

It would not have been any good grouping on just JOB_DESCRIPTION because then COUNT(*) would have contained, for example, the number of turners across ALL departments.

Selecting groups with HAVING

HAVING acts towards groups in the same way that WHERE acts towards table rows. Instead of a result being output for every group, only selected groups pass through the filtering effect of HAVING.

HAVING filters the groups.

Query 7.22 'List from the EMPLOYEE table all departments where the average age is under 27.'

```
1 SELECT DEPARTMENT, AVG(AGE)
2 FROM EMPLOYEE
3 GROUP BY DEPARTMENT
4 HAVING AVG(AGE) < 27 ;
```

which results in:

DEPARTMENT	AVG(AGE)
Accounts	26

Exercise 7.9

Write SQL queries for the following:

1. Which cities in CUS have a total customer balance of over $500?'

2. Which workshop groups in the GROUPS table have more than two members, and how many members do these groups have?'

If it is not required to output the results of the aggregate functions, they can be calculated in the HAVING clause itself. For example:

Query 7.23 'Which workshop groups have more than two members?'

```
1 SELECT TERM, GROUP_NO
2 FROM GROUPS
3 GROUP BY TERM, GROUP_NO
4 HAVING COUNT(*) > 2 ;
```

gives as output:

Only groups with more than two members are output.

TERM	GROUP_NO
1	1
1	2

Query 7.24 'List the number of employees and the average age in each department with three employees and an average age over 27.'
This requires a compound condition in the HAVING clause of the query and the required SQL is:

```
1 SELECT DEPARTMENT, COUNT(*), AVG(AGE)
2 FROM EMPLOYEE
3 GROUP BY DEPARTMENT
4 HAVING COUNT(*) > 3
5 AND AVG(AGE) > 27 ;
```

Compound HAVING condition in lines 4 and 5.

giving:

DEPARTMENT	COUNT(*)	AVG(AGE)
Billing	3	28

Exercise 7.10

Express in English what the following SQL query does:

```
1 SELECT DEPARTMENT, AVG(AGE)
2 FROM EMPLOYEE
3 GROUP BY DEPARTMENT
4 HAVING COUNT(*) > 1 ;
```

Sorting the output with the SQL ORDER BY clause

The order of the rows in the table in the database is not altered by ORDER BY, which simply changes the order of the output. The syntax of ORDER BY is:

ORDER BY sorts the output.

SELECT ...
ORDER BY {expr|posn} [ASC|DESC], ...

ASC is ascending, DESC is descending.

Query 7.25 'List the contents of the CUS table in alphabetical order of surname.'

```
1 SELECT *
2 FROM CUS
3 ORDER BY SNAME ;
```

Ascending order is the default, so the output appears in alphabetical order.

Query 7.26 'List customer surname and balance, in descending order of balance.'

```
1 SELECT SNAME, BALANCE
2 FROM CUS
3 ORDER BY 2 DESC ; <— '2' is the column number
```

Line 3 requests that the second output column (BALANCE) be chosen as the sort key, and that the output rows appear in descending order of BALANCE.

Query 7.27 'List the customer file in descending order of balance within ascending order of city name.'

```
1 SELECT *
2 FROM CUS
3 ORDER BY CITY, BALANCE DESC ;
```

Exercise 7.11

Using the CANDIDATE table, write SQL SELECT commands to perform the following:

1. List the details of all candidates not in the Labour party.

2. List the total number of votes in constituency number 1.

3. List the total number of votes for each party.

4. List the total number of votes for each party having a total vote of over 100.

5. List the total number of votes for each party in descending order of number of votes.

6. List the maximum number of votes.

7. List the number of votes for each party with more than 200 votes total, best first.

8. List the party with the maximum number of votes.

SELECT with JOINED TABLES

SQL can join rows from various tables.

All the queries so far described involve the use of only one table. In many practical situations it will be necessary to access information from two or more tables. All the join types described in Chapter 6 can be implemented in SQL. The main differences between selecting data from one table and selecting data from two tables are:

- The FROM clause contains reference to the two (or more) tables to be joined.
- The WHERE clause must contain one or more additional conditions ('join criteria') stating the test for deciding which rows from the tables are to be joined.

Query 7.28 'List the names, addresses and invoice details of all customers who have outstanding invoices.'

Here the output must contain information from both CUS and INVOICE tables; names and addresses from CUS and 'invoice details' from INVOICE.

```
1 SELECT TITLE, INITS, SNAME, STREET, CITY, POSTC,
2 INV_NO, INV_DATE, AMOUNT
3 FROM CUS, INVOICE
4 WHERE CUS.C_NO = INVOICE.C_NO;
```

A 'join criterion' is the test you apply to specify which rows from the tables will be joined.

In line 1, the list of column names required in the output is given. Note that this is a combination of column names from the two tables CUS and INVOICE; the first six columns come from CUS and the other three from INVOICE. Line 3 shows the two tables from which data values are to be drawn, and line 4 gives the join criterion, i.e. that the customer account numbers on the CUS and INVOICE tables should be equal. Notice that the identically named customer account numbers: C_NO in both tables, have to be qualified by prefixing them with their respective table names in order to avoid ambiguity. The output from this query is as follows:

TITLE	INIT	SNAME	STREET	CITY	POSTC	INV_NO	INV_DATE	AMOUNT
Mr	G.R.	Sallaway	12 Fax Rd	London	WC1	940	05-DEC-90	26.2
Mr	G.R.	Sallaway	12 Fax Rd	London	WC1	1003	12-JAN-91	16.36
Miss	P.	Lauri	5 Dux St	London	N1	1004	14-JAN-91	200
Mr	R.	Jackson	2 Lux Ave	Leeds	LE1 2AB	1005	20-JAN-91	510
Mr	M.	Dziduch	31 Low St	Dover	DO2 9CD	1002	12-JAN-91	149.23
Ms	S.Q.	Woods	17 Nax Rd	London	E18 4WW	1006	21-JAN-91	250.1
Mrs	C.	Williams	41 Cax St	Dover	DO2 8WD	1017	22-JAN-91	412.21

Note that data for Mr G.R. Sallaway appears twice because he has two outstanding invoices. Instead of using the full table name to qualify identically named column names in the two tables, it is possible to use table aliases, that is, alternative names for the tables. In the following query, A and B are table aliases:

> A 'table alias' is an alternative name for a table. The alias exists only for the duration of the query.

```
1 SELECT TITLE, INITS, SNAME, STREET,
2 CITY, POSTC, INV_NO, INV_DATE, AMOUNT
3 FROM CUS A, INVOICE B
4 WHERE A.C_NO = B.C_NO ;
```

Query 7.29 'List the account numbers, names, addresses and invoice details of all customers who have outstanding invoices.'

```
1 SELECT A.C_NO, TITLE, INITS, SNAME,
2 STREET, CITY, POSTC, INV_NO, INV_DATE, AMOUNT
3 FROM CUS A, INVOICE B
4 WHERE A.C_NO = B.C_NO ;
```

> Line 4 contains the join criterion.

Exercise 7.12

Write an SQL query for the following:

'List the names, addresses and invoice details of all London customers who have outstanding invoices with invoice amounts over $100.'

In the following example a 'greater than' join is performed. Suppose we have EMPLOYEE2 and JOB tables as follows:

> 'greater than' join.

EMPLOYEE2			JOB	
E_NO	NAME	SALARY	DESCR	STD_SALARY
1	Alan	10000	Clerk	9000
2	Bill	20000	Accountant	18000
3	Carol	30000	Manager	25000

Query 7.30 'For each employee, list the jobs which will give him or her a standard salary higher than his or her current salary.'

```
1 SELECT *
2 FROM EMPLOYEE2, JOB
3 WHERE STD_SALARY > SALARY;
```

This will give every combination of employee and job details where the STD_SALARY is greater than the current salary for that employee:

E_NO	NAME	SALARY	DESCR	STD_SALARY
1	Alan	10000	Accountant	18000
1	Alan	10000	Manager	25000
2	Bill	20000	Manager	25000

Self join

In a self-join, rows from a table are joined to other rows in the same table.

Query 7.31 'For each employee show all employees who are earning a higher salary.'

Assuming the same database as for the previous query, only one table, EMPLOYEE2, needs to be accessed since that is the source of all current salary data. For each employee it is required to inspect the salary of every other employee in the table to see if any of those employees receives a higher salary. The query SQL is as follows:

```
1 SELECT *
2 FROM EMPLOYEE2 A, EMPLOYEE2 B
3 WHERE B.SALARY > A.SALARY;
```

giving:

E_NO	NAME	SALARY	E_NO	NAME	SALARY
1	Alan	10000	2	Bill	20000
1	Alan	10000	3	Carol	30000
2	Bill	20000	3	Carol	30000

Exercise 7.13

Suppose there is a table on the database like this:

EMPLOYEE3

EMP_NO	NAME	SALARY	MGR_NO
1	Audrey	10000	3
2	Betty	20000	4
3	Carol	15000	2
4	Denise	15000	7
7	Erica	20000	

Write an SQL query for the following:

'List out all employees who are earning more than their manager.'

The table shows what people are earning and also who their managers are. It is assumed that MGR_NO is from the same 'domain' as EMP_NO, and that every manager will have an employee row in this table. Note that Erica does not have a manager so MGR_NO in her row is null.

A 'domain' is a set of values from which attribute values may be taken.

Joining more than two tables
Query 7.32 'List the account codes, names, and invoice payments for all customers.'

```
1 SELECT A.C_NO, SNAME, B.INV_NO, B.AMOUNT,
2 PMT_NO, PMT_DATE, C.AMOUNT
3 FROM CUS A, INVOICE B, PAYMENT C
4 WHERE A.C_NO = B.C_NO
5 AND B.INV_NO = C.INV_NO;
```

Complex queries often join more than two tables. Line 3 shows there are three tables being joined. Lines 4 and 5 show the join criteria.

The output from this query is as follows:

Joins are one method of 'navigating' from one table to another.

C_NO	SNAME	INV_NO	AMOUNT	PMT_NO	PMT_DATE	AMOUNT
1	Sallaway	940	26.2	2	12-DEC-90	13
1	Sallaway	940	26.2	3	19-JAN-91	10
3	Jackson	1005	510	1	14-JAN-91	510
6	Williams	1017	412.21	1	30-JAN-91	100

What is interesting about the output is the data that does NOT appear. Firstly, only three of the six customers appear. Secondly, only three of the seven invoices appear. Why? The answer is clear when the mechanism of the natural join is considered. In line 4, which is used for joining rows from the CUS and INVOICE tables, it is possible to imagine the temporary result before the matching PAYMENT rows are joined on in line 5.

C.NO	SNAME	INV_NO	AMOUNT
1	Sallaway	940	26.2
1	Sallaway	1003	16.36
2	Lauri	1004	200
3	Jackson	1005	510
4	Dziduch	1002	149.23
5	Woods	1006	250.1
6	Williams	1017	412.21

Every customer account appears in this intermediate result because every customer happens to have at least one outstanding invoice. If any customer did not have an outstanding invoice, that customer's details would be eliminated at this stage because the join criterion of line 4 would not have been satisfied. The next step in the SQL query is to join the payment details onto this intermediate result and this is performed in line 5. The join criterion in line 5 says that in order for a row from this intermediate result to be passed to the output, B.INV_NO, which is column 3 in the intermediate result, should match with a C.INV_NO in the PAYMENT table. The INV_NO of the first row of the intermediate result matches with the INV_NO of the first row of the PAYMENT table (both equal to 940) so a joined row consisting of the columns mentioned in lines 1 and 2 of the query are passed to the output. The second row of PAYMENT also matches the first row of the intermediate result so the projected columns of these rows are also joined, forming the second row of the output. There are no further payments for invoice 940 so the 'pointer' to the intermediate result table is incremented to point to its second row (INV_NO = 1003). There are no matches in the PAYMENT table for this intermediate table row so the row is abandoned and produces no output. Thus the invoice details of Sallaway's invoice number 1003 are lost and are eliminated from the output. Similarly, the intermediate data for Lauri, Dziduch and Woods is eliminated from the output because none of them has a payment to his or her credit.

It is not certain whether this was what was wanted when the English query was formulated since it is rather vague. If the query had been put in the form:

'List all current invoice and payment details for all of our customers'

then this SQL form of the query would definitely not be correct since:

- any customer with no current invoices would not be output and, more importantly,
- invoice details for any customer with current invoices having no payments would not be output.

Getting the correct output for this query involves the use of the outer join.

The outer join

In Query 7.32, details of all invoices with no payments were lost from the output. In the case where the only invoices sent to a customer were as yet unpaid, the customer details were also omitted from the output. Since the probable use of the output data would be to prepare monthly Statements of Accounts for customers, that query would result in customers only receiving acknowledgement of their payments and the reminder aspect of the statement would be lost.

The remedy for this problem is the outer join with the (+) being applied to the PAYMENT table. In the outer join version, an 'all null' row is appended to the PAYMENT table with the special property that it will join to any INVOICE row that can't find a matching PAYMENT. The 'all null' row is of course not actually appended. This is simply a useful way of describing the action of the outer join. The modified query is:

```
1 SELECT A.C_NO, SNAME, B.INV_NO, B.AMOUNT,
2 PMT_NO, PMT_DATE, C.AMOUNT
3 FROM CUS A, INVOICE B, PAYMENT C
4 WHERE A.C_NO = B.C_NO
5 AND B.INV_NO = C.INV_NO (+);
```

In line 5, the (+) sign signifies an outer join.

The only change is the addition of the (+). The output from this query is now as follows:

C_NO	SNAME	INV_NO	AMOUNT	PMT_NO	PMT_DATE	AMOUNT
1	Sallaway	940	26.2	2	12-DEC-90	13
1	Sallaway	940	26.2	3	19-JAN-91	10
1	Sallaway	1003	16.36			
2	Lauri	1004	200			
3	Jackson	1005	510	1	14-JAN-91	510
4	Dziduch	1002	149.23			
5	Woods	1006	250.1			
6	Williams	1017	412.21	1	30-JAN-91	100

All six customers and seven invoices are now accounted for. In the unlikely event of a statement being required for customers with no outstanding invoices, a (+) would be appended to line 4.

Exercise 7.14

1. Write an SQL statement to list details of all PRODUCTs and their deliveries (DELIVERY table).

2. Write an SQL statement to list details of all PRODUCTs which have not had deliveries. Use an outer join.

SELECT with subqueries

SQL contains the facility for nesting one SELECT command within another. The nested SELECT is called a subquery and it appears in parentheses in the WHERE clause of the outer SELECT statement as shown in Fig. 7.4.

```
SELECT ...        <—— Outer Query
FROM ...
WHERE ...
[AND ...]...
(SELECT ...       <—— Subquery
FROM ...
WHERE ... ) ;
```

Fig. 7.4   The position of an SQL subquery.

Values returned by the subquery are used in the main SELECT's WHERE clause.

The subquery consists of a SELECT statement which will retrieve a set of values from one or more tables in the database. It is these values which are then used in the selection criteria of the outer SELECT's WHERE or HAVING clause to determine which rows from the tables in the outer select (or from the intermediate grouped values in the case of HAVING) will appear at the output. Subqueries are in practice, for many programmers, a more 'natural' alternative to the join and there are some situations in which there is no alternative to using a subquery. There are also some situations in which there is no alternative to using a join. One important restriction in the use of subqueries is that the values selected by the subquery do not themselves appear at the output; they are simply used as part of the selection criteria of the outer SELECT. Joins and subqueries can be intermixed.

Figure 7.5 gives more detail with regard to the syntax of subqueries. In both Fig. 7.4 and Fig. 7.5, only the WHERE selection criteria are shown; very similar syntax is used when a subquery is used to filter groups using HAVING.

```
(a)      SELECT ...
         FROM ...
         WHERE col-exprn {comparison [AL I ANY ] I N I NOT IN]}
         (SELECT ...
         FROM ...
         WHERE ...
         [GROUP BY ...]
         [HAVING ...]) ;
```

(b)   SELECT ...
        FROM ...
        WHERE {EXISTS | NOT EXISTS}
           (SELECT ...
           FROM ...
           WHERE ...)
        [GROUP BY ...]
        [HAVING ...]
        [ORDER BY ...] ;

Fig. 7.5   The detailed format of subqueries.

The subquery is considered as part of the WHERE (or HAVING) clause of the outer SELECT and the outer SELECT may continue after the subquery's closing parenthesis with the usual GROUP BY, HAVING and ORDER BY clauses. An ORDER BY must not be included in the subquery itself. The 'comparison' is '=' or '<' or '>' or '>=' or '<=' or '!='.

Usually, a set of values is returned by the subquery.

If ALL, ANY, IN or NOT IN are included, then the subquery is expected to return a set of one or more values from a single column in the subquery. If none of these terms appears, then the subquery must return a single value. ORACLE SQL*PLUS has a useful additional feature which allows more than one column to be returned from the subquery and compared to corresponding columns in the outer query. There is an example of this below.

The WHERE and HAVING clauses in the subquery may themselves contain further subqueries. It is usual in most queries for the nesting of subqueries to go no further than four or five deep. Subqueries can be used as an alternative to joins in navigating around a database where the query is required to span several entity types in the logical schema. In such cases it is essential to have the entity-relationship diagram (in addition to the table definitions) available.

The normal procedure is to join adjacent tables in the navigation path by equating the primary key on the 'one' side of a one-to-many relationship with the corresponding foreign key on the 'many' side.

As a matter of interest, the SQL query interpreter, in its attempt to optimize the sequence of database search operations required, may convert SQL subqueries into joins as one of its early translation steps. All of the above points are demonstrated in the following examples.

Simple subqueries and their join equivalents
Query 7.33 'List the employees in the EMPLOYEE table who are in the same department as Karen.'
The EMPLOYEE table is as follows:

EMPLOYEE

EMP_NO	NAME	AGE	DEPARTMENT
1	Judy	23	Billing
2	Madge	27	Accounts
4	Karen	19	Billing
3	Terence	42	Billing
5	Grace	25	Accounts

The answer to this query could be obtained by first querying the **EMPLOYEE** table to establish which department Karen works in:

```
1 SELECT DEPARTMENT
2 FROM EMPLOYEE
3 WHERE NAME = 'Karen' ;
```

giving:

DEPARTMENT

Billing

and then querying the same table again:

```
1 SELECT NAME
2 FROM EMPLOYEE
3 WHERE DEPARTMENT = 'Billing';
```

giving:

NAME

Judy
Karen
Terence

Notice that 'Karen' appears in the output, since she is of course in the same department as herself!

Using a subquery, we can achieve these two steps in one:

```
1 SELECT NAME
2 FROM EMPLOYEE
3 WHERE DEPARTMENT =
4 (SELECT DEPARTMENT   <-- Subquery
```

```
5 FROM EMPLOYEE
6 WHERE NAME = 'Karen') ;
```

Lines 4 to 6 are the subquery, which must be enclosed in parentheses as shown. The subquery must be executed before the outer query so that it can deliver the value 'Billing' to the outer query's WHERE clause. This simple example illustrates the basic flavour of SQL subqueries. Note that the value 'Billing' from the subquery never appears at the output; it is simply used in the selection criteria of the outer query. This is true no matter how deep the level of nesting in a query; only the outer query delivers values to the output. That is a limitation of subqueries that joins do not have.

> The subquery is executed before the outer query.

The same result could have been obtained if the following self join had been used:

```
1 SELECT B.NAME
2 FROM EMPLOYEE A, EMPLOYEE B
3 WHERE A.DEPARTMENT = B.DEPARTMENT
4 AND A.NAME = 'Karen' ;
```

> Joins can often be used instead of subqueries.

This does a self join on EMPLOYEE on DEPARTMENT and then selects out rows where the first name is 'Karen'.

Query 7.34 'List details of all products which have had deliveries.'
The data required is contained in the two tables:

PRODUCT

PROD_NO	DESCR	QIS	MINQ	REORDQ	PRICE
1	Bat	10	5	10	12
2	Ball	5	5	20	2
3	Hoop	3	5	10	3
4	Net	2	5	10	20
5	Rope	1	10	10	6

DELIVERY

C_NO	PROD_NO	QTY	DEL_DATE
3	2	2	3-NOV-90
3	1	3	3-NOV-90
1	4	6	7-NOV-90
5	3	4	12-NOV-90
3	3	1	12-NOV-90

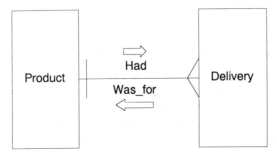

Fig. 7.6   Product-had-delivery (query 7.34).

Notice that PROD_NO in the DELIVERY table is a foreign key from PRODUCT. See Fig. 7.6. The query is as follows:

```
1 SELECT *
2 FROM PRODUCT
3 WHERE PROD_NO IN
4 (SELECT PROD_NO
5 FROM DELIVERY);
```

giving:

PROD_NO	DESCR	QIS	MINQ	REORDQ	PRICE
1	Bat	10	5	10	12
2	Ball	5	5	20	2
3	Hoop	3	5	10	3
4	Net	2	5	10	20

The subquery is executed first and delivers the list of values (2,1,4,3,3) from the DELIVERY table because this is the set of products that have been delivered. The value of PROD_NO in each row of the PRODUCT table is checked to see if it is contained in this set of values and if it is, the PRODUCT row is output. Note that this query could also have been implemented relatively simply as a join:

```
1 SELECT DISTINCT A.*
2 FROM PRODUCT A, DELIVERY B
3 WHERE A.PROD_NO = B.PROD_NO;
```

The DISTINCT is necessary here because some products may have been delivered twice and this would have resulted in those PRODUCT rows being output twice.

Query 7.35 'List details of all products which have had no deliveries.'
The only change required compared with the previous query is to replace IN
with NOT IN since what the query will now need to output is all products in
the PRODUCTS table whose product numbers do not appear in the list of
product numbers in DELIVERY:

```
1 SELECT *
2 FROM PRODUCT
3 WHERE PROD_NO NOT IN
4 (SELECT PROD_NO
5 FROM DELIVERY);
```

The join version of this query has to be an outer join:

```
1 SELECT A.*
2 FROM PRODUCT A, DELIVERY B
3 WHERE A.PROD_NO = B.PROD_NO (+)
4 AND B.PROD_NO IS NULL ;
```

Subquery with join in the outer SELECT
Query 7.36 'List the customer names and invoice amounts for invoices
which have been paid in January 1990.'
Clearly, CUS and INVOICE and PAYMENT must all be consulted to satisfy this query. See Fig. 7.7.

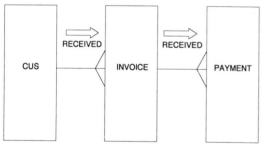

Fig. 7.7   CUS-INV-PMT (query 7.36).

A subquery version of the query is as follows:

The outer query
contains a join here
(line 2).

```
1 SELECT INITS, SNAME, AMOUNT
2 FROM CUS, INVOICE
3 WHERE CUS.C_NO = INVOICE.C_NO
4 AND INV_NO IN
5 (SELECT INV_NO
6 FROM PAYMENT
7 WHERE PMT_DATE BETWEEN '1-jan-90' AND '31-jan-90');
```

Where a join must be used instead of a subquery

The two tables CUS and INVOICE are joined in the outer SELECT since outputs are required from both tables. If any PAYMENT details, such as the payment amount for example, had been required to be output then all the tables would have had to be joined (and a subquery would not have been possible) since no data from a subquery can be output, as already mentioned.

Values returned by a subquery cannot be output.

The subquery in lines 5 to 7 specifies the set of invoice numbers to be considered by inspecting the payment dates. The relevant set of invoice numbers delivered by the subquery is (940, 1005, 1017). The 'owners' of these invoices are Sallaway, Jackson and Williams. The output from the whole query is thus:

INITS	SNAME	AMOUNT
Mr	Sallaway	26.2
Mr	Jackson	510
Mrs	Williams	412.21

Joins in the subquery

Query 7.37 'List the names of all customers who have made a payment before the invoice was sent.'

The general strategy in this query is to join the INVOICE and PAYMENT tables in the subquery so that the invoice and payment dates can be compared. The selected customer numbers are then fed to the outer query so the customer names can be output from the CUS table. The resulting SQL query is thus:

The subquery contains a join here (line 5).

```
1 SELECT SNAME
2 FROM CUS
3 WHERE C_NO IN
4 (SELECT C_NO
5 FROM INVOICE, PAYMENT
6 WHERE INVOICE.INV_NO = PAYMENT.INV_NO
7 AND PMT_DATE < INV_DATE);
```

The subquery joins tables INVOICE and PAYMENT where the INV_NOs are equal and the PMT_DATE is less than (before) the INV_DATE, and it delivers to the outer query the set of customer numbers (3) since this is the only customer who has paid before being asked. The output is:

SNAME
——
Jackson

because the payment date of payment number 1 of invoice number 1005 is earlier than its invoice date. The join in this example could have been replaced by another nested subquery.

Returning more than one column from the subquery

Query 7.38 'List employees in the EMPLOYEE1 table who have the same job in the same department as employee 12.'

The EMPLOYEE1 table contains the following data:

EMPLOYEE1

DEPARTMENT	EMPLOYEE_NO	JOB_DESCRIPTION
1	12	Fitter
1	19	Turner
1	14	Fitter
1	20	Miller
2	6	Turner
2	17	Miller
2	21	Miller

```
1 SELECT *
2 FROM EMPLOYEE1
3 WHERE (DEPARTMENT, JOB_DESCRIPTION) =
4 (SELECT DEPARTMENT, JOB_DESCRIPTION
5 FROM EMPLOYEE1
6 WHERE EMPLOYEE_NO = 12);
```

This feature is available in ORACLE SQL*PLUS

giving:

DEPARTMENT	EMPLOYEE_NO	JOB_DES
1	12	Fitter
1	14	Fitter

In this query the subquery returns two columns, which are then compared with the respective columns in the outer query. This ability to return more than one column in a subquery is available in ORACLE SQL*PLUS. However it is possible to obtain the same result without using this implementation-specific feature by utilizing a join, in this case a self join.

Exercise 7.15

Rewrite Query 7.38 in the form of a self join.

ANY and ALL

Query 7.39 'List the details of all employees in EMPLOYEE3 who are not receiving the maximum salary.'

The idea is that a given employee's details will be output if it is possible to find ANY employee who receives a higher salary. The data is:

EMPLOYEE3

EMP_NO	NAME	SALARY	MGR_NO
1	Audrey	10000	3
2	Betty	20000	4
3	Carol	15000	2
4	Denise	15000	
5	Erica	20000	

One way of writing the SQL version of this query is:

```
1 SELECT *
2 FROM EMPLOYEE3
3 WHERE SALARY < ANY
4 (SELECT SALARY
5 FROM EMPLOYEE3);
```

giving:

EMP_NO	NAME	SALARY	MGR_NO
1	Audrey	10000	3
3	Carol	15000	2
4	Denise	15000	7

Betty and Erica are removed from the output because there are no employees who receive a lower salary than they do. The operation of the ANY is to output a row from the outer query wherever there is at least one row in the subquery which makes the selection criterion TRUE. Here, for Audrey, for example, there is at least one employee (e.g. Betty but also Carol, Denise and Erica) who receives a higher salary.

Take care when using ANY and ALL.

Possible ambiguities with ANY and ALL
In spoken language the phrase 'less than any' may be given a similar meaning to 'less than all'. Care must be taken in formulating SQL queries using ANY and ALL that their precise meaning in SQL is understood. Since the difference between the functioning of the SQL versions of ANY and ALL is often misunderstood, another example of the use of ANY follows.

Query 7.40 'List details of all employees in EMPLOYEE3 for whom there is AT LEAST ONE employee who does not receive the same salary.'

```
1 SELECT *
2 FROM EMPLOYEE3
3 WHERE SALARY != ANY
4 (SELECT SALARY
5 FROM EMPLOYEE3);
```

giving:

EMP_NO	NAME	SALARY	MGR_NO
1	Audrey	10000	3
2	Betty	20000	4
3	Carol	15000	2
4	Denise	15000	7
5	Erica	20000	

which is the whole EMPLOYEE3 table! The reason is that unless all salaries are the same, there will always be at least one employee who does not receive the same salary as a given employee. Returning now to Query 7.39, it is worthwhile demonstrating an alternative SQL formulation.

Query 7.39 'List out the details of all employees in EMPLOYEE3 who are not receiving the maximum salary'.

Subquery with no join equivalent?

```
1 SELECT *
2 FROM EMPLOYEE3
3 WHERE SALARY !=
4 (SELECT MAX(SALARY)
5 FROM EMPLOYEE3);
```

which has identical output to the original SQL command but seems a clearer formulation.

Subquery with no join equivalent?

Exercise 7.16

Rewrite Query 7.39 as a join (if possible). If you do not think it is possible, say why.

ALL

ALL is quite different in its operation from ANY and is more intuitively obvious in its function. Staying with the EMPLOYEE3 table, consider the following query.

Query 7.41 'List details of all employees in table EMPLOYEE3 who earn the maximum salary.'

```
1 SELECT *
2 FROM EMPLOYEE3
3 WHERE SALARY >= ALL
4 (SELECT SALARY
5 FROM EMPLOYEE3);
```

which gives:

EMP_NO	NAME	SALARY	MGR_NO
2	Betty	20000	4
5	Erica	20000	

Betty and Erica earn the maximum salary. For each of them, their salary is greater than or equal to ALL employees in the table. If the '>=' 'had been replaced by a '>', no rows would have been selected because in order to have a salary higher than ALL employees in the table, they would have had to earn a higher salary than themselves! An alternative formulation for this query is:

```
1 SELECT *
2 FROM EMPLOYEE3
3 WHERE SALARY =
4 (SELECT MAX(SALARY)
5 FROM EMPLOYEE3);{
```

Correlated subqueries

In all the queries in the previous section, the subquery was executed once to return a set of one or more values.

Query 7.42 'List details of the employee in table EMPLOYEE who earns more than anyone else.'

To provide a correct SQL query here it is necessary to scan the table in the subquery once for each row in the outer query so that the row for every employee other than the current outer-query employee is tested. In a correlated subquery, the subquery is executed repeatedly, once for each row considered for selection by the outer query and its WHERE clause. The correct SQL SELECT command is the correlated subquery:

```
1 SELECT *
2 FROM EMPLOYEE A
3 WHERE SALARY > ALL
4 (SELECT SALARY
5 FROM EMPLOYEE B
6 WHERE B.EMP_NO != A.EMP_NO);
```

For each row in the outer query, the subquery inspects all other rows (line 6 does the 'other') to check that none has a higher salary.

How to recognize the need for a correlated subquery
For each row in the outer query, all rows in the subquery must be inspected.

How to recognize an already existing correlated subquery
A table alias which appears in both the outer query and the subquery.

In Query 7.42, the table alias A appears in both the outer query and the subquery. The B alias in lines 5 and 6 is not strictly necessary; the query would work just as well without it.

Query 7.43 'Which is the city in CUS with the maximum total outstanding balance?'
It is necessary to perform two scans of the CUS table; one to establish the maximum total balance for a city, and a second scan to list the city having that total balance.

```
1 SELECT CITY, SUM(BALANCE)
2 FROM CUS
3 GROUP BY CITY
4 HAVING SUM(BALANCE) =
5 (SELECT MAX(SUM(BALANCE))
6 FROM CUS
7 GROUP BY CITY) ;
```

giving:

CITY   SUM(BALANCE)

Dover 561.44

Note the use of the nested aggregate functions in line 5. Lines 5 to 7 establish the maximum total outstanding balance across all cities. Having established this figure, it is necessary to link this up with the city in the outer query. The outer query table does not immediately have this data available since there is no single row containing the total for the whole city. Consequently the outer query needs to recalculate the total balance for each city and match it with the figure delivered by the subquery.

Exercise 7.17

1. Using the CANDIDATE table, write an SQL SELECT statement to find the candidate with the most votes.

2. Using the same table, write a SELECT statement to find the candidate with the maximum number of votes and his or her number of votes.

3. Given the following tables, write an SQL query to answer the query 'Who has purchased something that is not an instrument?':

PURCHASE		INSTRUMENT	
CUS	PROD	PROD	PRICE
Alan	Violin	Violin	100
Betty	Book	Piano	500:

You might try using ANY or ALL. The correct output is of course:

CUS
Betty

UNION, INTERSECT and MINUS

UNION, INTERSECT and MINUS are the SQL counterparts of the 'union', 'intersection' and 'complement' (minus) operations covered in Chapter 6.

An SQL table can be considered as a set of rows. When a simple SELECT statement with a WHERE condition accesses a single table, data from a subset of the rows in the table is delivered to the output. If an AND condition is used, indicating two selection criteria, the resulting set of rows output is the intersection of the two sets of rows which would have resulted had the two conditions been entered separately in two SELECT statements. The same kind of relationship exists between OR and UNION, and AND NOT and MINUS. It is also possible to view the operation of some joins as similar in some ways to the intersection of the sets of rows from two or more tables, or even from one table considered twice (self join).

Some SELECT commands containing a 'WHERE NOT EXISTS' clause (page 209) can be considered as performing an operation similar to the complement operation – select all the rows from one table where there is no corresponding row in the second table.

These similarities are illustrated in some of the following examples. Despite the similarities mentioned, there are situations in which UNION, INTERSECT and MINUS are necessary and cannot be replaced by alternative code, particularly when two or more tables are involved in the query.

UNION, INTERSECT and MINUS are additional SQL commands which can make the formulation of some queries more straightforward than any equivalent joins or subqueries. Some of the examples will show alternatives to these commands and attempts will be made to find examples where there is no alternative.

UNION
The general format of a query using UNION is:

SELECT statement
UNION
SELECT statement
... ;

In its simplest form, a UNION of two or more tables simply appends the rows from one table to those of another to produce a set of rows for output. That is, it adds rows from the second table under the rows from the first table. The individual tables remain unchanged; the appending just occurs in the output from the query.

A UNION appends rows from two tables.

There are other issues to consider, such as attempting to find the UNION of tables which have a different number of columns, differently named columns, differently typed columns, identical columns in a different order, or duplicated rows. Various WHERE conditions, joins and subqueries can also be 'mixed in'.

Query 7.44 'Produce a list of students who play either violin or piano.'
The list is to be prepared from the separate class lists for violin and piano classes. Suppose the class lists are currently as follows:

VIOLIN   PIANO

STUD_NO	NAME	AGE	STUD_NO	NAME	AGE
1	Fred	10	2	Jane	12
2	Sally	11	4	David	10
4	David	10	5	Zena	11

The SQL for the query would be:

```
1 SELECT * FROM VIOLIN
2 UNION
3 SELECT * FROM PIANO;
```

giving:

STUD_NO	NAME	AGE
1	Fred	10
2	Jane	12
3	Sally	11
4	David	10
5	Zena	11

UNION eliminates duplicate rows from the output.

Note that, consistent with the definition of set union, SQL has eliminated the duplicate row (4,'David',10). It has to do this since the output is considered to be a set and by definition, sets contain no duplicates. In effect, the PIANO table has been 'appended' to the bottom of the VIOLIN table. This example illustrates the basic operation of UNION. Two or more SELECTs, no matter how complex, are separated by the word UNION.

Column homogeneity

The two tables VIOLIN and PIANO are said to be 'column homogeneous' since they contain the same column names, types and lengths. These 'attributes' of the columns in the tables can be shown by the SQL command:

DESCRIBE is used to list the attributes of a table.

```
1 DESCRIBE VIOLIN;
```

which gives:

NAME	NULL?	TYPE
STUD_NO		NUMBER(3)
NAME		CHAR(10)
AGE		NUMBER(3)

If required, who is a violinist and who is a pianist can be shown on the report as follows:

'Violin' and 'Piano' are dummy attributes.

```
1 SELECT STUD_NO, NAME, AGE, 'Violin' from VIOLIN
2 UNION
3 SELECT STUD_NO, NAME, AGE, 'Piano' from PIANO;
```

giving:

STUD_NO	NAME	AGE	VIOLIN
1	Fred	10	Violin
2	Jane	12	Piano
3	Sally	11	Violin
4	David	10	Piano
4	David	10	Violin
5	Zena	11	Piano

Note that David now appears twice because the artificially introduced column showing the instrument means the rows for David are no longer identical. The rather untidy column name for the instrument can be corrected by using a column alias:

```
1 SELECT STUD_NO, NAME, AGE, 'Violin' Instrument
2 FROM VIOLIN
3 UNION
4 SELECT STUD_NO, NAME, AGE, 'Piano' FROM PIANO;
```

giving:

STUD_NO	NAME	AGE	INSTRUMENT
1	Fred	10	Violin
2	Jane	12	Piano
3	Sally	11	Violin
4	David	10	Piano
4	David	10	Violin
5	Zena	11	Piano

Exercise 7.18

Write an SQL query to list the ten-year-old violinists and pianists.

Query 7.45 'Produce a list of students who play either violin or cello.'
1 DESCRIBE VIOLIN;
NAME NULL? TYPE

The columns in VIOLIN and CELLO are in a different order.

STUD_NO	NUMBER(3)
NAME	CHAR(10)
AGE	NUMBER(3)

1 DESCRIBE CELLO;
NAME NULL? TYPE

STUD_NO	NUMBER(3)
AGE	NUMBER(4)
NAME	CHAR(8)

The format of the CELLO table is different from that of the VIOLIN table; the number of columns and their names are identical to those of the VIOLIN table but they are in a different order and have different length attributes. The data in CELLO is:

CELLO
___

STUD_NO	AGE	NAME
4	10	David
6	11	Josey

The SQL query is:

```
1 SELECT * FROM VIOLIN
2 UNION
3 SELECT STUD_NO, NAME, AGE
4 FROM CELLO;
```

giving:

STUD_NO	NAME	AGE
1	Fred	10
3	Sally	11
4	David	10
6	Josey	11

Notice that the differences in format mentioned above have not caused any problems for SQL. It was simply necessary in line 3 to state the correct order of the columns in the CELLO table so that they would match those in VIOLIN.

Converting a data type to achieve column homogeneity
Query 7.46 'Produce a list of students who play either violin or flute.'

FLUTE is not column homogeneous with VIOLIN

```
1 DESCRIBE FLUTE;
```

NAME	NULL?	TYPE
STUD		NUMBER(3)
CNAME		CHAR(10)
AGE		CHAR(3)

The first two columns in FLUTE have different names from those in VIOLIN. The AGE column has a different data type. The data in FLUTE is:

FLUTE
___

STUD	CNAME	AGE
7	Ashfak	12

If the following query is attempted:

```
1 SELECT STUD_NO, NAME, AGE FROM VIOLIN
2 UNION
3 SELECT STUD, CNAME, AGE FROM FLUTE;
```

then an error of the following type results:

'expression must have same data type as corresponding expression'

which refers of course to the AGE column. No objection is made to the difference in column names. This can be remedied by using a character-to-number function to convert FLUTE.AGE to numeric:

No objection is made to columns with different names.

```
1 SELECT SELECT STUD_NO, NAME, AGE FROM VIOLIN
2 UNION
3 SELECT STUD, CNAME, TO_NUMBER(AGE) FROM FLUTE ;
```

The resulting output is then:

STUD_NO	NAME	AGE
1	Fred	10
3	Sally	11
4	David	10
7	Ashfak	12

which is correct.

INTERSECT <—- (ORACLE SQL*PLUS)

We now consider the intersection of the VIOLIN and PIANO sets of rows.

Some SQLs do not have INTERSECT.

Query 7.47 'List details of all students who play both violin and piano.'
Remembering the data for violinists and pianists are in two different tables VIOLIN and PIANO and that these tables have the same format, the query is:

```
1 SELECT * FROM VIOLIN
2 INTERSECT
3 SELECT * FROM PIANO ;
```

The set of students selected in line 1 is intersected with the set of students in line 3 and only those students in both sets appear at the output:

STUD_NO	NAME	AGE
4	David	10

As with UNION, the set of columns selected in both SELECTs must be of the same number and type.

Exercise 7.19

Write SQL to perform the following query:

'List the product numbers of all products which have current deliveries.'

1. using INTERSECT;

2. using a join.

Combinations of UNION and INTERSECT
Query 7.48 'List students who play the piano or both violin and cello.'

```
1 SELECT * FROM PIANO
2 UNION
3 (SELECT * FROM VIOLIN
4 INTERSECT
5 SELECT STUD_NO, NAME, AGE
6 FROM CELLO) ;
```

which gives:

STUD_NO	NAME	AGE
2	Jane	12
4	David	10
5	Zena	11

The parentheses are necessary to make it clear that the intersection occurs before the union in this query.

Exercise 7.20

1. Show the output that would result if the UNION and the INTERSECT were reversed in Query 7.48.

2. Express this query in English.

3. Find a join or subquery version of Query 7.48.

MINUS <— (ORACLE SQL*PLUS)

The MINUS operator delivers to the output data from all rows of the table(s) in the first query which do not have 'corresponding' rows in the second table. The tables, or at least the subset of columns projected for output, must be column homogeneous, as with UNION and INTERSECT. The MINUS operation is analogous to the 'complement' operation of Relational Algebra (Chapter 6).

Some SQLs do not have MINUS.
|

Query 7.49 'List students who play violin but not piano.'

```
1 SELECT * FROM VIOLIN
2 MINUS
3 SELECT * FROM PIANO;
```

giving:

STUD_NO	NAME	AGE
1	Fred	10
3	Sally	11

This query outputs rows for all students who are in the first set (violinists) but not in the second set (pianists). The SQL query is equivalent to the following subquery version:

```
1 SELECT *
2 FROM VIOLIN
3 WHERE STUD_NO NOT IN
4 (SELECT STUD_NO FROM PIANO) ;
```

All rows from table VIOLIN which do not have a corresponding STUD_NO in PIANO are delivered to the output. Care must be taken with parentheses when more than one logical (AND, OR and NOT) or set (INTERSECT, UNION, MINUS) operation are involved in a query. The parentheses ensure that the operations are applied in the required sequence, just as with arithmetic operations.

Exercise 7.21

1. Write an SQL statement to answer the query:

   'Who plays cello and either piano or flute but not both.'

2. You have a recipe book and some ingredients in your cupboard. The data is stored in two tables:

In this query, you need a sufficient quantity of all the required ingredients.

REC_BOOK(rec_no, ing_no, qty_reqd)
ING_IN_CBD(ing_no, qty_avail)

Write an SQL query to list out all the recipes you can make.

EXISTS and NOT EXISTS

EXISTS and NOT EXISTS are used in SQL SELECT statements to test, as their names suggest, for the existence or nonexistence of rows in a database table. The general structure of a query containing an EXISTS is shown in Fig. 7.8.

SELECT ...
FROM ...
WHERE ...
AND ...
...
AND EXISTS
(SELECT*
FROM ...
WHERE ...
...)

Fig. 7.8   Positioning of EXISTS in an SQL query.

A NOT EXISTS takes a corresponding position. Data from a row in the outer query is delivered to the output provided the WHERE selection criteria are all true, including the EXISTS or NOT EXISTS condition. Each row of the table in the outer query is tested. The EXISTS condition becomes true if the subquery can locate a row in its table(s) which satisfies the subquery's WHERE conditions and the NOT EXISTS condition becomes true if such a row cannot be located.

Where EXISTS and NOT EXISTS cannot be replaced by IN and NOT IN
EXISTS and NOT EXISTS are often replaceable by IN and NOT IN, but there are several situations in which they are not:

1. IN and NOT IN require some value to be passed from the outer query to the subquery for comparison; EXISTS and NOT EXISTS do not.

See query 7.38.
2. IN and NOT IN usually allow only one column to be passed to the subquery for comparison (there is an exception in the case of ORACLE SQL*PLUS which allows values of more than one column to be passed); in the case of EXISTS and NOT EXISTS, the values are passed directly into the WHERE conditions of the subquery and so the number of columns whose values are compared is not limited.

3. Where doubly nested subqueries are involved, EXISTS and NOT EXISTS allow values to be passed from the outer query to the second subquery, whereas IN and NOT IN do not.

EXISTS

Consider the following small three-table database concerning the purchases of products that customers have made:

CUST		PURCHASE		PROD	
CNO	NAME	CNO	PRNO	PRNO	DESCR
1	Alan	1	a	a	Apple
2	Bill	1	b	b	Ball
3	Charles	2	a		

The tables show who has purchased what; for example the first rows of each table show that Alan has purchased an apple.

Query 7.50 'List all customers who have purchased any product.'

```
1 SELECT *
2 FROM CUST
3 WHERE EXISTS
4 (SELECT *
5 FROM PURCHASE
6 WHERE CUST.CNO = PURCHASE.CNO);
```

giving:

CNO	NAME
1	Alan
2	Bill

Rows from CUST are selected in lines 1 to 3 only where there exists a row in PURCHASE with a matching CNO. Each row in the outer query is tested in turn to see if there is a corresponding row generated by the subquery, that is, that there is a matching customer number in the PURCHASE table. This simple example shows how EXISTS works in general and what it is intended for. Note that it will only ever be necessary to include a '*' in the subquery SELECT (rather than column names) since it is the existence or nonexistence of a matching row that is being tested for. The same result could have been obtained using IN:

Equivalent 'IN' version.

```
1 SELECT *
2 FROM CUST
3 WHERE CNO IN
4 (SELECT CNO
5 FROM PURCHASE);
```

In the EXISTS version the value passing is via the WHERE clause of the subquery whereas in the IN version, the value is passed via IN and the SELECT clause in the subquery.

NOT EXISTS

Query 7.51 'List details of all customers who have not purchased any product.'

See, for example Clocksin and Mellish (1984) for a short introduction to Predicate Calculus.

Any trace of ambiguity in the English version of this query could be removed by adopting the descriptive style of the Predicate Calculus and rewording it: 'List details of all customers for whom there does not exist a purchase.'

SQL EXISTS is closely analogous to the existential quantifier @E of the Predicate Calculus. As will be seen in a later example, there is not a direct SQL equivalent of the universal quantifier 'for all' $\forall$; this has to be simulated using a double NOT EXISTS. A Set Theory oriented form of the query would be:

'List details of all customers whose customer number is not a member of the set of customer numbers in the PURCHASE table.'

A numerical alternative is:

'List details of all customers for whom the number of purchases is zero.'

The query can also be performed using a join (an outer join), but the English equivalent of the join version is not very 'natural':

'Perform an outer join on the CUST and PURCHASE tables on CNO with the (+) sign against the PURCHASE.CNO and select out only the rows with a null PURCHASE.CNO.'

Each of these English formulations, biased towards a different approach, has its own SQL equivalent. These differing versions are now shown:

Four SQL versions of query 7.51.

NOT EXISTS

```
1 SELECT *
2 FROM CUST
3 WHERE NOT EXISTS
4 (SELECT *
```

```
5 FROM PURCHASE
6 WHERE CUST.CNO = PURCHASE.CNO);
NOT IN
1 SELECT *
2 FROM CUST
3 WHERE CNO NOT IN   (or '!= ALL')
4 (SELECT CNO
5 FROM PURCHASE);
COUNT
1 SELECT *
2 FROM CUST
3 WHERE 0 =
4 (SELECT COUNT(*)
5 FROM PURCHASE
6 WHERE CUST.CNO = PURCHASE.CNO);
OUTER JOIN
1 SELECT A.*
2 FROM CUST A, PURCHASE B
3 WHERE A.CNO = B.CNO (+) <-- (ORACLE SQL*PLUS)
4 AND B.CNO IS NULL;
```

In each case the result will be:

CNO	NAME
3	Charles

because Charles is the only customer who has not purchased a single product.

Query 7.52 'List customers who have purchased all products.'
As can be seen by inspecting the data, Alan is the only such customer. The way this can be seen (and this is of course only practicable with small amounts of data) is:

1. Inspect the PROD table and keep in mind the set of product numbers (a and b).
2. Inspect the PURCHASE table to see which customer number has purchased all product numbers a and b (1).
3. Inspect the CUST table to find the names corresponding to those customer numbers (Alan).

There is an 'ALL' operator in SQL, as we have seen, but it cannot be made to perform in the way that is required by this query. In fact what is required is a double NOT EXISTS (or a double NOT IN). In its NOT EXISTS form the query can be written in English as:

A double NOT EXISTS is used to implement the Predicate Calculus 'for all' ($\forall$) operator.

'List customers for whom there does not exist a product which they have not purchased'

or

'List customers for whom there does not exist a product for which there does not exist a purchase by that customer.'

This **NOT EXISTS** format can easily be translated into SQL as:

```
1 SELECT *
2 FROM CUST
3 WHERE NOT EXISTS
4 (SELECT *
5 FROM PROD
6 WHERE NOT EXISTS
7  (SELECT *
8 FROM PURCHASE
9 WHERE CUST.CNO = PURCHASE.CNO
0 AND PROD.PRNO = PURCHASE.PRNO)) ;
```

giving:

CNO	NAME
1	Alan

The query can be read as 'Select all columns from CUST rows where there does not exist (lines 1 to 3) any row from PROD where there does not exist (lines 4 to 6) a PURCHASE row for that customer and product (lines 7 to 10)'. In general, when the English version of the query contains the word 'all', there is a strong possibility that the double NOT EXISTS form will be appropriate. A Venn diagram showing the various sets involved in this query is shown in Fig. 7.9.

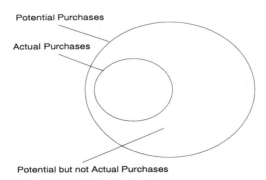

Fig. 7.9   Venn diagram for query 7.52.

Exercise 7.22

The following query has appeared before and was implemented using an outer join:

'List out all departments with no employees.'

The tables involved are:

DEPARTMENT   EMPLOYEE4

DEPT_NO	DEPT_NAME	EMP_NO	NAME	DEPT_NO
1	Sales	1	Alan	3
2	R & D	2	Bill	1
3	Billing	3	Corin	3
		4	Dennis	1

Implement this query using a NOT EXISTS.

Simulating an outer join using UNION and NOT EXISTS

We now have at our disposal the tools necessary (namely UNION and NOT EXISTS) to simulate the outer join command in SQLs that do not have it.

Query 7.53 'List details of products with any deliveries they may have had.'

```
1 SELECT P.PROD_NO, DESCR, C_NO, QTY
2 FROM PRODUCT P, DELIVERY XX
3 WHERE P.PROD_NO = XX.PROD_NO
4 UNION
5 SELECT P.PROD_NO, DESCR, 0, 0
6 FROM PRODUCT P
7 WHERE NOT EXISTS
8 (SELECT *
9 FROM DELIVERY XX
10 WHERE P.PROD_NO = XX.PROD_NO) ;
```

Lines 1 to 4 perform a join, matching up products with deliveries. Lines 4 to 10 append product rows with no matching deliveries.

Exercise 7.23

1. Write an SQL query to list out details of all CUSTOMERs who have INVOICEs with no PAYMENTs.

2. Write an SQL query to list out all customers who are the only customer we have in a city.

Chapter 8

File organization and indexing

In this chapter you will learn:

- ☐ to define alternative database file organizations;

- ☐ to relate these to the required access methods;

- ☐ to use the SQL CREATE INDEX command;

- ☐ to show where indexes are useful and where not.

Introduction

Having designed the logical schema, it is desirable to be able to specify the physical schema, that is, the way the database relations are to be stored on the storage medium. This is called the **file organization**. There are essentially two factors to consider. Firstly, how the records (rows) are to be physically mapped onto the storage medium, and secondly, which **indexes** (if any) are to be used and if so, which fields (attributes, columns) are to be indexed. Indexes are designed to increase the speed of access to required records.

The deciding factor in this is the access method (or access methods) which will be used to retrieve and update data on the database. The file organization should be decided on the basis of maximum speed of access, the type of access required and storage space considerations.

This chapter first describes the various file organizations currently in use and relates them to the access methods to which each is suited. This is followed by the SQL syntax that is employed to create indexes and gives advice on how to decide which indexes (if any) should be used in particular cases.

File organization

File organization is the way the physical records are physically mapped onto the storage medium, usually a disk in database applications. Data is stored on disks in cylinders, tracks, and sectors. See Fig. 8.1.

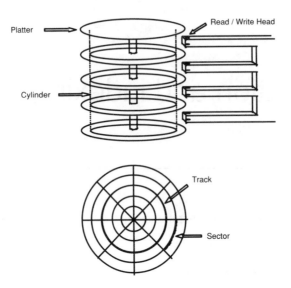

Fig. 8.1 Essential structure of a hard disk.

A disk contains a number of platters, each of which contains a set of concentric tracks on which the data is stored. Tracks are divided up into a number of sectors, and when a disk read is performed, one sector is read into memory. The sector is the smallest addressable component of a disk. A set of tracks, one on each recording surface of the platters, which are all equidistant from the centre of the disk, is called a cylinder.

The purpose of an index is to tell the DBMS where on the disk the required record is located. From the moment the DBMS is 'aware' of this address, there is a delay, called the access time, before the sector with the required record is read in and a copy of it is available in the buffer area of the computer's memory. Access time consists of four components:

Disk access time consists of four components.

'Seek time' is also called 'head movement time'.

'Seek area' is another name for 'cylinder'.

One nanosecond = 10^{-9} seconds.

- **Seek time**. This is the time it takes for the read-write heads of the disk to move to the required cylinder. All of the heads are physically connected, so they all move together. There is one head for each recording surface. The time taken is measured in milliseconds (thousandths of a second), which in computing terms is slow. In a millisecond, a typical CPU could execute thousands of machine-code instructions. Seek time depends on how far the heads have to move, so it is wise to have all the records an application will access in the same or adjacent cylinders if possible. Seek time is often the largest component of access time.
- **Head switching time**. Having moved all the heads into the correct cylinder, the correct head now has to be switched on so that reading or writing to the desired track can commence. This is done at electronic speeds (nanoseconds – billionths of a second) so it is not a significant part of access time.

- **Latency** (also called rotational delay time). Having moved the heads and switched on the right one, there is a delay while the disk rotates so that the required sector becomes available under the read-write head. On hard disks the disk rotates continually while it is switched on; on floppy disks (unlikely to be used in database work, even on PCs) there is also a startup delay while the disk gets up to speed for reading or writing. The rotational delay is, on average, the time taken for half a disk rotation. Thus if the disk were rotating 50 times per second, the latency would be a hundredth of a second: 10 mS (ten milliseconds).
- **Data transfer time**. This is the time taken to read or write the sector from/to memory. This is clearly dependent on the speed of disk rotation and the number of sectors that each track is divided into. If the disk rotates 50 times per second and there are 10 sectors per track, then the data transfer time is a tenth of a fiftieth of a second, i.e. 2 mS. The time it takes for the data to move from disk to CPU is minimal since this again is at electronic speeds (nanoseconds).

One millisecond = 10^{-3} seconds.

Exercise 8.1

A hard disk rotates at 3000 rpm (revolutions per minute). It has 10 recording surfaces, and 100 tracks per surface. Each track is divided up into 10 sectors, each of which stores 30 K (kilobytes) of data. Average head movement time is 50 mS.

1. Calculate the storage capacity of the disk.

2. Calculate the average access time.

We now consider the various file organizations.

Sequential file organization

In sequential file organization, the records are stored on the disk tracks in the sequence of one or more (usually one) record field, called the sequence field. For example, a customer file might be held in the sequence of the customer account number or the customer name. Clearly it would not be possible to hold records in both sequences. The sequence decided upon will be governed by the order in which the records are most often accessed. IBM calls sequential organization and the associated access method SAM (Sequential Access Method).

In traditional dataprocessing systems, data was held most often on magnetic tape. The only access method available was sequential access, that is, accessing the records in the sequence they were stored on the tape.

A sequential file is sorted on one or more sequence fields.

An unsorted file is called a 'serial file' or a 'heap'.

Batch processing

Instead of updating records as and when transactions (changes to the customer master file) arose in the real world, transactions were batched (i.e. stored up on another tape), then sorted into the same sequence as the master file. All updates could then occur, in the sequence of the sequence field, in one pass of the master file. This process was known as batch processing, because the transactions were batched.

Sequential file organization and batch processing are still appropriate for some applications on disk using DBMSs. The obvious disadvantage is that the 'master file' is rarely up to date, since there are transactions that are known about that have not yet updated the master file. In some applications this is not a great disadvantage. In applications which by their nature involve periodic update of a high proportion of the records on a file, sequential organization and batch update may be the best choice. The proportion of records that are updated in a single run of the update program is called the hit rate.

Insertions into sequential files can be slow.

Apart from the limited access method available with sequentially organized files, there are other disadvantages. If we wish to insert a new record somewhere in the middle of a sequential file, it is necessary to rewrite the entire file with the new record inserted. If an update results in the lengthening of a record, there will be a similar problem. In some databases, even with normalized files, record length is not fixed. Even though the number of fields is the same for each record in the file, the database may allow variable length fields, and hence variable length records. Other databases have fixed length records and reserve enough space in each field for the maximum number of bytes as defined in the CREATE TABLE (or similar) command.

Another disadvantage with pure sequential file organization is that the file will only be sequential on one field (possibly composite), as mentioned above, whereas different applications may want to process the data in a different sequence. In such a situation, there is no alternative but to sort the file on the new sort key and generate a temporary file with this new sequence field for the duration of the processing.

Sequential files may be stored in either ascending or descending order of the sequence field.

Exercise 8.2

Think of some applications which could profitably use sequential file organization and batch processing.

On-line real-time processing

With on-line real-time processing, updates are presented to the database table directly via a terminal as soon as they arise. For example, a customer sends in an order, the stock table is checked to see if sufficient stock is available for each order line, each order line is priced, the total order value is calculated, and the customer credit limit and current balance are checked. If the order can be filled, and the customer credit limit would not be exceeded by the order, the stock records are updated (quantity in stock is decremented) and the customer balance is incremented immediately.

Random access

Notice that no batching and sorting of the input 'transactions' occurs in on-line real-time processing. In fact there is no longer any necessity for a transaction file (although a record of transactions such as the orders mentioned above is often kept for other processing purposes). In order for this type of processing to be possible, random access to the records on the database file is required. This means that the records will no longer be accessed in the order in which they are stored. Transactions will not be sorted but will be presented to the computer 'randomly', in the order in which they arise in the real world. Random access is also known as direct access.

Some companies call disks DASDs, direct access storage devices. Disks were designed to provide direct access. The read-write heads are capable of moving directly to the track containing the desired record, rather than having to scan the entire file hoping for a match.

See Fig. 8.1.

In order to capitalize on this direct access capability of disks, one must first know where on the disk the desired record is! It is the purpose of the following file organization techniques to provide this information, for example, we may know we require to access the record for customer number 23, but where is it?

Indexing and hashing are ways of showing where on the disk the desired record is located.

We now discuss some file organizations which provide this information (without extensively searching the file itself).

Indexed sequential file organization

In this file organization method, random access is provided via a supplementary file called an index. If you are searching for a particular word in a text book, you look in the index because that will tell you the page numbers in which the word occurs. It gives you direct access, rather than having to sequentially scan the whole book looking for hits, which is a lengthy process. Instead, you sequentially scan the index, which is quicker because the index is smaller and in sequence.

In an indexed file, the index is in effect another table, stored in the database, containing two columns. The first column contains values of the indexed field, and the second column contains a pointer to one or more records. See Fig. 8.2.

In a dense index, every record on the indexed table has an entry in the index: every record is indexed. In a nondense index, only some of the records contain index entries. This is typically the case where there is more than one record contained in a sector. In this case, the key value of the last record in the sector is shown in the index.

In Fig. 8.2, the key (C-NO) value of the last CUS record (row) in the sector is shown in the index.

C_NO	Cylinder No	Track No	Sector No
10	5	1	1
23	5	1	2
34	5	1	3
44	5	1	4
56	8	4	2
60	8	4	3
70	8	7	2

Indexed Field ↘   Disk Address ↗

Fig. 8.2   Part of an index on C_NO for a customer file.

If the file is a long one, even a nondense index will be correspondingly long. Imagine a database table containing a record for each vehicle in the UK. There may be ten million records in such a table. Even assuming 100 records per sector, there will still be 100 000 sectors of data. In order to find the record for a particular vehicle, up to 100 000 index entries would have to be searched. This suggests that it would be advisable to have a second and possibly more levels of indexing.

In IBM's ISAM (Indexed Sequential Access Method), it is possible to have a volume index, a cylinder index, a track index and a sector index.

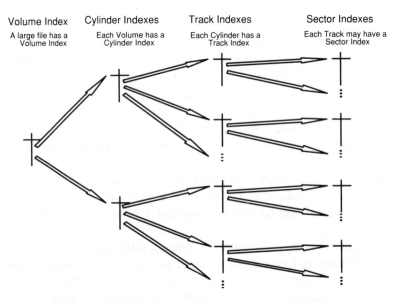

Volume Index	Cylinder Indexes	Track Indexes	Sector Indexes
A large file has a Volume Index	Each Volume has a Cylinder Index	Each Cylinder has a Track Index	Each Track may have a Sector Index

Fig. 8.3 shows a four-level ISAM index. INGRES, for example, allows ISAM storage structures.

Fig. 8.3   Four-level ISAM index.

A 'volume' is a physical storage device such as a disk. Large files may span several on-line disks. The volume index shows on which volume the required record will be found. The cylinder index shows on which cylinder in that disk the record will be found. This determines where the heads should be placed for access. The track index determines which head should be switched on, and the sector index, if used, shows the sector within the track which contains the required record (if indeed the record exists). The sector index in such a situation cannot speed up the access as the other levels of index do. It merely allows the CPU to be getting on with other processing during the latency time.

It is possible to have an indexed file with the physical placement of the records not held sequentially. In the vehicle file mentioned above, it is unlikely that sequential access would ever be required. (Is there any application you can imagine where a contiguous sequence of registration numbers would need to be accessed?) This means in practice that where more than one record is held in a sector, the records need not be sequential in that sector.

In many applications it is desirable to have both random and sequential access to the data in a file. Take a stock file in a mail-order warehouse for example, which holds one record for each type of stock item held. During the week, as orders come in, the stock records will be accessed 'randomly', depending on which items the customer wants to buy. In this case an index on stock number would be essential to quickly retrieve the desired stock records. Periodically however, it may be required to produce a sequential list of stock items. In this case it would be useful if the records were held sequentially so that no sorting would be required to produce such an inventory listing. If a large shipment of goods comes in from a supplier, a batch update (after sorting the deliveries on stock number) could be performed. This would tie the stock file up for less time than holding it 'open' while data entry staff type in the delivery data on-line.

> ISAM files allow both random access and sequential access.

Records can be updated in place by simply writing over the existing version of the record. Records can be deleted by marking them as deleted.

Overflow areas

Inserting new records requires a more complicated strategy. We want to insert a record in the right place so that the required sequence is maintained. One strategy is to leave free space in each sector for inserted records. Another is to leave free space on each track and rewriting the entire track after an insertion. This is not a complete solution of course since the sector or track may become full. Where this is possible, an overflow area can be used. The index entry for the set of records pointed at has an additional field, a pointer to the disk address of the first record in the overflow area. Records on the overflow area themselves also contain a pointer to the next record in the overflow area. Random access of a record in an ISAM file containing overflow areas is thus as follows:

1. Find the appropriate entry in the index.
2. Fetch the appropriate sector for the required record.
3. If not found, sequentially search the overflow area via the pointers.

Reorganizing indexed sequential files

Searching overflow areas can be slow.

If the number of inserts since the file was created is large, the time taken to retrieve records will be significantly increased by sequentially searching overflow areas. In this case, the file should be reorganized so that all the records are moved into the prime area (the non-overflow area) so that the benefits of indexing can be restored. This may be performed by the DBMS itself or 'manually' by simply renaming the file, and writing all the records to a file with the old name. In this process, all the records will be written contiguously and in sequence to the prime area, the overflow areas will be emptied, and the indexes will be updated accordingly to show the new positions of the records.

Inverted files

Another advantage of indexed files is that they can be indexed on more than one field. Sometimes, for example, it might be required to have random access on the customer number of a customer file. At other times, random access on customer name or city may be required. A separate index can be set up for each of these fields. A customer number index will point to the address of the customer with that customer number. There will be a single pointer because customer number is a candidate key. An index on the field CITY however would contain many entries in the disk address field of the index, since many customers will live in that city. Some queries such as:

'How many customers live in Bristol?'

can then be answered by accessing the index alone, and not retrieving the actual records.

In the extreme case, an index is set up on every field in the file. If there are 10 fields, there will be 10 indexes. In this case, the file is called a fully inverted file. If only a subset of the attributes are indexed, the file is partially inverted. The file is called 'inverted' because, instead of applying the value of the indexed field to obtain the other attributes by retrieving the record, you apply a value of one of the 'other' attributes to obtain the key value.

In many cases it will be the primary key that is the indexed field in a singly indexed file, although this is not necessary in modern databases. The fact that the value of the primary key uniquely identifies the record does not imply that it will always be known. If a customer rings in with an enquiry about his or her account, he or she might not know the account number and the correct record will have to be retrieved via, say, name and address (probably using fuzzy matching). If this is usually the case, indexing on one or more of these fields is desirable.

The LIKE operator can be used for fuzzy matches.

Indexes slow down updates

Although indexes are designed to give fast random access to required records so that they can be read, they can actually slow down updates, particularly insertions. In a dense index, the index (as well as the prime area and possibly the overflow area) will have to be updated when a new record is inserted. In a nondense indexed file, the index will also frequently need to be updated when records are inserted. Since the index is stored on the disk, an extra write operation will have to occur. It is true that the sector in which the insert will occur will be found more quickly, but the extra write may increase the time taken for the insert. This becomes more pronounced when the file is indexed on several fields. All of the indexes will be updated with a dense index, and are likely to have to be updated even with a nondense index.

All indexes have to be updated for an INSERT.

Hashing

In a situation where only random access and not sequential access is required, **hashing** may be a superior method of file organization than indexing. Instead of looking up an index table to find the required record, the value of the field by which the record is to be retrieved has a hashing algorithm applied to it to convert it directly to a disk address.

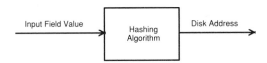

Fig. 8.4 Hashing algorithm.

No space is thus required for indexes and since the algorithm involves just a few mathematical and/or logical operations, which the CPU can perform quickly with no need to retrieve indexes from disk, hashing can provide very fast access. When storing a record, apply the hashing algorithm to find a disk address to store it. When retrieving the record, simply apply the same algorithm.

Access time is still limited by disk seek, latency and data transfer times.

A disadvantage of hashing compared to indexing is that a file can be hashed on only one field (possibly composite). It is thus advisable before considering hashing, to be sure that a large percentage of accesses will be on that field.

Hashed files are not good for sequential access.

Exercise 8.3

Think of some applications where hashing would be an appropriate method of file organization.

Hashing algorithms are essentially numeric, but can be applied to non-numeric fields by converting them into their equivalent ASCII values or using the numeric position (e.g. '1' for 'A', etc.).

The purpose of a hashing algorithm is to convert the field to be hashed (the 'hashed field') to a bucket address. A 'bucket' is the name given to a set of one or more disk sectors. In many cases, buckets contain just one disk sector. If the hashed field takes values from 1 to some integer N with no gaps, then the hashing algorithm can be very simple. The bucket address is simply the field value plus some offset, which is the start address of the first record. In this case, the address is called a relative address, because it is found 'relative' to the start address. Relative addressing would probably be suitable for an order file, since we allocate the order numbers consecutively. This would however only be satisfactory if all old orders were retained.

There are several disadvantages with relative addressing. Firstly, only one record will be inserted in each address. If a sector is 20 Kb and the record length is 1 Kb then a considerable amount of disk memory will be wasted. Secondly, the hashed field values may be non-contiguous, that is, there may be gaps in the set of its values. In that case, many buckets would be unused. The packing density is the proportion of space allocated to the file which is actually occupied by records. For these reasons, hashing algorithms which are more complex than simple relative addressing are used. The idea is that the algorithm should convert the range of values that the field can take, into a range of disk addresses that will be sufficient to contain the number of records.

Let us assume that we have a customer number C_NO as follows:

999 99999

The first three digits are the region number, which currently ranges from 000 to 099, although we plan to open more regions in the future. The next five digits are the customer number within region. The region with the most customers at present is London, which has 10 000 customers. A particular customer in London (in fact our first customer ever) has C_NO 00000000. Our latest London customer (our ten-thousandth – there was a small party!) has C_NO 00009999. The Outer Hebrides, which is our latest conquest, was allocated region number 099. We currently have 10 customers there.

If we were to adopt relative addressing, we would need one hundred million hash addresses, and we have only 100 000 customers at last count. The packing density would be:

$$100\ 000 \div 100\ 000\ 000 = 0.1\%$$

Only a thousandth of the allocated area would contain records. Even assuming we invested in all the necessary disk space, it is unlikely that it would ever become full since, for example, it is unlikely that we will ever have a hundred thousand customers in the Outer Hebrides.

For this reason, a hashing scheme will have to map the large range of values of the hashed field to a smaller range of hash addresses. A perfect hashing algorithm would map each value to its own address. However, this is usually not possible. Two different values may be converted to the same address. This is called a collision, and the two values are called synonyms. A good hashing algorithm is one that produces addresses that fit the range, provides a fairly uniform distribution of records, and minimizes collisions.

Unfortunately, the best hashing algorithm for one field and its distribution of values will not necessarily be the best for another. It should be possible to produce a tailor-made hashing algorithm for each field, assuming we have complete knowledge of the distribution of values. However, the distribution may change (the Outer Hebrides may really 'take off'). In practice, there are several standard hashing algorithms that work reasonably well in many situations.

Choosing an appropriate hashing algorithm requires a good knowledge of the data.

Division/remainder

In this algorithm, the hashed field value is divided by a certain number (the 'divisor') and the remainder is taken as the hash address. In our customer number example, since we have 100 000 C_NO values, we need 100 000 hash addresses. If we divide the customer number C_NO by 100 000, the remainder will range from 0 to 99 999. The remainder will simply be the last five digits of C_NO. If we adopted 100 000 as the divisor, the first customer in each region would be mapped to the same bucket – clearly not ideal; there would be too many synonyms for address 00000 and thus too many collisions.

In practice, it has been found that a prime number (a number with no factors) slightly less than the number of addresses available gives a more even distribution of hash addresses.

Designing a general-purpose hashing algorithm is a job for a mathematician!

Folding

In this algorithm, the field value is split into parts which are then added. In our example, the first four digits could be added to the last four,

```
 9,999
+9,999
───────
19,998
───────
```

yielding a hash address in the range 0 to 19 998, approximately twenty-thousand addresses. There would thus be, on average, five synonyms per bucket. If the bucket size (the number of records that can fit in a bucket) were five, this may be a satisfactory algorithm. However, there is no guarantee that the distribution of addresses would be uniform across the buckets. Some buckets may have no records and others may quickly become full.

Bucket overflow

One approach to buckets which become full is simply to increase the bucket size. This however is only a temporary measure.

Another method is forward search, in which, when the correct bucket is full, the record is located in the next bucket with available space. However, when the packing density becomes high, this can result in long sequential searches, which detracts from the aim of hashing – fast access. In practice, if a predetermined number of buckets are inspected and there is no available space, the file is too dense in that region and the file will have to be reorganized, a lengthy process.

An alternative is to use overflow areas, as described in the section on ISAM files. The last record in an overflowed bucket contains a pointer to the first record in the overflow area. The overflow records are chained by themselves having a pointer to the next overflow record.

Exercise 8.4

We have a file with up to 1000 records with a key field K on which we wish to hash. The range of K is from 0 to 1 000 000.

1. Show how a division/remainder and a folding hashing algorithm can be applied to this file.

2. Devise a hashing algorithm of your own. You might find experimenting with a calculator useful here.

Linked lists

Linked lists are used extensively in CODASYL databases and some relational databases.

If it is required to keep the records in a volatile file (i.e. one with frequent updates) in sequence, without having to continually move records or re-sort the entire file; or to show special relationships between specific records, then linked lists may be advantageous.

The idea is that each record contains one or more pointers. In the simplest case, the singly linked list, each record contains one pointer, which points to the next record in the sequence. See Fig. 8.5(a).

The records need not be held in contiguous areas, because the pointers can point anywhere on the disk. The sequence can be easily maintained, since insertions can be made at the correct place [Fig. 8.5(b)] by doing the following:

1. Find the first record with a key value higher than the one to be inserted (7).

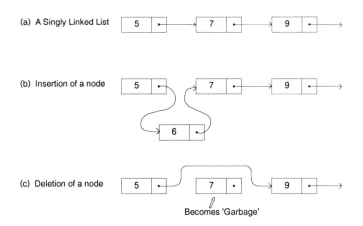

Fig. 8.5 Linked lists.

2. Find an available space and store the new record.
3. Put the pointer address that was held in the previous record (5) in the new record. (6) now points to (7).
4. Put address of the new record in the previous record pointer. (5) now points to (6).

Deletions from a singly linked list are also simple. See Fig. 8.5(c). Suppose we wish to delete record (7). The procedure is simply to make the pointer of the previous record (5) point to where the deleted record (7) now points (9). Nothing now points to record (7) and so it cannot be accessed via the links. It still occupies space however. Such records are called garbage. The space occupied by these records can be reused by performing garbage collection, where the deleted records are placed in another linked list – the 'garbage' list. When a new record is to be inserted, the first record in the garbage list (the head of the list) is used.

It is necessary of course to keep a record of the address of the head of both the data list and garbage list so that they can be accessed at all. The address of the head of the garbage list will move forward for each insertion and the tail will be extended for each deletion from the data list. If this list were visible, it would be seen to crawl through unused disk space (backwards)!

It is possible to make the last record in a list point back to the first one. Such a list is called a ring or circular- linked list. One use to which circular-linked lists have been put in database work is to link records of one type with those of another type. In Fig. 8.6 there is a circular-linked list from Constituency 1 (CO1) to all of the candidates (CA1, CA2) and back to the constituency (CO1). The advantage of linking the 'member records (CA1, CA2) back to the 'owner record' (CO1) like this is that we can answer both the following queries:

Fig. 8.6 shows circular linked lists being used in a CODASYL database.

'Which candidates are there in this constituency?'
'Which constituency is this candidate in?'

Without the pointer from CA2 back to CO1, the second query would be difficult to answer.

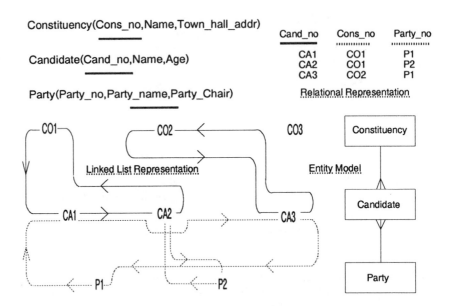

Fig. 8.6   Linked lists in CODASYL database schema.

In Fig. 8.6, the Candidate record type contains two pointers in each record. There is a pointer chain to associate a Constituency and its Candidates, and another pointer chain to associate a Party and its Candidates.

Relational databases do not present this view to the user, although the underlying physical schema may be like this. In the earlier CODASYL databases, this was the view presented to the user/database programmer. Notice that in a relational representation, the link between a Constituency record and the Candidates in it would be by a foreign key Cons_no in Candidate and the link between Part and Candidate would be by the foreign key Party-no, in Candidate. In the CODASYL version, these relationships are represented by disk address pointer chains and the foreign keys are removed from Candidate.

An alternative to circular-linked lists that also allows two-way travel along the list is the doubly linked list, which has one pointer in each record for the 'forward' direction and one for the 'backward' direction.

A singly linked list is incidentally a good way of maintaining the overflow records of an indexed sequential file in order.

Exercise 8.5

Show how the CUSTOMER-INVOICE-PAYMENT records and relationships can be represented in a CODASYL schema.

B trees

A 'B' tree is a specialized indexing system widely used in contemporary relational databases. A tree is a hierarchy of nodes. The top of the tree is called the root node which points to a set of child nodes. These in turn may point to lower-level nodes. The nodes at the bottom of the tree that have no children are called the leaves of the tree, or leaf nodes. Each node has one parent node, that is, the node which points down to it. The depth of a tree is the number of nodes on the longest path from root to leaf. The degree of a tree is the maximum number of children that a node may have. A binary tree for example has degree two. The top node is at level 0, its child nodes are at level 1, theirs at level 2, etc.

ISAM indexes, as we have seen, can form a type of tree. The volume index points to a number of cylinder indexes, the cylinder index points to a number of track indexes, and the track index may point to a number of sector indexes. The reason for having this tree of indexes was to make it unnecessary to search a large proportion of the index entries, which itself takes time, in order to find the desired record.

A potential disadvantage of ISAM indexes is that if the data is unevenly spread throughout the range of values on which the records are stored, some indexes will be more dense (contain more entries) than others.

A tree is said to be balanced when every path from the root node to a leaf has the same length. A B tree (the 'B' stands for 'balanced') is a tree of index nodes which has a built-in mechanism for maintaining it in a balanced condition, even for data which is unevenly distributed.

> 'B' stands for 'Balanced'.

> In a binary tree, each node has two child nodes (except the leaves).

B+ trees

There are several variations on the B tree idea. We discuss B+ trees, which are the type of B tree implementation used in IBM's VSAM ('Virtual Storage Access Method') file organization method and in DBMSs such as INGRES and ORACLE.

B+ indexes consist of two parts, the sequence set and the index set. See Fig. 8.7.

The sequence set

The sequence set runs along the bottom of the tree and contains a linked list of nodes which together contain entries for every data value on the file. Each entry on the node contains the 'key' data value (we use the term 'key' here to mean the attribute (possibly composite) on the data record that is

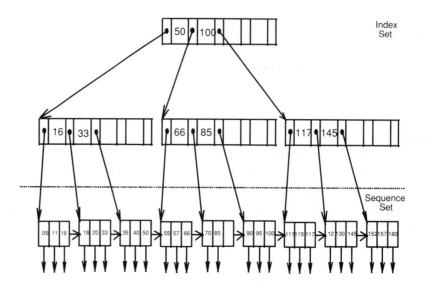

Fig. 8.7   B+ tree.

Pointers are shown as
arrows in Fig. 8.7.

being indexed) and a pointer to the record on the disk. Each sequence set
node is linked to the next node by a horizontal pointer.

The key values in the sequence set are maintained in sequential order, so
if sequential access to the file on the key value is required, it is merely necessary to access the records via the sequence set. Note that as with sequential and indexed sequential files, only one sequence is supported.

Insertions and deletions to/from the sequence set benefit from the speed
and simplicity of these operations on linked lists already mentioned earlier.
Nodes usually contain a fixed number of cells each of which may either
contain a key or be empty. When the nodes are full, it is merely necessary to
link in a new one. (This might necessitate changes to the index set, as we
shall see on page 251.)

The sequence set could be used on its own to find records. There is sufficient information there. However, if there are a large number N of records,
there will also be N index entries in the sequence set that must be searched.

The index set

The purpose of the index set is to quicken the search. In the B+ tree of Fig.
8.7, the procedure used to find the address of the record with key value 57 is
as follows:

1. Access the root node. 57 is greater than 50 but less than 100, so follow
   the pointer to the middle second-level node.
2. 57 is less than 66 so follow the left-most pointer to the sequence set and
   search the sequence node for a match (which here exists – a successful
   search).
3. The pointer in the '57' cell shows the address of the required record.

In this search, three nodes were accessed. If the sequence set had been used and a linear search performed, four nodes would have been visited. If the key value required had been 157, linear search of the sequence set would have entailed visits to nine nodes, but using the index set just three nodes. For larger B+ trees and larger data files, the advantage would be even more pronounced.

For a balanced tree, any access would require just 3 visits.

Insertions into a B+ tree

One great advantage of the B tree is that it remains balanced, even after insertions. An unbalanced tree has greater depth in some areas than others. If the record you want is at the foot of a long chain of nodes, while other leaf nodes are quite close to the root, you will suffer greater access time while all those nodes in the long chain are inspected. Maintaining the same number of levels throughout the tree (i.e. keeping it balanced) is an achievement of B trees.

Let us consider some insertions into the current tree.

Firstly, we wish to insert a record with key value 88. Tracing through the tree from the root as before, we can see that there is a free space in the appropriate leaf node. 88 goes in there, and a pointer to the actual data record appended.

Now let us suppose that we wish to insert key value 135. See Fig. 8.8.

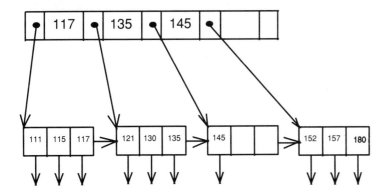

Fig. 8.8   Inserting value 135 into B+ tree.

We have only shown the part of the tree affected. First, the Nodes in the sequence set are all full, so 135 is placed where 145 was, to maintain sequence, and a new sequence node inserted in the list, with some spare spaces. Next, the appropriate second-level node has the new value 135 inserted (since it is now the highest value in a sequence node) in a spare space. It is usual to allow the number of entries in a node to fall between N/2 and N, where N is called the order of the tree. Here N is 4.

Now let us suppose that the tree has grown somewhat, due to insertions, and that the current situation in this part of the tree is as shown in Fig. 8.9.

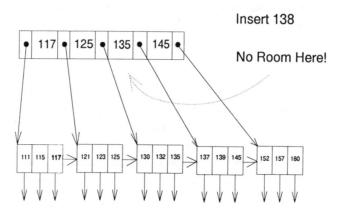

Fig. 8.9   B+ tree with full node.

Suppose we now wish to insert key value 138. The sequence set is modified as before by inserting a new node since all sequence nodes are full. However, there is no room in the parent node since it is also full. This node is therefore split and the 'middle' value (135) pushed up to the next higher node. In this case there is room in that node for 135 to go. The key values in the second-level nodes are rearranged and the pointers to the sequence nodes updated. The situation after the insert is shown in Fig. 8.10.

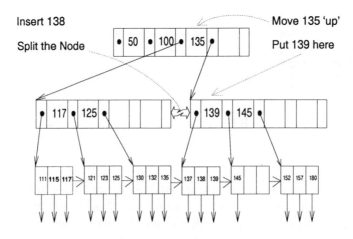

Fig. 8.10   Inserting value 138 results in a node split.

This splitting process is the essence of B trees and is the mechanism that keeps them balanced even when a large number of insertions occur in a localized area. In the example above, if there had been no room for 135 at the root node, it also would have been split, creating a new root node and hence an extra level to the tree.

Exercise 8.6

1. Construct a B+ tree index of order 4 containing the following values:

{10,11,14,20,25,61,1000,1001,1003,1006,1008,1010}

Note that it is up to you which values you place initially in the nodes. It would be sensible to just place two values in each index set node to start with (leave space for the additional two), and try to choose values which divide up the range of values fairly evenly.

2. Experiment with insertions. (Try {12, 500, 1002, 1020}.)

The SQL CREATE INDEX command

In SQL, there are two main objectives that indexing seeks to achieve:

- increasing the execution speed of queries;
- ensuring that given columns have 'unique' values.

An SQL index entry contains on its left-hand side the item required, and on the right-hand side, one or more locations (ROWIDs) in which the item can be found. A ROWID (Row Identifier) is the address in the database where that row resides.

With large tables, the use of an index can considerably reduce the time taken to find particular items.

In dBASE IV, the use of an index also gives an apparent change of sequence of the rows, so that if one index is in use a LIST command lists out rows in one order, while choosing another index will cause the rows to be listed in another order.

In SQL, including the dBASE IV, ORACLE and INGRES variants and in standard SQL, the DBMS itself decides which indexes if any are to be used in the execution of a query. The listed sequence of rows is determined by the ORDER BY clause as we have seen.

Indexes are created by the user if granted appropriate privileges, otherwise by the DBA. There is a tendency for users to create indexes for a variety of reasons, usually as an experiment to see if the speed of particular queries can be improved. This can lead to an unjustified proliferation of indexes and it might be better, where large shared databases are in use, for the DBA to control the creation of indexes. Indexes can in some circumstances actually slow down database updates involving INSERT and DELETE and UPDATE commands. When a new row is inserted for example, not only the base table but also the index (in fact every index related to that base table) must be updated with a new index entry.

At this point it is also worthwhile dispelling two database myths. Some programmers believe that

- primary keys must be indexed because
- that is how you retrieve rows – via the primary key.

Both beliefs are false. Primary keys can be indexed but it is not mandatory. As we have seen, the selection criteria in the WHERE clause may involve any number of columns, key and nonkey. In a query like:

```
1 SELECT *
2 FROM CUS
3 WHERE BALANCE > 100 ;
```

only the BALANCE column will be inspected; the primary key C_NO will not be considered. Even if there were an index on C_NO, it would not be used in this query.

It is possible to ensure the 'uniqueness' of the primary key using SQL indexes. The reason for wanting to ensure this uniqueness is just so we can have a handy, short identifier for each row in the table and for the real-world object that the row models. If (in the roughly ISO 9075 and ANSI 86 SQLs under discussion) no index has been created on what the DBA considers is the primary key in a table, or the UNIQUE option has not been used in such an index, then there is nothing to stop duplicate primary key values emerging. Later versions and standards of SQL address this and other database integrity issues.

Basic syntax of CREATE INDEX
The basic syntax of the CREATE INDEX command is:

CREATE [UNIQUE] INDEX index-name
ON table-name (column-name [ASC I DESC], ...) ;

An index may use more than one index column. You may create different indexes for different combinations of columns in the table, and different indexes with the same columns in a different order. These indexes will be used for different purposes.

Remember that each time you create an additional index you are going to further slow down the updates (in general – there may be some cases where the additional time to update the index is more than compensated for by the reduction in time taken to find the row or rows to be updated).

Every index must have a unique system-wide name, which is another reason for allocating index-creating responsibilities to the DBA.

The user does not name the index to be utilized in a particular SELECT statement; that is left to the query interpreter. Naming the index is necessary so that it can subsequently be DROPped (by name) if required.

Note that the index entries may be in ASCending or DESCending order so that when the DBMS decides to use an index, the rows will be processed in that order.

Improving speed of access
Example 1

```
1 CREATE INDEX INV_C_NO
2 ON INVOICE (C_NO) ;
```

This creates an index table called INV_C_NO whose left-hand side contains a list of C_NOs in ascending (ascending is the default) order. This will be useful in a query in which a particular customer's invoices are required, or one in which a JOIN involving, say, CUS and INVOICE on C_NO is required. Whether or not this index does improve the speed of access to invoices on customer number is best tested by experiment.

The DBMS may decide not to use an index in a high hit-rate join, opting instead for a sort/merge.

Query 8.1 'Get all the invoices for Sallaway.'

```
1 SELECT INV_NO, INV_DATE, AMOUNT
2 FROM CUS A, INVOICE B
3 WHERE SNAME = 'Sallaway'
4 AND A.C_NO = B.C_NO ;
```

Here, the query interpreter and optimizer in the DBMS will do the relational algebraic select (also known as restrict) on CUS first to retrieve the C_NO of Sallaway. This value (1) will then be fed into the INV_C_NO index (the optimizer will 'decide' this) to quickly locate all the ROWIDs for INVOICE rows containing that C_NO value. This is faster than sequentially searching the whole INVOICE table for rows with matching C_NOs.

Note that any SQL query will work (provided it is syntactically and semantically correct) and give the same output whether or not there is an index; the only difference will be in execution time of the query.

See Codd's Rule 8 page 25.

For a small table the execution time of a query might be increased because two tables then have to be accessed – the index table and the base table. The point at which an index becomes profitable is best determined experimentally. The ORACLE SQL*PLUS User's Guide for example recommends indexing if the table has more than 'a few hundred' rows.

Index not useful here

Query 8.2 'Get the details of customers who have outstanding invoices dated before 1st Jan 1991.'

```
1 SELECT *
2 FROM CUS
3 WHERE C_NO IN
4 (SELECT C_NO
5 FROM INVOICE
6 WHERE INV_DATE < 1-jan-91');
```

Here, the index will probably not be useful. The query interpreter should decide not to use the index because the INVOICE table should first be scanned on INV_DATE to retrieve the required set of C≤NOs. The CUS table rows will then be scanned to retrieve CUS rows. The INV_C_NO index does not contain the required kind of information. Only if the query interpreter decided to do a full join of CUS and INVOICE first would the INV≤C≤NO conceivably be of any use. This decision would only be wise if both tables were large and there was likely to be a high hit rate (proportion of rows accessed) on INVOICE due to the fact that many invoices were for dates before 1-jan-91. Of course it is unlikely the query interpreter will know this *a priori*.

Enforcing uniqueness

Example 2

```
1 CREATE UNIQUE INDEX CUS_C_NO
2 ON CUS (C_NO) ;
```

The UNIQUE option will ensure that no two rows of the CUS table shall have the same value of C_NO. If you attempt to insert a new row with a duplicate value of C_NO, an error will result:

```
1 INSERT INTO CUS
2 VALUES (6, 'Mr', 'Jones', ... ) ;
```

'Error : DUPLICATE VALUE IN INDEX'

One should not overestimate the powers of UNIQUE to support database integrity. Various types of primary key anomaly are not prevented by this option. For example, it is still possible to assign a customer more than one C_NO. It is still possible not to assign a customer a CUS record at all. It is still possible for a C_NO to be assigned to a customer that does not exist. UNIQUE really only prevents you from assigning two customers the same C_NO. One out of four.

Specifying uniqueness in ANSI-86 and ISO 9075 SQL

In the ANSI-86 and ISO 9075 standards, the UNIQUE option is specified in the CREATE TABLE command and in the latter, 'UNIQUE' can be replaced by 'PRIMARY KEY' (unless of course you want to specify a column or group of columns as unique and you have not chosen that group of columns as the primary key, i.e. it is a candidate key but is not used as a primary key).

The CREATE INDEX command does not appear in either standard, but it does appear in ORACLE, INGRES and dBASE IV with the syntax shown here.

Indexing on a combination of columns

Example 3

The syntax description shown above suggests that an index can be built out of more than one column. In example 3, it is desired to create an index on the primary key since it is expected that the rows will often be retrieved via the primary key. The primary key is a composite key consisting of INV_NO and PMT_NO. (See the definition of the PAYMENT table in Appendix A.)

```
1 CREATE UNIQUE INDEX PMT_INV_NO_PMT_NO
2 ON PAYMENT (INV_NO, PMT_NO DESC) ;
```

The left-hand side of the index will notionally contain the concatenation of invoice and payment numbers with, for a given invoice number, the highest payment number first (because of the use here of the DESCending option).

Dropping indexes

It might become necessary to remove an index, either as part of general 'housekeeping' duties to remove apparently unused indexes (the identity of the creator of the index can usually be found in the data dictionary), or in order to modify it (in which case you DROP it and reCREATE it). In either case, dropping the index will save space and speed up INSERTs, DELETEs and UPDATEs on the indexed column(s) and since it is unused it will not have any effect on queries. For example:

```
1 DROP INDEX INV_C_NO ;
```

Exercise 8.7

It is assumed that you have available and are familiar with the SQL and other manuals that come with your DBMS. Find out from the manuals which of the file organizations and indexing methods mentioned are available and how you specify which ones you want.

Chapter 9

Database administration facilities

In this chapter you will learn:

- [ ] to explain the roles of the DBA;

- [ ] to explain the options that the DBA has in order to improve the speed of the database, including file organization, indexing and query optimization;

- [ ] to explain the options that the DBA has in order to improve the security of the database, including views and the granting of privileges.

The role of the database administrator

In any large shared database installation there will be a job role called Database Administrator (DBA). The DBA is responsible for the efficient and secure operation of the database. In practice, the DBA may control a team of analysts and database programmers. Since the DBA has overall responsibility for the security and efficiency of the database, members of the DBA team are likely to be found in board meetings, steering committees and program specification walkthroughs. It is vital in large shared databases that alterations to the database schema are controlled centrally and that all database users, particularly analysts and programmers, are fully aware of any changes that are made to the schema, and the implications of those changes. No less important than this is that end users, managers and decision makers are aware of what the database contains, so that they know what questions are capable of being answered by querying it. The stages in the life cycle of a database in which the DBA team are usually involved are outlined below.

Schema design and maintenance
The DBA may be involved from the very outset in the design of the database schema. What entity types are to be included, the attributes that need to be stored for each entity type, and the relationships between the entity

types, are all considered in the light of the likely set of applications the database will have to support.

As time passes, new applications will be required and the schema may have to be extended to accommodate them. New entity types, attributes and relationships will be added. It is also likely that alterations to the existing schema will have to be made in the light of actual experience with the database and its applications. It is important that program changes to the existing set of applications are minimized when this happens, that is, that program-data independence is maximized.

If a new column is added to a database table, this is unlikely to affect many applications. In a traditional COBOL program-file system, adding a new field would require a change to the FD (file definition) statement for every application using that file. In many database applications, this will not be necessary, since the attribute names are the means of accessing data; the DBMS itself decides where to find the data linked to those names. If an SQL query asks for the name of a particular customer using the SELECT statement:

```
SELECT NAME FROM CUS
WHERE C_NO = 5;
```

then the DBMS itself 'knows' (via its data dictionary) not only where the CUS table is located, but also where the NAME and C_NO attributes are located within it. If the DBA decided to insert a new attribute between C_NO and NAME, the data dictionary would be updated to reflect this, and the query would still work.

The DBA is closely concerned with the contents of the Data Dictionary.

If an attribute were to be deleted from a table, then despite the fact that the record length would change, only applications that used that attribute would be affected.

In many cases, changes to existing applications can be minimized when the schema changes by having the old application access a view rather than the base table. Views and the SQL CREATE VIEW command are discussed on page 263. The view can make the new table 'look' like the old table. There are limitations to this approach, since if the schema change involved vertically splitting a table into two, with a subset of the attributes in each table, then it is unlikely that changes to programs that update this section of the database can be avoided, since it is in general impossible to update a view based on more than one table.

Choice of file organization

There are several choices here. Each is outlined below. File organization was discussed in Chapter 8. This discussion, expanded here, is from the point of view of database administration.

Serial organization

In a serial file organization, the records are stored in the order in which they are input. No sorting is involved and the records are in no particular sequence. One application for serial organization is a collection of statistical data, such as the preferred breakfast cereal of respondents questioned in a survey. Individual records are unlikely to be accessed in isolation; the only significance of the data in an individual record is its contribution to the statistics, such as the most popular cereal. If there is no attribute whose value distinguishes one record from another, then duplicates are likely to occur, and, theoretically at least, such a file cannot be placed on a relational database, because there is no entity integrity. In such cases, a primary key may be introduced to ensure entity integrity. A serially organized file is often called a heap.

Exercise 9.1

Think of other applications for serially organized files.

Sequential organization

With sequential organization, the records in the file are maintained in the sequence of one or more attributes. A serial file can be converted to a sequential file by sorting on those attributes. The attributes on which the file is sorted are called the sort key. The sort key may be the primary key or some other attribute(s). Files may be sorted into ascending order (start small, get bigger), or descending order. The sort key can be numeric or non-numeric. It is possible to sort on one key within another. For example, in the DELIVERY table (see Appendix A), it would be possible to sort the records on PROD_NO within C_NO. C_NO would then be called the major sort key and PROD_NO the minor sort key. The result would be:

C NO	PROD NO	QTY	DEL DATE
1	4	6	7-NOV-90
3	1	3	3-NOV-90
3	2	2	3-NOV-90
3	3	1	12-NOV-90
5	3	4	12-NOV-90

Exercise 9.2

1. Re-sort DELIVERY on descending order of C_NO (minor sort key) within ascending order of PROD_NO (major sort key).

2. We have considered ascending and descending order. Are there any other orders you can imagine? Why?

When a record is inserted into a sequential file, some means of 'creating a gap' into which the new record will be placed is necessary. In low volatility files, that is, files which have few changes over time, it may be practicable simply to read and rewrite the file with the new record in place, deleting the old file. In high volatility files, a linked list may be used so that the sequence can be maintained without moving any records. The sequence set in a B+ tree is an example of this.

B+ trees are discussed on page 249.

It is only possible to maintain a sequential file in the sequence of one of its attributes (possibly composite). If an application requires the data in a different order, then the file will have to be sorted. In traditional COBOL (and other 3GL) applications, the SORT utility was frequently the most-used program in many installations, and a great deal of effort was put into designing efficient sort routines for different situations. If there was sufficient main memory available, an internal sort would be performed. The entire file would be read into memory and sorted there. There are many algorithms for internal sorts. One popular internal sort is the bubble sort in which pairs of records in the wrong order are continually swapped until a complete scan of the file requires no further swaps.

Where there is insufficient memory to contain the whole file, a sort merge is performed. Strings of records are read into main memory, sorted, and written to temporary files on disk or tape. Pairs of sorted strings are then merged to produce sorted strings of double the length. These are then merged. The process is repeated until there are just two long strings remaining. These are then merged and the process is completed. Since file merging only requires two records at a time to be compared and one to be written out, the sort merge routine solves the problem of excessive memory usage in sorts. However, reading and writing from/to disks or tapes is a relatively slow process, and the number of merges can be reduced by making the original string size as large as possible.

A sort-merge is often implemented by the SQL interpreter when a join of two large tables is to be performed. If the hit rate (that is the proportion of records accessed) on the tables to be joined is high, it is often faster to perform a sort of both files on the join attributes and then merge them than to use random access via an index on the second table. For example, suppose that we wish to join the CUS and INVOICE tables (see Appendix A) on C_NO, and there are a large number of tuples in each table, and we wish to produce end-of-month Statements of Account for every customer. The best policy would be to sort both CUS and INVOICE on C_NO first, rather than having to search for each INVOICE record for a given CUS. Even using an index on INVOICE.C_NO would probably be slower than the sort merge, since every INVOICE tuple must be accessed (100% hit rate) and a great deal of disk head movement is likely to slow up the processing.

Indexed organization

This has been covered in Chapter 8. The major choice that the DBA will have to make is between ISAM and B tree. If a relatively large proportion of the activity in a file is sequential access, ISAM is likely to be chosen, since the records are arranged sequentially. If most activity is random access, a B tree is the likely choice.

Hashed organization

This too was covered in Chapter 8. If all of the file activity is random access, hashed file organization will give the fastest access. A file can however only be hashed on one attribute (possibly composite), so all the accesses will have to be on that attribute to achieve the speed advantage.

Views

As previously mentioned, views can be created to give the user or the application a 'view' of parts of the database which is more suitable than the actual schema definition. Using a view can make the writing of the application simpler. Views can also be used to limit access to parts of the database only, when used in conjunction with access privileges. The DBA should be the one responsible for creation of views and access privileges. Both of these subjects are discussed below. It is possible, using views, to define database subschema, which are parts of the database to which a set of users and/or a set of applications can have access. Views are created using the SQL CREATE VIEW command.

Security

The DBA should ensure that only prescribed users are able to access the database and that within this set of users, only the parts of the database that concern each user are accessible. This is achieved using the SQL GRANT and REVOKE commands, described on page 278.

Query optimization

Database accesses involve the relational algebraic selects (σ), projects (π), joins ($\times$), unions ($\cup$), intersections ($\cap$), and minus ($-$) operations. In many cases, the same output data will result even if the order of these basic operations is changed. However, some orders will result in far greater processing effort than others. Which order is fastest and uses least intermediate storage depends on database statistics, such as the number of tuples in tables, the likely hit rate for the query, and other factors to do with the database extension existing at any one time. The issues concerning query optimization are covered later in this chapter (page 284).

Views

Views allow the user to 'see' parts of the database in a way that is oriented towards his or her own interests, needs or perspectives. Using SQL, a database 'view' can be set up which will encompass data derived from selected columns and rows from one or more database tables. The tables on which views are defined are called the base tables of the views.

There are several situations in which an SQL VIEW can be used to advantage.

Schema changes

Both the end user and the database applications programmer often inherit a situation in which the database schema has already been designed and will not be altered radically in design throughout the lifetime of the database. Those early decisions concerning the tables and the attributes that constitute the database consequently have a powerful and continuing effect on the subsequent data processing activities in the organization, and even on the picture that the organization has of itself. SQL VIEWs can allow 'new' views of the existing base tables (i.e. the tables as originally defined and physically stored on the database and represented in the schema) to evolve without changing the structure of the underlying base tables and without duplicating any data.

A change to the underlying base tables can be made transparent to application programs by using views.

Little storage overhead with views

No data is actually stored in a view. The 'virtual table' that a view represents is reconstructed by the DBMS each time a query or program names it. This is transparent to the user and the process; it is as if the virtual table actually existed. No (or very little) additional storage overhead is required since the data in the view is derived from data in the base tables. Note however that each time a query uses a view, the virtual table has to be regenerated, incurring a time penalty. In some applications, it may be preferable to create a temporary table once and work with that. However, this is really only suitable for situations in which the data involved will not be updated during the life of the temporary table; updates to the base tables will not of course be reflected in the temporary table.

A temporary table may sometimes be used instead of a view.

Views and updates

When data values in the base tables are updated, the views defined on those tables automatically reflect the new values. In some cases the reverse is also true; a view can be updated (that is, the database can be updated via a view) and the base tables (and any other views deriving from those base tables) are updated. What really happens is that the relevant base tables are updated and the views built upon those base tables simply reflect the changes. It is even possible to create a new view in terms of existing views. There are

Updates to views are restricted.

some restrictions upon updating and querying of base tables via views. Examples illustrating these restrictions are shown below.

Views and security

A view may be used to restrict access to parts of tables.

Another use for views is to restrict the access to the database that different classes of end user will have, to those tables, rows and columns that relate to the type of processing they require and are allowed to perform. This bestows enhanced security on the database as a whole, both from the aspect of protecting the secrecy of certain data 'facts' which might require confidentiality among different classes of user within an organization, and as a way of protecting certain data values in a database against unsolicited modification, including changes, insertions and deletions. If collections of views are suitably protected by passwords and those passwords are distributed selectively to the different classes of user, the database can effectively be partitioned into several overlapping subschema, reflecting the data needs and privileges of these users.

Using the built-in facilities of SQL, data can be partitioned both vertically and horizontally, that is, in terms of both columns and rows, using views. If the DBA grants suitable privileges to a user, he or she can be restricted to accessing table data via a certain view and thus to a certain subset of the data. For example, a particular category of user in the Payroll section (defined by the allocation of account codes and passwords) might be allowed to read the name, staff number and age of everyone on the payroll, to read in addition his or her own salary value but nobody else's, and to change but not read certain other data items such as the monthly pay rate.

Views can make programming easier

Apart from giving users a simpler view and restricting access to defined areas, SQL VIEWs can also help the database SQL programmer to break down a complex query into several smaller steps, each VIEW presenting the programmer with a 'view' of the database closer to the way he or she would like to see it in order to make subsequent SELECT statements easier. An alternative method in this situation is to create and drop temporary tables.

SQL VIEWs are commonly used to:

- restrict rows
- restrict columns
- rename columns
- restrict rows and columns
- calculate summary data
- group data
- join tables
- contain subqueries.

Creating a view

Suppose we want to create a VIEW called LONCUS, which just shows the London rows of the CUS table (see Appendix A). The restriction is on the rows of the CUS table only; all columns are to be visible in the view. The SQL CREATE VIEW command to do this is:

```
1 CREATE VIEW LONCUS AS
2 SELECT *
3 FROM CUS
4 WHERE CITY = 'London';
```

Views and single-table queries

LONCUS can now be treated as a new table in its own right. Suppose that the base table CUS contains:

C_NO	TITLE	SNAME	INITS	STREET	CITY	POSTC	CRED_LIM	BALANCE
1	Mr	Sallaway	G.R.	12 Fax Rd	London	WC1	1000	42.56
2	Miss	Lauri	P.	5 Dux St	London	N1	500	200
3	Mr	Jackson	R.	2 Lux Ave	Leeds	LE1 2AB	500	510
4	Mr	Dziduch	M.	31 Low St	Dover	DO2 9CD	100	149.23
5	Ms	Woods	S.Q.	17 Nax Rd	London	E18 4WW	1000	250.1
6	Mrs	Williams	C.	41 Cax St	Dover	DO2 8WD		412.21

Then the query:

Query 9.1 'List the contents of the view LONCUS'
can be simply implemented as:

```
1 SELECT *
2 FROM LONCUS ;
```

which will output just the London rows:

C_NO	TITLE	SNAME	INITS	STREET	CITY	POSTC	CRED_LIM	BALANCE
1	Mr	Sallaway	G.R.	12 Fax Rd	London	WC1	1000	42.56
2	Miss	Lauri	P.	5 Dux St	London	N1	500	200
5	Ms	Woods	S.Q.	17 Nax Rd	London	E18 4WW	1000	250.1

Similarly, a view SHORTCUS can be set up which lets all the rows through but restricts the columns:

```
1 CREATE VIEW SHORTCUS AS
2 SELECT C_NO, CRED_LIM, BALANCE
3 FROM CUS;
```

The query:

Query 9.2 'List the contents of view SHORTCUS'
can be implemented as:
```
1 SELECT *
2 FROM SHORTCUS;
```

with the result:

C_NO	CRED_LIM	BALANCE
1	1000	42.56
2	50	200
3	500	510
4	100	149.23
5	1000	250.1
6		412.21

It is allowable to give new names to the columns in the view, so for example:

This view gives new names to the columns.
```
1 CREATE VIEW SHORTCUS (ACCOUNT, LIMIT, BALANCE)
2 AS
3 SELECT C_NO, CRED_LIM, BALANCE
4 FROM CUS ;
```

creates the same view but with the column names changed to ACCOUNT, LIMIT and BALANCE. These are column aliases for the original column names.

The query:

Query 9.3 'List credit details of London customers'
can be achieved in various ways. Suppose that 'credit details' means the three columns of view SHORTCUS. Clearly there is no way of using SHORTCUS itself to answer Query 9.3 since data about CITY is absent. We could use the LONCUS view:

```
1 SELECT C_NO, CRED_LIM, BALANCE
2 FROM LONCUS;
```

which performs the required relational algebraic project operation to give the required columns and utilizes the relational algebraic select intrinsic to the LONCUS view to select the required subset of rows. The output is thus:

C_NO	CRED_LIM	BALANCE
1	1000	42.56
2	500	200
5	1000	250.1

It is also possible to create a view LONSHORT (try to keep table and view names more self-explanatory than this) which delivers just these three columns for London customers. This effects a relational algebraic select and project in one view:

```
1 CREATE VIEW LONSHORT AS
2 SELECT C_NO, CRED_LIM, BALANCE
3 FROM CUS
4 WHERE CITY = 'London';
```

The query output is identical.

Defining one view in terms of another

The view LONSHORT could have been defined in terms of view LONCUS instead of table CUS. Line 4 would then be unnecessary since the relational algebraic select it represents has already been performed in LONCUS:

Defining one view (LONSHORT1) in terms of another (LONCUS).

```
1 CREATE VIEW LONSHORT1 AS
2 SELECT C_NO, CRED_LIM, BALANCE
3 FROM LONCUS;
```

The query:

```
1 SELECT *
2 FROM LONSHORT1;
```

has the same result as above.

Interdependency between views

For this query to work, both views LONCUS and LONSHORT1 must be in place on the database. If for example the view LONCUS is dropped:

```
1 DROP VIEW LONCUS;
```

and an attempt is made to use the view LONSHORT1 by repeating this query, then an error of the following type will occur:

'Table or view does not exist.'

This might appear puzzling since LONSHORT1 itself was never dropped. But a view on which it was based was dropped, and that caused the error.

Checking view definitions in the data dictionary

A record should be kept in the data dictionary of which views exist and how they are derived. In ORACLE for example, a record of the text used to create each view is kept in the ORACLE data dictionary. The data dictionary can be queried by the DBA and selected users, depending on their privileges.

The following query looks at the part of the data dictionary concerned with views:

Query 9.4 'Which VIEWs on the database start with 'LON' ?'

```
1 SELECT *
2 FROM VIEWS
3 WHERE VIEWNAME LIKE 'LON%';
```

This gives:

VIEWNAME	VIEWTEXT	<—— ORACLE allows you to see a summary of the views

The ORACLE Data Dictionary stores the definition of views.

VIEWNAME	VIEWTEXT
LONCUS	SELECT * FROM CUS WHERE CITY = 'London'
LONSHORT	SELECT C_NO, CRED_LIM, BALANCE FROM CUS WHERE CITY = 'London'
LONSHORT1	SELECT C_NO, CRED_LIM, BALANCE FROM LONCUS

This is a very useful way of checking how a view was created. It can be seen clearly here that if the LONCUS view is dropped then LONSHORT1 will also be unavailable, with the result that any reference to LONCUS or LONSHORT1 will give the error shown above. However, even after LONCUS is dropped, the definition of LONSHORT1 is still contained in the data dictionary item VIEWS, so that:

```
1 SELECT *
2 FROM VIEWS
3 WHERE VIEWNAME LIKE 'LON%';
```

gives:

VIEWNAME	VIEWTEXT
LONSHORT	SELECT C_NO, CRED_LIM, BALANCE FROM CUS WHERE CITY = 'London'
LONSHORT1	SELECT C_NO, CRED_LIM, BALANCE <— View is FROM LONCUS still there

If LONCUS is ever reinstated, all the views built on it will work again.

Summary views

One common and very useful purpose to which VIEWs can be put is in the construction of summary data. For example we may want to create a view containing summary financial data on our customer accounts.

A view may be used to contain summary data.

```
1 CREATE VIEW SUMMARY1 AS
2 SELECT CITY, SUM(CRED_LIM) MAX_RISK,
3   SUM(BALANCE) DEBT
4 FROM CUS
5 GROUP BY CITY ;
```

Query 9.5 'List the summary financial data on customer accounts.'
```
1 SELECT *
2 FROM SUMMARY1;
```

In line 2 of the CREATE VIEW command an alternative way of specifying column aliases (rather than having them in the CREATE VIEW line) is shown. Notice that here we have a GROUP BY in a view, the totals being grouped by city. The column aliases are in fact mandatory here, since the aggregate functions SUM(CRED_LIM) and SUM(BALANCE) are not valid column names. The output from Query 9.5 is:

CITY	MAX_RISK	DEBT
Dover	100	561.44
Leeds	500	510
London	2500	92.66

which is a very useful summary report. The means of obtaining the summary (such as the details of the GROUP BY) need not be remembered by end users since the logic is encapsulated in the view; all that is required in fact is to remember the VIEW name. In this way the end user can be insulated from the more involved aspects of the database queries, which can be left to the programmer or DBA to develop and test. The VIEW is always up-to-date because whenever the view is used, its built-in SELECT command is rerun.

Views of joined tables

One of the major uses for views is to give the database user the impression that the database contains tables that are in precisely the format that he or she requires for the application in hand. This makes thinking about the problem and the formulation of SQL queries simpler. Quite often, as we have seen in previous chapters, a query will require more than one database table to be accessed to produce the desired output. In many such cases, associated queries would be easier to write and reports easier to generate if the relevant data appeared to be all in one table.

In Chapters 3 to 5, the processes of Entity Analysis and Normalization tended to split data into separate tables, each table corresponding to a 'real-world' object type. The major object in doing this was to eliminate data redundancy and the associated insertion, deletion and update anomalies. In creating views of joined tables, we are apparently reversing this process and 'denormalizing'. However, remembering that views do not actually store any data, no data duplication will result, and we will obtain the advantage of having a single table which contains all relevant data items.

> A view based on a join can present its user with a 'denormalized' view of the data.

One common requirement in accounting systems, in particular the sales ledger subsystem, is to provide customers with a monthly statement of account. A typical statement is shown in Fig. 9.1.

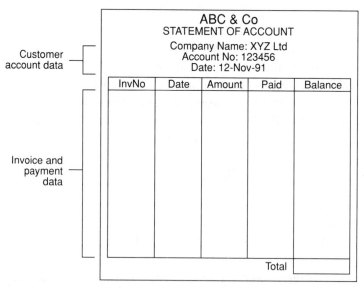

Fig. 9.1 Customer statement.

The data required in the statement consists of:

1. Customer Account data.
2. Invoice data.
3. Payment data.

Assuming this data is contained in the tables CUS, INVOICE and PAY-MENT, it is possible to create a view, based on a join of corresponding rows in the tables, which will make the writing of a report program to print statements considerably simpler. The necessary view can be created by the following CREATE VIEW command:

```
1 CREATE VIEW STATEMENT AS
2 SELECT A.C_NO, SNAME, B.INV_NO, B.AMOUNT
3   INV_AMOUNT, PMT_NO, PMT_DATE, C.AMOUNT
4   PMT_AMOUNT
5 FROM CUS A, INVOICE B, PAYMENT C
6 WHERE A.C_NO = B.C_NO
7 AND B.INV_NO = C.INV_NO (+);
```

The view created here makes it easy to print statements such as that shown in Fig. 9.1.

Note the use of column aliases in lines 3 and 4 to prevent the attempt being made to create a view with two identically named columns 'AMOUNT'.

INGRES has a special feature called 'joindefs' which facilitates the generation and storage of such multitable views.

Joining views
It is possible to join a view to a table or another view. For example we may wish to join CUS to SUMMARY1 on CITY:

Query 9.6 'Produce a report that shows me each customer's debt as against the corresponding city debt.'

```
1 SELECT C_NO, SNAME, A.CITY, BALANCE
2   DEBT, ROUND((BALANCE / DEBT) * 100, 2) PROPORTION
3 FROM CUS A, SUMMARY1 B
4 WHERE A.CITY = B.CITY ;
```

In line 3, a base table CUS is joined to a view SUMMARY1.

The output from this query is:

C_NO	SNAME	CITY	DEBT	PROPORTION
4	Dziduch	Dover	149.23	26.58
6	Williams	Dover	412.21	73.42
3	Jackson	Leeds	510	100
1	Sallaway	London	42.56	8.64
5	Woods	London	250.1	50.77
2	Lauri	London	200	40.6

In line 3 it can be seen that the table CUS has been joined to the view SUMMARY1.

Similarly, one view can be joined to another. The report column 'PRO-PORTION' is a calculated column showing the proportion of the total city debt each customer's balance represents. The ROUND function rounds PROPORTION to two decimal places.

Views may produce duplicate rows

It is possible that the introduction of a view will result in duplicate rows. Take for example the DELIVERY table:

DELIVERY

C_NO	PROD_NO	QTY	DEL_DATE
3	2	2	3-NOV-90
3	1	3	3-NOV-90
1	4	6	7-NOV-90
5	3	4	12-NOV-90
3	3	1	12-NOV-90

If we define a view CUS_DELS containing just C_NO and DEL_DATE:

```
1 CREATE VIEW CUS_DELS AS
2 SELECT C_NO, DEL_DATE
3 FROM DELIVERY;
```

then the first two rows in the view are duplicated. This is not in theory allowed on a relational database where every table represents a relation which is a set of tuples and a set is by definition not allowed to contain duplicates. Whether or not a view (not defined in the mathematical theory of relations) is allowed to contain duplicates is open to debate. Clearly in practical DBMSs they are allowed to:

```
1 SELECT *
2 FROM CUS_DELS;
```

gives:

C_NO	DEL_DATE
3	03-NOV-90
3	03-NOV-90
1	07-NOV-90
5	12-NOV-90
3	12-NOV-90

There are duplicate rows in this view.

The first two rows are identical. In relational database theory (as distinct from the mathematical theory of relations – the former is an extension of the latter) one guarantee of no two rows being identical is the notion of the primary key. Every relation should have one. A primary key 'identifies' a row in the sense that no two rows are allowed to contain the same value of the primary key column or columns. In many practical tables it will be only this value (or some other candidate key) which is guaranteed to distinguish rows from each other. Clearly then, if a view definition omits all or part of the primary key then there is the potential for duplicate rows to occur.

Because in relational database theory the idea of a duplicate row is confused with the idea of duplication of data, measures are often taken to remove such duplication. It could be argued on the other hand that two occurrences of a phenomenon is basically different from one occurrence of the phenomenon and duplicate rows should be allowed, just as duplicate values are allowed in statistical data. The whole question turns on the notion of 'identity'. Do, for example, two 'identical' objects have the same 'identity'? Why is it sometimes necessary to invent a primary key (i.e. an identifying attribute)?

Exercise 9.3

The question of identity need not be dismissed as merely philosophical. It is true that philosophers have failed to give a satisfactory (clear, generally accepted and useful) answer through many centuries of speculation on the notion of identity. Perhaps it is now up to computer science to help to provide this answer, in a similar way to its contribution of fresh ideas and computer-derived terminology to some of the questions of cognition. 'Mundane' questions asked by data analysts are often surprisingly similar to 'profound' questions asked by philosophers. It may be that attempts to improve database technology will lead to improvements in our understanding of other aspects of the world by demonstrating in practice the inviability of some philosophical notions that had previously held sway, and positing better alternatives. Entity Relationship Modelling and the new terminology and practice of Object Oriented Analysis can both be viewed in this light. This is one of the things that makes ours such an interesting subject.

> 'Mundane' questions asked by data analysts are often surprisingly similar to 'profound' questions asked by philosophers.

Discuss.

Updating views

All updates to a base table are automatically reflected in all views that encompass that base table. For example if the balance of a certain customer in the CUS table is increased by £100 then the view LONCUS based on CUS will show this:

```
1 UPDATE CUS
2 SET BALANCE = BALANCE + 100
3 WHERE C_NO = 5 ;
```

will update the base table CUS, and;

```
1 SELECT C_NO, BALANCE
2 FROM LONCUS
3 WHERE C_NO = 5 ;
```

will produce the output:

C_NO	CRED_LIM	BALANCE
5	1000	350.1

which shows that the balance of C_NO 5 has been increased by £100.

Similarly, if the view is updated, then the base table will reflect the change:

```
1 UPDATE LONCUS
2 SET BALANCE = BALANCE + 100
3 WHERE C_NO = 5 ;
```

```
1 SELECT C_NO, BALANCE
2 FROM CUS
3 WHERE C_NO = 5 ;
```

The query will show the increased balance in the base table CUS.

Restrictions on updates via views

There are several restrictions commonly encountered concerning updates to database tables via views.

1. DELETES

   (a) The view must be based on one table only.
   (b) The view must not contain a GROUP BY or DISTINCT

2. UPDATES
   as above, plus

   (c) The view must contain no calculated column expressions.

3. INSERTS
   as above, plus

   (d) All columns in the base table which were defined as NOT NULL by the CREATE TABLE command should be in the view.

All of these restrictions make sense. If an attempt was made to delete from a join view, then the number of rows deleted in each of the joined tables may be unexpected. If a row from a view containing a GROUP BY were deleted, then should all the rows in the base table that contributed to the summary data be deleted? This is also the situation with DISTINCT; more than one base table row may have 'contributed' to a view row. These problems, or closely related ones, could occur if it was legal to perform updates and inserts on a view.

If an UPDATE were attempted on a calculated column in a view, then what should happen to the values of the columns in the view and the base tables from which the calculated column is derived? If an attempt were made to INSERT a row into a view containing a projection of a base table and some of the columns in the base table which were NOT NULL were not included in the view, then the values in the base table that were left out would end up with null values.

Note that it is possible to delete a whole row from a base table via a view defined as a projection of that base table.

Views as programmers' stepping stones
Some queries are made much easier to write by breaking them up into separate parts and using a view as a 'stepping stone' between the individual queries. Consider the following query:

Query 9.7(a) 'Which party won the election?'
Assume a table with the following structure and data:

CANDIDATE

CAND_NO	NAME	CONS_NO	PARTY	NO_OF_VOTES
1	Fred	1	Labour	100
2	Jim	1	Cons	120
3	Peter	1	Liberal	50
4	John	2	Labour	150
5	Mike	2	SLD	50
6	Jane	2	Cons	100
7	Mary	2	Green	150
8	Keith	1	Ind	150
9	Sue	1	SDP	160

Note that the winning party is the one which obtains the most won constituencies, not necessarily the most votes overall across the country.

This query is quite difficult to implement 'in one go'. It can with advantage be broken down into the following steps:

Query 9.7 is broken
down into steps using
intermediate views.
Query 9.7(b) 'Get the winning party in each constituency.'
Since the output from this query will be useful in the next step, the output
will be 'saved' in a view:

```
1 CREATE VIEW CONS_WINNERS AS
2 SELECT CONS_NO, PARTY
3 FROM CANDIDATE A
4 WHERE NO_OF_VOTES =
5   (SELECT MAX(NO_OF_VOTES)
6   FROM CANDIDATE B
7   WHERE A.CONS_NO = B.CONS_NO) ;
```

Note the use of a correlated subquery. Winning candidates are selected by
inspecting all other candidates in the same constituency and checking that
none has a higher number of votes.
The view CONS_WINNERS which results will contain in this instance:

CONS_NO	PARTY
1	SDP
2	Labour
2	Green

Note that here two parties have both 'won' in constituency 2. The next
step is to tot up the number of won constituencies that each party obtained.

Query 9.7(c) 'Get the number of constituencies won by each party.'
This can be achieved by creating another view:

```
1 CREATE VIEW WON_CONSTITS
2 (PARTY, NO_OF_CONSTITS) AS
3 SELECT PARTY, COUNT(*)
4 FROM CONS_WINNERS
5 GROUP BY PARTY ;
```

which will in this case produce the output in view WON_CONSTITS:

PARTY	NO_OF_CONSTITS
SDP	1
Labour	1
Green	1

Note that here we have three joint winners, an unusual event which
should nevertheless be accommodated in the query design. The next step is
to list out the party (parties) with the highest number of won constituencies.
This takes us back to the original Query 9.7(a):

```
1  SELECT PARTY
2  FROM WON_CONSTITS
3  WHERE NO_OF_CONSTITS =
4     (SELECT MAX(NO_OF_CONSTITS)
5      FROM WON_CONSTITS) ;
```

which in a normal situation would yield the one winning party.

Exercise 9.4

1. Using any of the above views, write an SQL command to answer the following query:

   'List each party and the number of constituencies won, best first.'

   Note that the ORDER BY has to be performed by the query itself, since it is not possible to define an ORDER BY condition in a view.

2. Create a view which shows for each INVOICE, the invoice details and all PAYMENT details, even for those invoices which have received no payments.

3. Create a view which shows the name and age (just once) of every musician in the VIOLIN, PIANO, CELLO and FLUTE tables.

View proliferation
The use of views in step-by-step formulation of queries should be the exception rather than the rule. It is wise for the query writer to look around for a suitable existing view to base the query upon. If the query is going to be stored and re-used, the DBA should ensure that the continued existence of the view (or views) is assured. Casual creation of new views can result in their uncontrollable proliferation and in some installations the DBA will reserve such privileges for himself or herself.

Justifying the use of a view
The creation of a view can be justified by:

- The continued need for a query which needs such a view as a 'stepping stone'.
- A convenience. Several tables are frequently used together in queries or reports.
- A security device. Access to data items in the database can be precisely specified.

Security is now discussed.

Security

The GRANT command

The GRANT command gives access privileges to users.

The facilities and syntax associated with GRANT vary from one DBMS and Standard to another. ORACLE is given as a representative example here. The GRANT command is used by the DBA to provide two basic types of security: user security, which is concerned with three general levels of access privilege that each user can have with respect to the database as a whole; and data security, which grants users privileges with respect to individual tables and views. It is possible for the DBA to pass on the ability to grant privileges to other users, as we shall see. There are consequently two forms of the SQL GRANT command.

The first form of the GRANT command

The first form of the GRANT command gives various levels of access to named users. The privileges are
- CONNECT
- RESOURCE
- DBA.

The first form of GRANT command is used by the DBA to enrol and drop users from the DBMS. Every user must have a username and a password. The syntax of the first form of the GRANT command is:

GRANT { CONNECT I RESOURCE I DBA } TO <username>
[IDENTIFIED BY <password>]

This shows that there are three broad classes of database privilege: CONNECT, RESOURCE, and DBA. (Not in the ISO 9075 Standard. The DBA grants these privileges to users with the given username and password. There is nothing the DBMS can do to stop several users sharing the same username and password and of course a given user may have several usernames and passwords that he or she uses for different purposes. The allocation of people to usernames and passwords is an organizational problem carried out by the DBA. The (username, password) to person mapping is normally expected to be 1:1.

CONNECT privilege

CONNECT privilege is the most basic privilege and in granting it to a user, the IDENTIFIED BY clause must be used. The CONNECT privilege permits:

1. Access to the DBMS.
2. The ability to SELECT, INSERT, DELETE and UPDATE other users' tables and views (provided such other users have granted the corresponding privileges to this user – see the second form of GRANT).
3. The creation of views and synonyms.

However, the user with only CONNECT privilege cannot create any tables or indexes.

Example 1
```
1 GRANT CONNECT TO SALLY
2 IDENTIFIED BY ARMY ;
```

Having been 'connected' to the system, username SALLY can now access certain tables and views. Assuming JOHN had granted SELECT privilege to his table CUS, SALLY could perform the query:

```
1 SELECT *
2 FROM JOHN.CUS ;
```

Here, the user SALLY, who has only CONNECT privilege, is retrieving data from a table CUS owned by JOHN. SALLY could create a synonym, to give this table another name:

```
1 CREATE SYNONYM CUSTOMER
2 FOR JOHN.CUS ;
```

The query could then be written:

```
1 SELECT *
2 FROM CUSTOMER ;
```

with the same effect.

A user with CONNECT privilege can change his or her own password at any time using GRANT CONNECT:

```
1 GRANT CONNECT TO SALLY
2 IDENTIFIED BY MANDER ;
```

so MANDER is SALLY's new password.

CONNECT privilege is sufficient for the majority of database users such as operational staff, managers, etc. who will only want to inspect and update data. What they can inspect and update can be precisely defined by the second form of the GRANT command. For many application programmers, who will not need to create tables and views, but will just write programs and queries to access existing ones, CONNECT will also be sufficient.

RESOURCE privilege

Users with RESOURCE privilege have all the privileges they obtained when they received CONNECT privilege, and in addition they can:

1. CREATE tables and indexes.
2. GRANT privileges on those tables and indexes to other users (using the second form of GRANT) and REVOKE those privileges.

REVOKE is how privileges are removed. If there is not a single corporate database, and users will be experimentally creating and dropping their own tables in a variety of small applications, then these users will need RESOURCE privilege. Typical users requiring RESOURCE in addition to CONNECT would be the development team of database designers in the design phase of the system life cycle, DBAs when the system has been implemented but still requires changes and extensions to the design, and students working on a large number of completely separate projects.

DBA privilege

DBA privilege bestows all the powers of CONNECT and RESOURCE, and in addition it allows the owner of this privilege to:

1. Access any user's data, with the ability to perform any SQL operations on it.
2. Use the first form of the GRANT command to grant CONNECT, RESOURCE and DBA privileges.
3. Create PUBLIC synonyms.
4. Perform detailed auditing and disk space allocation, organization, and backup functions.

A DBA can also remove privileges from a user using REVOKE:

```
1 REVOKE CONNECT FROM JOHN ;
```

Any tables created by John will remain, but he will not now have access to the database.

In a similar way, DBA, RESOURCE and CONNECT privileges may be selectively revoked.

The second form of the GRANT command

The second form of the GRANT command gives users access to tables and views.

This form of the GRANT command grants privileges to users with respect to tables or views. The syntax is:

GRANT { privilege, ... | ALL } ON table-or-view
 TO { user | PUBLIC } [WITH GRANT OPTION] ;

The privileges can be any combination of SELECT, INSERT, DELETE, UPDATE, ALTER and INDEX to a table, and just the first four to a view. ALL grants all of the privileges possessed by the granter. UPDATE may be followed by a list of columns, limiting the grantee to updating just those columns in the table or view.

Limiting the ability to see certain columns and rows is achieved using the definition of the view and then granting SELECT privilege to the view rather than the base table(s).

PUBLIC grants the specified privilege to all users. The optional WITH GRANT OPTION authorizes the grantee to grant all or part of these privileges in turn to other users.

Example 1
```
1 GRANT ALL
2 ON CUS
3 TO SALLY
4 WITH GRANT OPTION ;
```

This grants all the privileges that the granter has to user Sally on table CUS. It also allows her to pass any of these privileges on to other users.

Example 2
```
1 GRANT SELECT,
2 UPDATE (NAME, POSTC)
3 ON CUS
4 TO BRIAN ;
```

This allows Brian to see all columns and rows in table CUS but to only update the two columns NAME and POSTC.

Example 3
```
1 CREATE VIEW CUSVIEW1 AS
2 SELECT C_NO, NAME, POSTC
3 FROM CUS
4 WHERE CITY = 'London' ;
```

```
1 GRANT SELECT
2 ON CUSVIEW1
3 TO FRED ;
```

```
1 GRANT UPDATE (CRED_LIM)
2 ON CUS
3 TO FRED ;
```

In this sequence, a view CUSVIEW1 is created to limit the rows and columns of CUS that Fred is allowed to see. (He has no SELECT privilege on CUS itself; his 'view' is being limited by the VIEW.) He is however allowed to update the value of CRED_LIM on any row, without seeing it.

Should it become necessary to limit the rows of CUS in which Fred is allowed to update the CRED_LIM column, say to the London customers only, it would be necessary to revoke the update privilege on CUS and to grant it through the view CUSVIEW1 (suitably modified to include CRED_LIM) instead:

```
1 REVOKE ALL
2 ON CUS
3 FROM FRED ;


1 GRANT UPDATE (CRED_LIM)
2 ON CUSVIEW1
3 TO FRED ;
```

Now Fred can only see C_NO, NAME and POSTC and only update CRED_LIM. Here is an example of Fred updating the credit limit of Mr Sallaway:

```
1 SELECT *
2 FROM CUSVIEW1
3 WHERE UPPER(NAME) = 'SALLAWAY' ;
```

This checks that there is only one Sallaway. Assuming Fred is now confident he has his man, he can update Sallaway's credit limit (without seeing what it was):

```
1 UPDATE CUSVIEW1
2 SET CRED_LIM = 2000
3 WHERE UPPER(NAME) = 'SALLAWAY' ;
```

Fred might alternatively use C_NO for Sallaway to reduce typing in line 3:

```
3 WHERE C_NO = 1 ;
```

Listing your privileges using ORACLE SQL*PLUS

Listing your privileges

There are many system tables of interest in the data dictionary. The names of these tables vary from one DBMS to another but they will in general contain tables showing which tables and views exist, who the owners are, what privileges users have, etc. In ORACLE, you can find what your privileges are on other users' tables and views by:

```
1 SELECT GRANTOR, TNAME, A, D, I, S, U
2 FROM SYSTABAUTH
3 WHERE GRANTOR != USER
4 AND GRANTEE = USER ;
```

USER evaluates to your current log-in ID. GRANTOR is the person who granted you access and you are the grantee. SYSTABAUTH is the data dictionary table that contains this data. TNAME is the name of the table or view, and the letters in line 1 stand for ALTER, DELETE, INDEX,

SELECT and UPDATE. If you have the privilege, a G will appear under that column. Line 3 restricts the output to other people's tables.

To find out who has access privileges on your tables and views, type:

```
1 SELECT GRANTEE, TNAME, A, D, I, S, U
2 FROM SYSTABAUTH
3 WHERE GRANTOR = USER
4 AND GRANTEE != USER ;
```

Security and views

Suppose we have on the database a table EMPLOYEE with the following structure:

GRANT can be used to enhance security using views.

E_NO	NAME	JOB	SALARY	DEPT
1	Alan	Manager	2000	1
3	Carol	Accountant	1700	1
2	Brian	Clerk	1200	1
4	Dianne	Manager	2300	2
5	Lena	Clerk	1500	2

It may be required to allow all employees to be able to 'see' all data except salaries. This can be achieved by the DBA by the following two steps:

```
 CREATE VIEW EMP1 AS
2 SELECT E_NO, NAME, JOB, DEPT
3 FROM EMPLOYEE ;

1 GRANT SELECT < — Granting privileges
2 ON EMP1    on a view.
3 TO PUBLIC ;
```

This means that, assuming PUBLIC has no privileges over EMPLOYEE, then their only window into EMPLOYEE is via the view EMP1 which does not contain the SALARY column of the EMPLOYEE base table.

Another security requirement may be to allow only managers to 'see' salaries, and then only of their own departments. The following view definition assumes that every manager has an account code equal to his or her name and that that name is 'unique', i.e. nobody else in the organization has that name. The view can be modified to remove these constraints. The code employed is:

```
1 CREATE VIEW EMP2 AS
2 SELECT *
3 FROM EMPLOYEE
```

```
4 WHERE DEPT =
5 (SELECT DEPT
6 FROM EMPLOYEE
7 WHERE NAME = USER   < —- System Variable
8 AND JOB = 'MANAGER') ;


1 GRANT SELECT
2 ON EMP2
3 TO PUBLIC ;
```

The subquery in lines 5 to 8 delivers the department number provided the user is the manager of the department. The outer query delivers all columns (including the salary) of all rows in that department. The actual security inherent in this example depends on knowing the password of the departmental manager.

Query optimization

Query optimization is concerned with 'tuning' queries so that they run fast and minimize storage use.

The purpose of query optimization is to perform the sequence of relational algebraic selects (σ), projects (π), joins ($| \times |$), unions ($\cup$), intersections ($\cap$) and minus ($-$) operations in an SQL statement, and to use indexes appropriately, so that the amount of processing is minimized and thus the speed of the query is maximized. Achieving this also usually achieves a minimization of the amount of intermediate storage used, between executing the query, and obtaining the output.

The translation of the SQL query into the sequence of operations is performed by the query interpreter. The query interpreter has to use its 'knowledge' of database statistics and the indexes in existence to 'decide' how to execute the query. The sequence of RA operations performed is called the query execution plan.

Example 1
Suppose we have the following database tables:

PRODUCT						DELIVERY			
PROD_NO	DESCR	QIS	MINQ	REORDQ	PRICE	C_NO	PROD_NO	QTY	DEL_DATE
1	Bat	10	5	10	12	3	2	2	3-NOV-90
2	Ball	5	5	20	2	3	1	3	3-NOV-90
3	Hoop	3	5	10	3	1	4	6	7-NOV-90
4	Net	2	5	10	20	5	3	4	12-NOV-90

with the following database statistics:

Number of PRODUCT tuples = 1000
Number of DELIVERY tuples = 1000
Number of DELIVERY tuples for C_NO 1 = 10

Clearly, only a small section of these database tables is shown here. Now suppose we wish to perform the following SQL query:

Query 9.8 'List the description of all products delivered to customer number 1.'
One SQL SELECT statement that could be used here is:

```
1 SELECT DESCR                    <--- π
2 FROM PRODUCT P, DELIVERY D      <--- ×
3 WHERE P.PROD_NO = D.PROD_NO
4 AND C_NO = 1;                    <---- σ
```

There is a select (σ), a project (π), and a natural join ($|\times|$) in this query. The order in which they are carried out radically affects the query performance.

Query execution plan 1: Join, select, project
In this Query Execution Plan (QEP), a join of all matching tuples in the two tables is followed by a select where C_NO is 1, and a project onto the PRODUCT.DESCR attribute.
The relational algebraic expression for this QEP is:

The query interpreter/optimizer generates QEPs (query execution plans).

$$\pi_{DESCR} (\sigma_{C\_NO=1} (PRODUCT \ |\times| \ _{PROD\_NO} \ DELIVERY))$$

A query tree for this QEP is shown in Fig. 9.2.

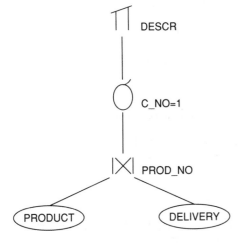

Fig. 9.2 Query tree for QEP 1.

The query tree is read from the bottom up. The tables involved are shown in ellipses.

The query statistics for this interpretation of the query are as follows:

Join: Each of the 1000 PRODUCT rows is joined to matching DELIVERY rows. For each PRODUCT row, every DELIVERY row will be retrieved and tested for a match. The number of databases accesses is thus:

PRODUCT accesses: 1000
DELIVERY accesses: $1000 \times 1000 = 1\,000\,000$

Every DELIVERY row will match with one PRODUCT row, so the resulting number of intermediate joined rows is 1000.

Select: Each of these 1000 rows is then inspected to see if $C\_NO = 1$. The number of accesses to perform this step is thus:

PRODUCT $| \times |_{PROD\_NO}$ DELIVERY accesses = 1000

We know that the number of deliveries to C_NO 1 is 10 (see above).

Project: Each of these 10 rows is projected onto DESCR, duplicates (delivery of same product to C_NO 1) being removed. The number of accesses for the project is thus:

Project accesses = 10

The total number of accesses for this QEP is thus:

$1000 + 1\,000\,000 + 1000 + 10 = 1\,002\,010.$

Query execution plan 2: Select, join, project
In this QEP, the select is performed first, followed by the join and then the project.

The relational algebraic expression for this QEP is:

$$\pi_{DESCR} (PRODUCT \; | \times |_{PROD\_NO} (\sigma_{C\_NO=1} DELIVERY))$$

The query tree for this QEP is shown in Fig. 9.3.

The query statistics for this interpretation of the query are as follows:

Select: Each of the 1000 DELIVERY rows is accessed and the 10 deliveries for C_NO 1 retrieved. The number of database accesses is thus:

DELIVERY accesses: 1000

Join: Each of the 1000 PRODUCT rows is accessed and 10 joins occur:

PRODUCT accesses: 1000

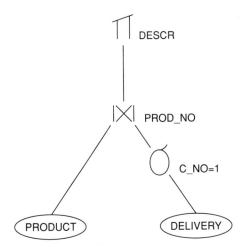

Fig. 9.3   Query tree for QEP 2.

Project: Each of the 10 rows is projected onto DESCR, duplicates being removed. The number accesses for the project is thus:

Project accesses: 10

The total number of accesses for this QEP is thus:

$1000 + 1000 + 10 = 2010$

If this is compared with the 1 002 010 accesses of QEP1, it is clear that the order of the relational algebraic expressions is highly significant in query optimization.

Using indexes further improves performance
We now consider how using appropriate indexes can further improve query performance for this query.

Select: Suppose there is an index on C_NO in DELIVERY. The index will give direct access to all deliveries for C_NO 1. The number of database accesses is thus:

DELIVERY accesses: 10

Join: Suppose there is an index on PROD_NO in PRODUCT. The index will give direct access to each product number from DELIVERY in PRODUCT. The number of database accesses is thus:

PRODUCT accesses: 10

Project: Each of the 10 rows is projected onto DESCR, duplicates being removed. The number accesses for the project is thus:

Project accesses: 10

The total number of accesses for this QEP is thus:

$10 + 10 + 10 = 30$

By producing an efficient Query Execution Plan, the query interpreter has reduced the number of database accesses from over a million to thirty.

We may have been a little unkind on QEP 1. The query interpreter may have performed a sort merge when joining PRODUCT and DELIVERY, which would have taken extra time for the sort, but reduced the overall number of disk accesses. Even in this case, all 2000 PRODUCT and DELIVERY rows would have been accessed. One further factor which should be mentioned and which would affect the above argument is that an 'access', that is, a disk access, will often retrieve more than one tuple into a buffer. Retrieving data from a buffer in RAM is much faster than retrieving it from disk. However, this is true for all of the above examples.

Joining three or more tables
Suppose we have three tables which we wish to join:

A | × | B| × | C

We assume each join is a natural join, so there is no need to state explicitly what the join attributes are (although we have been doing so to aid clarity).
Suppose A | × | B is a high hit-rate join (there is a high proportion of matches) and B | × | C is a low hit-rate join.
If A | × | B is performed first, a large number of intermediate joined tuples will result. A small proportion of these will then be joined to rows of C.
If B | × | C is performed first, a small number of intermediate joined tuples will result. This small number of intermediate tuples will then be joined to rows of A. Thus intermediate storage is saved. Used in conjunction with appropriate indexes, performing the low hit-rate join first will also further enhance execution speed.

General guidelines for producing efficient query execution plans
1. In a query involving a join, perform selects and projects as early as possible to reduce the number of rows that will have to be joined. (A project can reduce the number of rows because it removes duplicates.)
2. Use indexes for low hit-rate selects.

3. Use indexes for low hit-rate joins.
4. Use sort-merge for high hit-rate joins.
5. In joins involving three or more tables, first perform the join that produces the minimum number of intermediate rows.

Chapter 10

Recovery and concurrency

In this chapter you will learn:

☐ to use techniques for database recovery;

☐ to use techniques for database concurrency.

Recovery

A database may be damaged by a number of events. Program bugs could cause the program to abort, leaving incomplete updates, or to introduce incorrect data onto the database. An interruption to the power supply or hardware faults involving the network, the CPU or the backing storage could occur while data is being processed. The DBMS must be able to restore the database to some correct state following such a catastrophe. This process is called recovery.

Batch processing

Batch processing is a traditional method of file processing still applicable for some applications.

In a batch processing environment, a master file is updated by a program using a transaction file which contains a batch of updates (insertions, deletions and modifications). A backup copy of the master file should be made before the update so that if any error occurs while processing, the situation can be recovered by:

1. Finding and correcting the source of the error (hardware, power, program, data).
2. Copying the backup copy over the master file.
3. Rerunning the whole update process.

PC databases

In a single-user PC database, recovery is left up to the user, who is expected to take regular backups and, in the event of a database failure being detected, to restore the database to the latest backup version and repeat the updates since that point. Since there is no log of the updates, knowing which transactions need to be rerun can present a problem.

Shared database updates

In most large database environments, there may be several concurrent users interactively applying updates to various parts of the database. If the database is destroyed at 4:00 pm and the backup was taken at 10:00 pm the previous day, it would be inconvenient to have to ask the users to reinput all the transactions for that day. Not only is there a duplication of effort, but input of all current transactions must be delayed.

The DBMS must provide the following facilities to recover from such situations:

1. Backup.
2. Journalling.
3. Recovery.

Transactions, commit and rollback

A transaction is an indivisible unit of work containing a set of inserts, modifications, deletions (here, collectively called 'updates'), commits, and rollbacks. If a commit occurs, the updates up to that point are made permanent. If a rollback is asked for, the updates since the previous commit are disabled and do not take effect.

COMMIT makes updates permanent. ROLLBACK disables updates since the previous COMMIT.

It may be that the transaction contains only one independent update involving one record. However, a transaction may contain several interdependent updates. All of the updates contained within one transaction must succeed or else the whole transaction should be aborted in order to prevent database inconsistency. This principle is known as transaction atomicity. Atomicity is the responsibility of the DBMS. Transaction correctness, ensuring that the database is in a consistent state after the successful completion of the transaction, is the responsibility of the programmer.

A transaction which updates two records

As an example, consider a program that inserts INVOICE records and consequently updates the CUS.BALANCE field value. (See Appendix A for definitions of the INVOICE and CUS tables). There are two steps:

Step 1: Insert the INVOICE record.
Step 2: Update the customer balance so that:

These two steps should be combined into an individual transaction.

CUS.BALANCE = CUS.BALANCE + INVOICE.AMOUNT

These two steps are (or should be) indivisible. Either both or neither should occur. If any event occurs during the transaction that allows step 1 to occur but not step 2 (such as a system crash or fatal program error), then there will be a database inconsistency. These two steps are thus lumped together conceptually into a single transaction.

It can be argued that such a database dependency should not occur in a fully normalized database. However, it is convenient and common practice to keep summary data such as CUS.BALANCE on the database. (Imagine the speed penalty of having to recalculate CUS.BALANCE from all past invoices and payments every time it is required!) Step 2 may be executed automatically by a database rule and procedure in DBMSs such as INGRES. However, the fact remains that both or neither update should occur.

A program may contain several transaction types

Some update programs will execute a single transaction. Others will contain a loop executing several transactions of the same type. Still other programs may contain code performing a variety of transaction types under different conditions. Consider for example the pseudo-code fragment in Fig. 10.1.

```
FOR EACH input INVOICE record
        IF CUS record for this customer does not exist
                PERFORM INSERT_CUS_RECORD routine
        ENDIF
        Insert the INVOICE record
        Update CUS.BALANCE (as above)
END FOR
```

Fig. 10.1   Transaction contains a conditional insert.

Here, the insertion of all new invoices is done in one program and insertions of new customer records is only performed where necessary.

Backup

Periodically, the DBMS will make a copy of the current state of the database - a backup copy. This copy will be used with the stored transactions to regenerate the database in the event of a failure, without having to reinput all transactions since the last backup.

Journalling

Journalling involves keeping a copy of essential data concerning updates in a log file (also called a journal). There are several recovery policies that can be used, and the contents of the journal vary according to the policy used by the particular DBMS.

Incremental log with immediate updates

The recovery scheme described here is called incremental log with immediate updates. Alternative schemes are described on page 294.

Contents of a log file

Typically, the log file will contain the following data:

1. **Transaction ID**. A system-wide name for the transaction. Different runs of the same transaction type will be distinguished in this ID.
2. **Date and time** of the start of the transaction.
3. For each update within the transaction:

   - **Action type**: insert, modify, delete, commit, rollback.
   - **Object of action**: which record was affected.
   - **Before image**: what the affected record looked like before the update.
   - **After image**: what the affected record looked like after the update.

The contents of a log file vary from one system to another.

Sample operation of a log file

Suppose that in a particular period, there are two transaction types running:

Trans ID	Transaction description
INV1	Add an Invoice and Update Customer Balance
PMT1	Add a Payment and Update Customer Balance{{XTAB}}

The log file over this period may appear as shown in Fig. 10.2.

Trans ID	Time	Action	Before Image	After Image
INV1,1	9:00	Start		
PMT1,1	9:01	Start		
INV1,1	9:02	Insert INVOICE 1018		(New Values)
PMT1,1	9:03	Insert PAYMENT (940, 4)		(New Values)
INV1,1	9:04	Update CUS 2	(Old Values)	(New Values)
INV1,1	9:05	Commit		
PMT1,1	9:06	Update CUS 1	(Old Values)	(New Values)
PMT1,1	9:07	Commit		

Fig. 10.2 Sample log.

The transaction ID INV1,1 means that this is the first transaction type INV1 to be run. Several INV1 transactions may be running concurrently (two users both entering invoices) and they must be distinguished from each other. The times shown would in practice be more precise (e.g. 30-dec-93 16:10:56). Note that for an insert operation there is no before image. For a delete, there would be no after image. The transactions INV1,1 and PMT1,1 are interleaved here. One user is running an INV1 transaction type to input an invoice 1018 for customer 2, and the other user is running a PMT1 transaction to input a payment (940, 4) which is the fourth payment that customer 1 has made against invoice 940. (Check this in Appendix A.)

Recovery
The use of before images

Suppose that in processing transaction PMT1,1 the transaction aborts due to a program error or user error. For example, it may be discovered at commit time (9:07) that invoice 940 does not exist and the program has not allowed for this. A database procedure has however detected this erroneous condition. All updates for this transaction must be undone. The before image for CUS 1 must be applied to the database. The insert of PAYMENT (9:03) must then be undone by deleting it.

The use of after images

Suppose now that at 9:08 a system crash destroys the current version of the database. First, the cause of the crash is found and removed. The most recent backup copy will then be used to overwrite the current copy of the database. Next, all of the after images up to the time of the crash are applied to restore the database. The transactions that were being processed at the time of the crash can be discovered by inspecting the log for transactions with no commit action. Any such transactions will instead have the before images applied.

Log entries are written to disk before database updates

Log entries are written before database updates are written to disk.

If the database updates occurred before the log entries were saved to disk, and a crash occurred between these two events, there would be no log entries for these updates. Since the transactions running at the time of the crash were incomplete, database inconsistencies are likely to have been caused by these partial updates. It would be impossible to restore the before images, because they would have been lost in the crash. Consequently, log entries are written before the database updates are written to disk.

Forward and backward recovery

Forward recovery is starting from the backup copy and applying after images to restore the database to its position just before the error. This (possibly lengthy) process can be speeded up by prescanning the log file and only applying the most recent after image for a given disk area.

With **backward recovery**, the backup copy is not used. Instead, the log is processed backwards, using the before images to undo changes that were made by transactions that were not committed.

Checkpointing

It is convenient to halt the input of all new transactions for a few moments periodically and to save the log and the database updates so that the log and the current state of the database are known to be consistent with each other. This process is known as checkpointing and may be performed by the DBMS several times per hour. In the event of a system crash, it is then only necessary to trace back through the log to the most recent checkpoint and recover from there.

Alternative recovery strategies

In all of the above, we have been assuming that for each update within a transaction, the log entry is made and the update immediately follows. Incomplete transactions at the time of a crash are undone.

Differential files

Instead of updating the actual database records, it is possible to use a differential file, which contains all the changes to the database. When a user inputs a new update, the differential file is scanned to see if the record the user wants to update is there. If it is, the most recent version of it in the differential file is updated. If it is not, the actual database record is read into a buffer in the usual manner, but the updated version of the record is placed in the differential file. Periodically, after a specified number of complete transactions have occurred, the differential file is run against the actual database and, similar to a batch update, all relevant records are updated. There is thus less of a problem with partial updates brought about by incomplete transactions, and most of the time the actual database is 'protected' by being read-only. The disadvantage of this scheme is that response time may be increased by the need for each update to first scan the differential file.

Shadow writing

Updates are written to a separate disk area and the indexes that point to the updated records are not updated until the transaction commits. In this way, the updates are present on the disk but are not effective until the transaction successfully completes.

Mirroring

Two or more identical copies of the database are held on different secondary storage devices. If a device error occurs on one, service is continued with the others. If more than two copies are maintained on line, a voting (also known as polling) system can be used where one of the copies shows different data from the others. This system is in use at the London Air Traffic Control Centre where the current positions of aircraft are held on a database and absolute reliability must be maintained. In this instance, there are three CPUs and three copies of the database.

Fallback areas

A variation on mirroring is the scheme in which two disks A and B each have a primary area and a fallback area. There are also two disk controllers, each of which can be switched to either disk. The data in disk A's primary area is mirrored in the fallback area of disk B and vice versa. In normal usage, since there are two disk controllers, the primary areas of each can be searched in parallel, yielding a speed advantage. If one of the disks or disk controllers 'goes down', processing can continue since each disk contains all the data.

Incremental log with deferred updates

In this scheme, updates are not immediately applied to either the database buffers or the actual database. Updates are written to the log. When a transaction is about to commit, the commit is written to the log, the log is written to the disk, and the transaction is committed. Only then is the database actually updated and it is updated from the log itself. There is no need for the before image in this recovery scheme.

Two-phase commit

Either both or neither database should be updated to ensure consistency.

Suppose there are two databases A and B which must both be updated from a single set of transactions. (This situation often occurs with distributed databases where there is no single central database and a given transaction may affect records in several of the databases. For example, a fund transfer from an account at one site to an account in another is a single transaction affecting two databases.) If the transaction completes successfully, then both databases must be updated. If only one is updated, there will be an inconsistency. Either both databases or neither (in the case of an error) should be updated. The local systems at sites A and B we shall call resource managers and the system responsible for controlling the transaction execution and ensuring both sites remain in step we shall call the coordinator. The coordinator or either of the resource managers 'going down' during a transaction should not result in inconsistency. This is the purpose of the two-phase commit protocol.

Suppose the transaction completes successfully and issues a COMMIT. The two phases are as follows:

Phase 1. The local resource managers A and B each write appropriate log entries for the transaction. Each resource manager reports back to the coordinator whether or not this step was successful. Note that no database updates are made in Phase 1.

Phase 2. If both resource managers report success, the coordinator writes COMMIT in its own log. Otherwise it writes ROLLBACK. The coordinator informs the resource managers of its decision. For a COMMIT, both databases will now be updated, otherwise rolled back.

If an error occurs at any point during these two phases, the local COMMITs will not be executed. Assume phase 1 was successful and both sites have a correct log entry. If they cannot report this back to the coordinator because of, say, a network error, no COMMIT will be issued. If they do both report back success from phase 1 and the coordinator crashes, then no COMMIT will be issued and no local database updates occur. If the coordinator successfully responds and sends a COMMIT, but only one resource manager A receives it, then other measures will have to be taken. At least the site B has the log entry from which the local update can be made when the cause of the fault is removed and clearance is given.

Some sample embedded SQL code

Programs involving interdependent SQL INSERT, UPDATE and DELETE commands are written with these commands embedded in either 4GL or 3GL code. INGRES, for example, has its own procedural language usually called 'INGRES 4GL'. ORACLE has 'trigger' features in its SQL*FORMS utility, and dBASE IV and similar PC-based DBMSs have their own procedural database languages. These can all be called 4GL features (although the usage of the term '4GL' varies). Alternatively, the SQL commands can be embedded in 3GL code such as COBOL, C or FORTRAN code. Examples of SQL embedded in several different 3GLs and 4GLs are contained in Carter (1992). The code in which the SQL statements is embedded is called the host language code.

The fragment of embedded SQL code shown in Fig. 10.3 implements the 'insert an invoice and update customer balance' transaction mentioned above:

```
1 EXEC SQL WHENEVER SQLERROR GOTO error_label;
2 EXEC SQL INSERT INTO INVOICE
        VALUES (:inv_no, :c_no, :inv_date, :amount);
3 EXEC SQL UPDATE CUS
4       SET balance = balance + :amount
5       WHERE cus.c_no = :c_no;
6 EXEC SQL COMMIT;
7 goto finish_label;
8 error_label:
9   EXEC SQL ROLLBACK;
10 finish_label:
11   return;
```

This transaction inserts an INVOICE and updates CUS balance.

Fig. 10.3 Simple update illustrating COMMIT and ROLLBACK.

Line 1 says that should any database error occur throughout this transaction, control is passed to error_label, where a ROLLBACK occurs. This means that if either the INSERT or the UPDATE is unsuccessful, both updates are 'rolled back', that is, undone. No updates to the database will have occurred. Line 2 inserts the new invoice values (obtained from elsewhere and contained in host variables :inv_no, etc.) into the INVOICE table. Host variables are variables accessible to both the host code and the SQL commands. Lines 3 to 5 update CUS.BALANCE. If both the INSERT and the UPDATE are successful, line 6 COMMITs (makes permanent) the changes to the INVOICE and CUS tables.

Note that in a program such as that in Fig. 10.1, which contains a loop in which several transactions are processed, a COMMIT or ROLLBACK can be implemented for each transaction. If five transactions are each committed and an error is detected on the sixth, that will be rolled back and the first five made permanent.

Exercise 10.1

1. Draw up a limited entry decision table showing which actions the program in Fig. 10.1 should take for each possible combination of the conditions:
   (a) CUS exists (y/n)
   (b) CUS insert succeeds (y/n)
   (c) INV insert succeeds (y/n)
   (d) CUS update succeeds (y/n).

The possible actions are:

(a   COMMIT CUS insert
(b) ROLLBACK CUS insert
(c) COMMIT INV insert
(d) ROLLBACK INV insert
(e) COMMIT CUS update
(f) ROLLBACK CUS update

2. Modify the pseudo-code of Fig. 10.1 to implement your chosen policy. Simplify your code as much as possible.

3. Convert your pseudo-code to the form shown in Fig. 10.3.

4. Identify the transactions in your design.

Concurrency

Locking is used to remove problems related to concurrency.

A concurrency control mechanism is necessary in shared databases to ensure that simultaneous (concurrent) transactions do not interleave with each other in such a way as to cause incorrect data to be written to the database. We describe three problems related to concurrency and show how locking can remove these problems.

Concurrency problems
The lost update problem
Consider the following sequence of events:

1. Transaction A fetches the CUS record for CUS 2. The balance is £200.
2. Transaction B fetches the same record.
Transaction A is a lost update.
3. Transaction A adds £100 to BALANCE.
4. Transaction B adds £50 to BALANCE.
5. Transaction A writes the CUS 2 record back to the database with a BALANCE of £300.

6. Transaction B writes the CUS 2 record back to the database with a BALANCE of £250.

CUS.BALANCE is now £250 and it should be £350. The effect of transaction A has been lost.

The uncommitted dependency problem

Consider the following sequence of events:

1. Transaction A updates CUS.BALANCE for CUS 2 from £200 to £300. The update is written to the database but is not yet committed. (This assumes the incremental log with immediate update protocol described on page 292).
2. Transaction B fetches the CUS 2 record and adds £50 to BALANCE, giving £350.
3. Transaction A performs a ROLLBACK because of some condition arising in subsequent processing. CUS.BALANCE is momentarily restored to its original value of £200 on the database.
4. Transaction B updates the BALANCE of CUS 2 to £350 and commits.

CUS.BALANCE is now £350 and it should be £250. Transaction B was 'dependent' on the effect of transaction A even though transaction A had not committed and in fact had to roll back.

The inconsistent analysis problem

Consider the following sequence of events, in which transaction A is summing CUS balances and writing the result to a SUMMARY table, and transaction B is transferring £100 from CUS 2 to CUS 6:

1. Transaction A sums the CUS.BALANCE fields of customers 1 to 5 to get, correctly, £1151.89.
2. Some time during step 1, Transaction B transfers £100 out of CUS 2's BALANCE into CUS 6's BALANCE, making the latter £512.21. Transaction B successfully completes and COMMITs.
3. Transaction A adds £512.21 from CUS 6's BALANCE to its total to get £1664.10. It writes this incorrect figure to the SUMMARY table.

The SUMMARY table now contains £1664.10 whereas it should contain £1554.10. This is because in calculating the sum, it used the old value of CUS 2's balance and the new value of CUS 6's balance. Transaction A has performed an inconsistent analysis of the CUS table, because it was changing while the analysis occurred.

Serializability

Serial execution of a set of transactions means that the transactions are executed one after another, without any interleaving of updates. Only one transaction is executing at any one time. Providing each transaction is correct, the database cannot be left in an inconsistent state. If a set of transactions executes concurrently, the schedule (sequence) of updates is said to be 'correct' if it produces the same result as some serial schedule. In the cases above, each schedule of operations was non serializable because it resulted in incorrect results, results that would not have occurred if a serial schedule had been executed. Note that for a set of n transactions, there are $n!$ [that is, $(n*(n-1)*(n-2)*...*2)$] possible serial schedules. In some cases different serial schedules may result in different results. For example, adding £100 to BALANCE in transaction A and then multiplying BALANCE by 1.1 in transaction B would have the result 1.1*(BALANCE+100), which is not the same result as if the order of the transactions is reversed: (1.1*BALANCE)+100.

A schedule of transactions is said to be serializable if it produces the same results as some serial schedule. A serializable schedule will avoid the problems described above. There are two popular ways of ensuring a schedule of transactions is serializable: locking and timestamping.

Locking

One solution to the update problems above is for the first transaction to update an object to lock the object against further transactions until it successfully completes. Locking can occur at database level (the whole database is locked), at table level (all of the records in the table being updated are locked), at record level (just the records involved in the transaction are locked) or at field level (just the fields involved in the transaction are locked). In the following discussion, record locking is assumed.

There are two types of lock:

S lock: A 'shared' lock. This is applied to the record when a FETCH (read) occurs.
X lock: An 'exclusive' lock. This is applied to the record when an update is to occur.

Several transactions can have an S lock on a record at the same time. Having an S lock disallows other transactions from applying an X lock, so if transaction A is reading CUS 2's record and transaction B wishes to update it, transaction B will be queued until transaction A has completed.

If transaction A is updating CUS 2's record, it applies an X lock on it. This means that no other transaction can apply either type of lock and so cannot either read or update the record until transaction A has completed.

Locking solves all of the problems described above; however, unless suitable precautions are taken, **deadlock** can occur.

Deadlock

Consider the following sequence, which is an attempt to solve the lost update problem on page 298, using S and X locks:

1. Transaction A fetches the CUS record for CUS 2. An S lock is applied.
2. Transaction B fetches the same record and also applies an S lock.
3. Transaction A adds £100 to BALANCE and tries to update, requesting an X lock on the record. This request fails because of the S lock of transaction B.
4. Transaction B adds £50 to BALANCE and tries to update, requesting an X lock on the record. This request fails because of the S lock of transaction A.
5. DEADLOCK!

In general, deadlocks may involve one or more loops of update contentions. See Fig. 10.4, which shows two wait-for graphs.

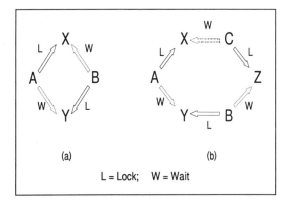

(a)   (b)

L = Lock;   W = Wait

Fig. 10.4   Wait-for graphs.

In Fig. 10.4 (a), transaction A has locked record X in some table and transaction B has locked record Y in the same or possibly another table. (In the case discussed above X and Y were the same record.) A waits for Y to be released and B waits for X to be released. In Fig. 10.4(b), there are three transactions all deadlocked in a loop.

Exercise 10.2

Will deadlocks always form simple loops of the type shown in Fig. 10.4? Draw wait-for graphs of more complexity in which some transactions are waiting for more than one resource and some resources are directly holding up two or more transactions.

Dealing with deadlocks

Deadlock prevention

In this method a transaction puts exclusive locks on all records it will require and only releases them when the transaction is complete. The problem with this approach is that it might not be possible to predict at the beginning of a transaction exactly which records on the database will be accessed. It might be necessary for example to read a record in one table to retrieve sufficient data to decide which record in another table to update.

Deadlock resolution

In this method, deadlocks are allowed to occur but are then resolved. Before deadlocks can be resolved, they must first be detected. A matrix as shown in Fig. 10.5 can be maintained by the DBMS and periodically inspected for deadlocks using a suitable algorithm. There is a deadlock in each of the matrices in Fig. 10.5 corresponding to the wait-for graphs of Fig. 10.4.

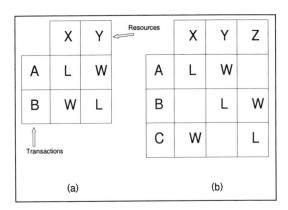

Fig. 10.5   Deadlock matrices.

When a deadlock is detected, one of the transactions in the loop is temporarily rolled back. For simple loops (the vast majority of cases) this is sufficient. When the other transactions have completed, the rolled-back transaction can restart.

Exercise 10.3

1. Develop a pseudo-code algorithm for detecting simple loops involving *n* deadlocked transactions.
2. In nonsimple wait-for graphs (see Exercise 10.2), is it ever possible to roll back one transaction and remove two or more deadlock loops?

Timestamping

Timestamping is an alternative concurrency control mechanism to locking. Since no locks occur, deadlocks are no longer a problem. Each transaction is timestamped with the exact starting time or starting sequence number of the transaction. Updated data items are write timestamped and read timestamped. Multiple copies of the data items with their associated timestamps are kept. When a read of a data item is requested by a transaction, the version of the data item that has the latest write timestamp prior to the transaction's timestamp is used. If a transaction B with a later timestamp than transaction A reads the data item which transaction A needs to update, transaction A is rolled back and given a later timestamp. These measures ensure serializability.

Optimistic techniques

In this technique, all transactions are allowed to go ahead as if no conflicts could arise due to interleaving. Just before the transaction commits, a check is performed to see if a conflict occurred. If so, the transaction is simply rolled back. No locking and hence no deadlocking occurs. In situations in which the probability of two separate transactions concurrently accessing the same record is small, optimistic techniques have considerable potential. If rollback occurs frequently, one of the alternative techniques mentioned above should be adopted.

Appendix A

Table definitions

CUS

C_NO	TITLE	SNAME	INITS	STREET	CITY	POSTC	CRED_LIM	BALANCE
1	Mr	Sallaway	G.R.	12 Fax Rd	London	WC1	1000	42.56
2	Miss	Lauri	P.	5 Dux St	London	N1	500	200
3	Mr	Jackson	R.	2 Lux Ave	Leeds	LE1 2AB	500	510
4	Mr	Dziduch	M.	31 Low St	Dover	DO2 9CD	100	149.23
5	Ms	Woods	S.Q.	17 Nax Rd	London	E18 4WW	1000	250.1
6	Mrs	Williams	C.	41 Cax St	Dover	DO2 8WD		412.21

INVOICE

INV_NO	C_NO	INV_DATE	AMOUNT
940	1	5-DEC-90	26.2
1002	4	12-JAN-91	149.23
1003	1	12-JAN-91	16.26
1004	2	14-JAN-91	200
1005	3	20-JAN-91	510
1006	5	21-JAN-91	250.1
1017	6	22-JAN-91	412.21

PAYMENT

INV_NO	PMT_NO	PMT_DATE	AMOUNT
940	2	12-DEC-90	13
1005	1	14-JAN-91	510
1017	1	30-JAN-91	100
940	3	19-JAN-91	10

PRODUCT

PROD_NO	DESCR	QIS	MINQ	REORDQ	PRICE
1	Bat	10	5	10	12
2	Ball	5	5	20	2
3	Hoop	3	5	10	3
4	Net	2	5	10	20
5	Rope	1	10	10	6

DELIVERY

C_NO	PROD_NO	QTY	DEL_DATE
3	2	2	3-NOV-90
3	1	3	3-NOV-90
1	4	6	7-NOV-90
5	3	4	12-NOV-90
3	3	1	12-NOV-90

VIOLIN STUD_NO	NAME	AGE	PIANO STUD_NO	NAME	AGE	CELLO STUD_NO	AGE	NAME
1	Fred	10	2	Jane	12	4	10	David
2	Sally	11	4	David	10	6	11	Josey
4	David	10	5	Zena	11			

FLUTE STUD	CNAME	AGE	CUST CNO	NAME	PURCHASE CNO	PRNO	PROD PRNO	DESCR
7	Ashfak	12	1	Alan	1	a	Apple	
			2	Bill	1	b	b	Ball
			3	Charles	2	a		

GROUPS TERM	GROUP_NO	MEMBER	CANDIDATE CAND_NO	NAME	CONS_NO	PARTY	NO_OF_VOTES
1	1	1	1	Fred	1	Labour	100
1	1	2	2	Jim	1	Cons	120
1	1	3	3	Peter	1	Liberal	50
1	2	4	4	John	2	Labour	150
1	2	5	5	Mike	2	SLD	50
1	2	6	6	Jane	2	Cons	100
2	10	3	9	Sue	1	SDP	160
2	10	2	7	Mary	2	Green	150
2	1	5	8	Ulrike	1	Indep	150
2	1	7	10	U Li	3	Red Guards	150
			21	Rosa	3	Simbianese	30
			29	Patty	3	Simbianese	12
			41	Astrid	3	Liberal	3
			50	Gordon	3	Labour	160
			52	Ben	1	Green	70

Appendix B

Answers to selected exercises

Chapter 2
Exercise 2.1: Aggregate functions such as MAX ignore NULLs.

Chapter 3
Exercise 3.1(1):

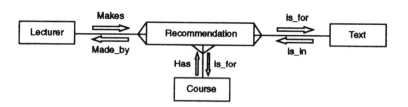

Exercise 3.2:

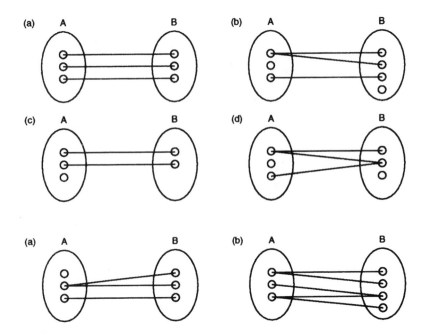

Exercise 3.3(1):

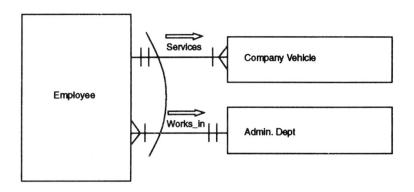

Exercise 3.4:

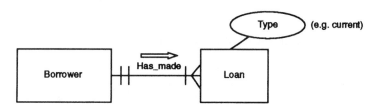

Exercise 3.8(3):   (a) In this example, each person must like someone, but needn't necessarily be liked. The arrows represent the 'like' relationship.

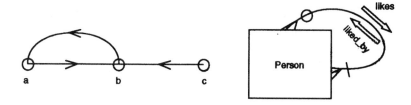

(b) Here, there is a rule saying that everyone must like someone and be liked by someone.

Chapter 4

Exercise 4.3(2):   Because in a relation, all attribute names must be different.

Exercise 4.7(2):   In this example, only B.a_no is nullable.

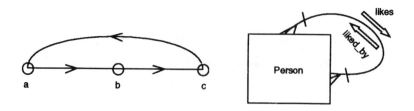

Exercise 4.11(1): If an INV.INV_NO changes, then every related PAYMENT.INV_NO should be changed accordingly.

Exercise 4.12:   They allow any program accessing R3 to know how many occurrences of the group to expect.

Exercise 4.18:   Because value x1 occurs twice.

Exercise 4.19(1): Whenever a value of (A,B) repeats, it always maps to the same value of Y (at least in this sample extension).

Exercise 4.26:   *Hint:* Play around with Surname, Initials, Jobname, Title and any convenient assumptions.

Chapter 5

Exercise 5.1(3): If EMP_NO with CHILD_NAME is the primary key, SALARY is partially dependent on it; it is functionally dependent on EMP_NO only.

Chapter 6

Exercise 6.1(1): English version:
```
SELECT CUSTOMER WHERE CITY ≠ 'London' and CITY ≠
'Birmingham' GIVING TEMP
PROJECT TEMP OVER (NAME, POSTC)
```
Greek version:
$$((\sigma_{city \neq \text{'London'} \text{ and } city \neq \text{'Birmingham'}} (CUSTOMER)))$$

Exercise 6.1(2): Not in this case.

Chapter 7

Exercise 7.5(1): $\Pi_{prod\_no, descr, price} (\sigma_{price > 5} (PRODUCT))$

Exercise 7.14:   List the average age of departments having more than one member.

Exercise 7.17(1): `SELECT CAND_NO, NAME FROM CANDIDATE`
`WHERE NO_OF_VOTES =`
`(SELECT MAX(NO_OF_VOTES)`
`FROM CANDIDATE);`

Exercise 7.18: `SELECT * FROM VIOLIN WHERE AGE = 10`
`UNION`
`SELECT * FROM PIANO WHERE AGE = 10;`

Chapter 8

Exercise 8.1(1): Capacity = $10 \times 100 \times 10 \times 30$ K = 300 Mb

Exercise 8.1(2): Seek time = 50 mS
Latency
3000 rpm = 3000/60 = 50 revs per second
∴ Rotation time = 1000/50 = 20 mS
∴ Latency = 20 mS/2 = 10 mS
Data transfer time
10 sectors per track
∴ transfer time = 20 mS/10 = 2 mS
∴ total average access time =
50 + 10 + 2 = 62 mS

References

Ashworth, C. and Goodland, M. (1990) *SSADM: A Practical Approach*, McGraw-Hill.

Avison, D.E. and Fitzgerald, G. (1988) *Information Systems Development*, Blackwell Scientific Publications.

Carter, J.R. (1992) *Programming in SQL with Oracle, Ingres and dBASE IV*, Blackwell Scientific Publications, Prentice-Hall.

Chen, P. P-S. (1976) The entity-relationship model – towards a unified view of data. *ACM Trans. on Database Systems*, **1**, 9–36.

Clocksin, W.F. and Mellish, C.S. (1984) *Programming in Prolog*, 2nd edn, Springer-Verlag.

Codd, E.F. (1970) A relational model of data for large shared data banks. *Comm. ACM*, **13**, 377–87.

Codd, E.F. (1974) *Recent Investigations in Relational Data Base Systems*, Information Processing 74. North Holland, Amsterdam, pp.1017–21.

Codd, E.F. (1985) Is your DBMS really relational? *Computerworld*, October 14, 1985.

Daintith, J. and Nelson, R.D. (1989) *Dictionary of Mathematics*, Penguin.

Date, C.J. (1986) *An Introduction to Database Systems*, 4th edn, Addison-Wesley.

Date, C.J. (1990) *An Introduction to Database Systems*, 5th edn, Addison-Wesley.

Downs, E., Clare, P. and Coe, I. (1992) *Structured Systems Analysis and Design Method*, 2nd edn, Prentice-Hall.

Eva, M. (1992) SSADM Version 4: A User's Guide, McGraw-Hill.

Fagin, R. (1977) Multivalued dependencies and a new normal form for relational databases. *ACM Trans. on Database Systems*, **2**, 262–78.

French, C.S. (1989) *Computer Science*, 3rd edn, DP Publications.

Ricardo, C. (1990) *Database Systems*, Macmillan.

Index